HMS *Glo*ı

The Untold Story

GLOUCESTER

" PRORSUM "

In honour of all who served on
HMS Gloucester 1939–41, and
to the memory of those who never came home.

HMS *Gloucester*

The Untold Story

Ken Otter

Pen & Sword
MARITIME

First published in 1999 by GAM Books, England
Second edition published in 2001

Published again in hardback format in 2004 by Pen and Sword Books
and again, in paperback format, in 2017 by
Pen and Sword Maritime

An imprint of
Pen & Sword Books Ltd
47 Church Street
Barnsley
South Yorkshire
S70 2AS

ISBN 978 1 52670 211 1

Typeset in 10/12pt Palatino by
Mac Style Ltd

Printed and bound in England
By CPI Group (UK) Ltd, Croydon, CR0 4YY

Pen & Sword Books Ltd incorporates the Imprints of Pen & Sword
Aviation, Pen & Sword Family History, Pen & Sword Maritime, Pen &
Sword Military, Pen & Sword Discovery, Pen and Sword Fiction, Pen
and Sword History, Wharncliffe Local History, Wharncliffe True Crime,
Wharncliffe Transport, Pen & Sword Select, Pen & Sword Military
Classics, Leo Cooper, The Praetorian Press, Seaforth Publishing and
Frontline Publishing

For a complete list of Pen & Sword titles please contact
PEN & SWORD BOOKS LIMITED
47 Church Street, Barnsley, South Yorkshire, S70 2AS, England
E-mail: enquiries@pen-and-sword.co.uk
Website: www.pen-and-sword.co.uk

CONTENTS

Foreword

KENSINGTON PALACE
LONDON W8 4PU

Her Royal Highness The Duchess of Gloucester, GCVO

I have very happy memories of 2nd November 1982 when I had the honour of launching the tenth HMS GLOUCESTER in Southampton. Not only because this was a new breed of Guided Missile Destroyer, which would enhance the capacity of the Royal Navy but also because this magnificent new Ship followed in a long and distinguished line of Ships carrying our shared name.

Very much in everyone's thoughts on that autumn day, nearly twenty years ago, was the courageous and proud service which her predecessor had offered and those many members of her Ship's Company who had lost their lives on 22nd May 1941 in the Battle of Crete.

Princess Alice, Duchess of Gloucester, my mother-in-law, had commissioned the ninth HMS GLOUCESTER in 1939. Her sinking was indeed a very tragic event and the pain of the survivors and the families of those who were killed was shared by my family, who have greatly valued the relationship which has developed and continued over the years.

Princess Alice joins me in sending warmest wishes to all members of 'The Fighting 'G' Club'; I trust that this second edition of 'HMS GLOUCESTER: The Untold Story' will act as a moving reminder of many shared memories.

Introduction

I was seven months old when my father, Fred Otter, was killed during the battle of Crete. He had been in the Royal Navy since he was fifteen and eventually became the Chief Yeoman of Signals aboard the cruiser, HMS *Gloucester*.

I often used to wonder what sort of life he had led aboard ship and what circumstances had led to HMS *Gloucester* being sunk. Whenever I came across a book about the Second World War, I would flip through the index to see if the name *Gloucester* was mentioned. I was never able to find much detail and when I did come across information it was often limited to a few lines.

After school I spent two years in the Royal Navy and went on to join the Metropolitan Police Force in 1960. An absorbing career, marriage and three children, studying for promotion, and playing too much football, cricket and golf, left the mystery of my father's fate, and the story of his ship, on the back burner.

In my early forties, however, I made a more determined effort and managed to contact John Stevens, one of the few men who had survived the sinking in 1941. By a happy coincidence he was in the process of organising the first ever reunion of survivors and families of men who had served on HMS *Gloucester*. The group took on the ship's nickname: The Fighting "G".

I went to the first reunion, held in Plymouth, which is where HMS *Gloucester* was built. I didn't know what to expect but I soon met Roy Tremaine and Les Thomas, who had served under my father on board the ship. They were able to tell me things about my father that I had never known; that he had a wonderful sense of humour, his compassion for the welfare of men under his command and his distinct weakness for cream cakes! It was clear to me that they had thought him a wonderful man. I was not emotionally prepared for the things I was being told and found that I could hardly speak to them and the other survivors, let alone ask the many questions to which I had longed to know the answers. Forty-two years of pent up emotions had suddenly and unexpectedly come to the surface.

The following year I was able to return and be better prepared. I asked the survivors about their life at sea, what they remembered about the sinking of the ship and their traumatic experiences as prisoners of war. It soon became evident that the story of HMS *Gloucester* was both fascinating and devastating and should be written for future generations to read and understand the tragedy of war. Not one of the men I spoke to glorified war and their graphic testimonies are evidence that the appalling conditions under which they lived have left everlasting impressions on them.

Every year I returned to their reunion and every year there were fewer survivors than the previous year. It was obvious that the story of HMS *Gloucester* could soon be lost forever, however at that point I could find no time to fully research and write their story.

When I retired from the Metropolitan Police Force I went to Durham University to read history and the degree which I was awarded gave me the confidence to begin writing this book.

I set off, travelling around Britain, to interview men who had served on the ship and survived the sinking and searching out the families of men who had perished. The more interviews I conducted the more I was amazed at the story which was unfolding. The contrast of their lives on board ship before they became engaged in action in the Mediterranean could not have been greater than that which they experienced after the spring of 1940. These men, who by now were in their seventies and eighties, had lived through times which will never be experienced by future generations of sailors. There will never again be such a sustained war at sea as the men of the Royal Navy faced in the Second World War, particularly those who served in the Mediterranean.

I travelled to the Greek Island of Kythira, where the men were first taken when they were rescued. Here I discovered more details of the story and was fortunate enough to meet some wonderful Greek people who witnessed the sea battle in 1941 and one man in particular who risked his own young life to feed our sailors.

In this book I have, wherever possible, used the invaluable personal testimony of the people I interviewed. Many of those who served on the ship have now passed away, but some left written accounts of their service, and I was able to use these sources. This book is the story of the men who lived and died on HMS *Gloucester*. It is their story, not mine.

Many people have given me invaluable help, both in my research and in writing the book. The men and the families who I interviewed were most kind, inviting me into their homes and showering me with hospitality. To have the advice and encouragement of such an accomplished author as Wendy Robertson has been invaluable. Gill Richardson gave me the advantage of her constructive advice. The staff at Bishop Auckland Library, the Public Records Office at Kew, the Imperial War Museum and the National Maritime Museum at Greenwich, have all shown remarkable patience with me and their help was of considerable assistance. The *Navy News* proved an invaluable source in contacting men who had served in the Eastern Mediterranean Fleet. Efthia and Andy, who are 'The Greek Experience', made my visit to Kythira unforgettable. My friends Chip, Tanya and Chris 'Cats', from Colorado Springs, were extremely helpful in explaining the mysteries of computer technology and managed, most of the time, to keep straight faces whilst watching over me.

Many members of 'The Fighting G Club' have sent me photographs and documents or have written letters of encouragement and I thank them all for their kindness. In particular Frank Moulder, who gave me access to his remarkable collection of photographs, documents and memorabilia. John Stevens, President of 'The Fighting G Club', has been my guiding light in the accumulation of details of the ship's history: without his help it is doubtful whether I could have produced this book.

Above all else I thank Judy, my wife, without whose editing and typing skills, and constant encouragement, this book would not have seen the light of day.

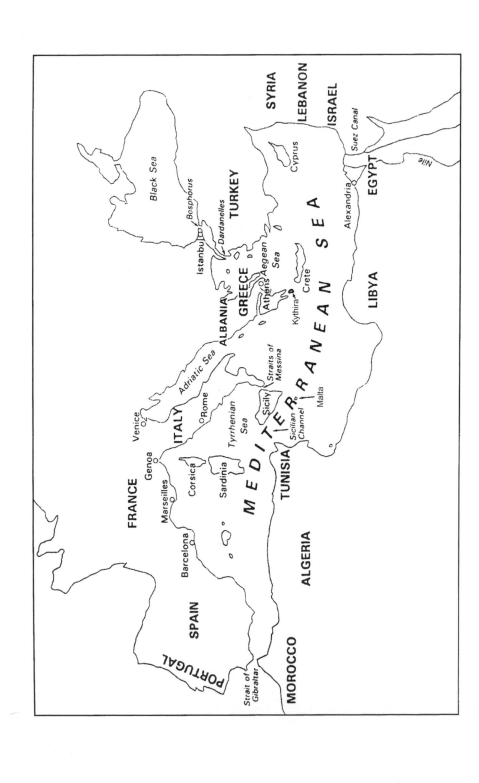

CHAPTER ONE

Launch to Commissioning

On Tuesday 19 October 1937, the *Western Morning News* reported a memorable day. Thousands of people turned out to attend the launching of the ninth HMS *Gloucester* from the South Yard of Devonport Dockyard, Plymouth. The Duke and Duchess of Gloucester attended the ceremony and among the crowds gathered for the launch were many local schoolchildren.

Fourteen-year-old Ernie Evans came along from King Street school. He was thrilled to watch the launch of the ship he had seen built and had heard so much about from his father, who had been working on her in the dockyard. Three years later, Ernie joined the Royal Marines and was eventually drafted to serve on HMS

Gloucester *in Plymouth Sound.*

Gloucester. He was one of only eighty-five men, from a ship's company of eight hundred and ten, who survived when the ship was destroyed on 22 May 1941. Ernie's future shipmates included many other West Countrymen and some from much further afield.

Bill Howe grew up in the village of Manaton on Dartmoor, where he had been working as a farmer's boy. When he was eighteen years old he joined the Royal Navy as a stoker and after training was drafted to serve on *Gloucester*. When the ship sailed from Plymouth, Bill had no idea that it would be six years before he would see the green hills of Devon again.

In 1935, Billy Grindell had been made redundant from the local steelworks in his hometown of Cardiff. He enlisted in the Navy and became a stoker, like Bill Howe. After *Gloucester* was lost in May 1941, Billy Grindell, Ernie Evans and Bill Howe were among the eighty-five men taken prisoners.

Fred Farlow, from Torquay, enlisted in the Royal Navy in January 1937 as a boy seaman, at the age of fifteen. *Gloucester* was the first ship he served on but he left the ship in July 1940 after being severely wounded when *Gloucester* was first attacked.

Michael Noonan travelled from his home in Cork, Ireland, in a cattle boat in order to join the Royal Navy as a boy of fifteen. He was later drafted to *Gloucester*. Ossie Lang, a Welshman, enlisted into the Royal Navy in January 1938. Ossie had wanted to enlist in the Physical Training Branch because he was good at sport, but was wrongly persuaded by the recruiting officer to enlist as a cook, which is what he remained for the rest of his service.

Dennis White grew up in Salisbury and left school to become a telegram boy attached to the local post office. When he was seventeen he decided he wanted to see more of the world so he went along to the Naval Recruiting Office where he was advised that he would be ideal material for the telegraphist branch. Dennis was always amused that the navy should find his experience in delivering telegrams on a bicycle suitable training for working with telegraphy equipment.

Roy Tremaine left his home in Plymouth at the age of fifteen to join the Navy as a boy seaman. Later he transferred to the signals branch and joined *Gloucester*, as a leading signalman, when she was commissioned in 1939.

By Friday 27 January 1939, everything was in place for the commissioning of HMS *Gloucester*. The new ship was the latest 'Southampton' class cruiser and displaced 9,600 tons. She had an overall length of 591 feet 6 inches and a beam of 62 feet 4 inches.

Her main armament consisted of twelve × six-inch guns, eight × four-inch guns, sixteen pom-poms, two triple torpedo tubes and a number of .5 machine guns. The armour plating ranged from 3 to 4 inches on the sides of the ship (between bulkheads 7 and 18), 4 inches around the Control Tower and between 1 and 2 inches around the gun turrets. In addition, *Gloucester* was fitted out to carry three Walrus aircraft. The ship was powered by Parsons turbines, with four shafts producing an SHP of 82,500, which was capable of producing a speed of 32.3 knots. She could carry 1,970 tons of oil fuel. A notable feature of the *'Southampton'* class ships was that the centre gun on the six-inch turrets was mounted slightly further back than the other two. The raking funnels and masts were a particularly attractive feature and distinctive of this class of ship.

The Duke and Duchess of Gloucester returned to Devonport for the commissioning ceremony during which Princess Alice, Duchess of Gloucester, referred to the ship as 'Our *Gloucester*' and thereafter the ship's company always referred to her as 'Our Alice'.

Whilst many of the new ship's company originated from the West Country, some came from further afield in the United Kingdom and Ireland. Most of them had spent several weeks in the Royal Naval barracks at Devonport preparing for their draft to the new cruiser. On the day of the commissioning they were marched from the barracks, in procession behind a blue jackets band, to their new ship. Boy seaman, Michael Noonan recalled the event as a proud moment;

'When I first saw the ship I felt so proud to be joining her. She was immaculate and sparkling in the winter light'.

Ship's company marching from Devonport Barracks to join HMS Gloucester.

The man who had been given command of the new ship and her young crew was Captain Freddie Garside CBE RN. He had joined the Royal Navy at Dartmouth as a thirteen-year-old cadet, seen action in the Battle of Jutland and his already distinguished career had led to him being awarded the CBE in the recent New Year's Honours list. The captain's wife, Peggy, was on board before the ship sailed. She and Freddie had married in 1931 after meeting one another in a party that had gathered for Ayr races.

The two months following the commissioning was spent 'working up' the ship in the Channel. This was a vital period for Captain Garside to forge the ship's company into an efficient team and for them all to become familiar with the ship's capabilities. On 15 March 1939 the ship prepared to sail. Families came to see their loved ones leave and some were invited on board to take tea on the messdecks. Boy seaman Fred Farlow's parents were there and he bought a crest of the ship for 1/6d in the NAAFI. The horseshoe on the crest is upside down, which is traditionally thought to depict the luck running out of it. It was a portentous purchase for Fred.

Bill Howe's sister and their parents came down from the village of Manaton, on Dartmoor. They took tea on the messdeck and were amazed at the limited space that the men had to live in.

When 'hands to stations for leaving harbour' was piped and the last visitor had left the ship, *Gloucester* sailed off on her great journey to the East Indies. The band of the Gloucestershire Regiment was assembled on the quay playing the song from the Walt Disney film, Snow White, 'Hi Ho, Hi Ho, It's off to work we go'. The song became the ship's signature tune and was played by the Royal Marine band whenever *Gloucester* visited ports around the Indian Ocean. The new ship looked resplendent in the cold spring sunlight as she sailed passed Devils Point, her crew lined up along the forecastle, amidships and on the quarterdeck.

Boy seaman Michael Noonan was making his maiden voyage. He recalled that as the ship passed between Drake's Island and the Hoe, the Commander in Chief's band was on the Hoe playing, 'Hearts of Oak' and 'A Life on the Ocean Wave'.

Chief Engine Room Artificer Charles Jope's wife and young daughter, Yvonne, stood on the Hoe waving to him as he sailed away on

Captain F.R. Garside CBE RN.

Gloucester *at Devils Point.*

Gloucester. They would never see him again. Many other families visiting the ship that day would never see their boys again. Even the 'lucky' ones would have to wait over six years before the few survivors came home from German prison camps.

The Ship's band.

Captain Garside welcomes HRH The Duchess of Gloucester aboard for the ship's commissioning on 27 January 1939. Captain Garside and Commander D'Aeth (second left) were both killed on 8 July 1940.

CHAPTER TWO

Ceremonies and Spices

On-board *Gloucester* there were about sixty boys, aged between fifteen and eighteen years old. They were not allowed to mix socially with the rest of the ship's company and their own messdeck was strictly segregated from the older sailors. Divisional Officer Lieutenant R S Brooke and Petty Officers, Robert Philpott and Sydney Press, were responsible for their welfare and training. The discipline on board was particularly strict for the boys; smoking was forbidden and when ashore the boys' leave ended at 1800, any transgressions being harshly dealt with. Ted Mort, a boy seaman from Newport, south Wales, recalled that if anyone was caught drinking, smoking or bullying they were given 'cuts', which were strokes from a cane, administered by the Master at Arms.

Gloucester sailed from Plymouth Sound into the Channel and on to the Bay of Biscay. Despite the younger sailors having been warned of its possible horrors, the voyage south through the Bay around Gibraltar and into the Mediterranean was an uneventful one and the sea remained calm. At that time the Spanish Civil War

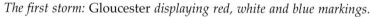

The first storm: Gloucester *displaying red, white and blue markings.*

Going into Malta.

was still being fought and HMS *Gloucester*, in order to avoid being wrongly identified by the warring Spanish factions carried red, white and blue identifications on her topside to mark her as a British ship.

On 19 March 1939 *Gloucester* entered the Mediterranean, heading for Malta. Here she encountered one of the worst storms she would sail through during the whole of her commission. The gale whipped up the sea to such an extent that many of the ship's boats were damaged.

Fred Brisley, a Royal Marine bandsman, was sick for three days but his friends continued to bring him his daily 'tot', which was the only thing he was able to keep down.

Dennis White remembered the ferocity of that storm;

'I've never forgotten that first gale which made me so horribly seasick. The bows of the ship kept disappearing in the waves'.

When *Gloucester* reached Malta it was Easter and Fred Farlow had a powerful recollection of the strong smell of incense wafting across the harbour and of colourful religious parades passing through the narrow streets.

In Malta, *Gloucester* had to be put into dry dock for repairs to the forecastle deck and to the condensers, which had been damaged in the storm. The break in Malta gave the men an opportunity to have some

In dry dock: Telegraphists aloft on the main mast.

time ashore and it was a chance to visit 'The Gut': a long street containing many bars in Malta's capital, Valetta, and famous to sailors for many decades as a drinking haunt.

Billy Grindell and his pals headed for 'The Gut' via Mary's bar which was run by two sisters. They were served a meal of chicken and chips with a glass of Ambeach wine and a cigar for 10d. After their meal the men continued along 'The Gut', and went to play the tombola in Vernons Club, then on to the American Bar and finished off in the Egyptian Queen Bar, where there was always a band playing.

James Simmons and his brother George went ashore in Malta and had a chance reunion with their other brother, Alfred, whose own ship, *Grenade*, had also arrived at Malta. The three Irish boys, from County Mayo, had a grand night out but it was the last time that Alfred would see his brothers, both of whom were killed when *Gloucester* went down on 22 May 1941.

On 7 April 1939, the political situation in the Mediterranean became more tense when Italy invaded Albania. Cyril Pearson, a store's rating from the ship, was in a cinema in Valetta on that day when a message was flashed across the screen ordering all *Gloucester* men to return on board immediately. *Gloucester* left Malta, heading towards the Suez Canal and her eagerly anticipated tour of the Indian Ocean, with little knowledge of the terrors she and her company would face when they next entered Mediterranean waters.

As the ship sailed south the temperature rose higher and at night most of the men slept on camp beds on deck but still the heat was so intense that many of them did not sleep well. *Gloucester* took over as the flagship of the East Indies station when she reached Aden and with Rear Admiral Ralph Leatham now aboard, additional messages were being received from the Admiralty in London, Colombo in Ceylon and from other ships on the East Indies station.

As the ship sailed further south towards the equator the ceremony of 'crossing the line' was an exciting event for the young sailors who had not experienced such a ceremony before. A canvas bath full of water was placed on the forecastle and a stage built next to it where 'King Neptune', dressed in all his finery, would sit in his chair holding a trident. He was accompanied by a band of 'pirates' made up from the older ratings, who had been initiated in crossing the line before. The 'pirates' ran around the ship capturing uninitiated sailors to be brought before 'King Neptune', who charged them with daring to enter his kingdom. All were found guilty and sentenced to receive punishment. The guilty parties were then put in a dentist's-style chair and subjected to a mock shave

Crossing the Line: Always a popular occasion.

with a huge wooden razor and liberal amounts of soap, which inevitably found its way into their mouths. The chair was then tipped up and the miscreants would shoot into the canvas bath where the 'pirates' made certain they got a good soaking. After their initiation the 'victims' received a certificate for 'Crossing the Line'.

As flagship of the East Indies station, *Gloucester* now was based at Colombo in Ceylon. From here she patrolled the east coast of Africa and islands such as the Seychelles, Maldives, Mauritius and the Chagos Archipelago in the Indian Ocean. Captain Garside, always keen to ensure the welfare and education of his young crew, used the opportunity of cruising in tropical waters to point out exciting and unusual sights.

Signalman Les Thomas, a Welshman, recalled one such occasion;

'I remember the captain's voice coming over the tannoy, telling us to look out for a huge water spout, caused by a freak wind, which was off the starboard side. There was a high fountain of water shooting up from the surface of the sea and the sun made it sparkle like a chandelier. He often pointed out unusual things to us and I remember that I first saw flying fish after the captain told us where to look'.

In the summer of 1939 their first visit was to Mombassa, Kenya where the ship docked at Kilindini Island, the port of Mombassa. The boy seamen were taken, by their Divisional Officer Lt Brooke, on an expedition up a creek, in two boats, until they beached on a remote shore. They swam in the warm waters and some played about in an old dugout canoe which they had found.

Michael Noonan recalled;

'We were larking about in the water when someone called out that there were crocodiles close by. Within seconds everyone had scrambled ashore before we realised that it was a hoax'.

On Saturday 17 June, the ship left Mombassa, bound for Dar Es Salaam, capital of Tanganyika. This was a favourite visit for many of the ship's company. The aroma of spices wafted through the air, reaching the ship well before she arrived at the port. She anchored and was further secured, by ropes, to the base of coconut trees to prevent her from swinging about in the strong currents. Dar Es Salaam was on the route of the Empire Flying Boats which brought rich and famous people to the port on flights from Southampton, via Marseilles, Alexandria and Khartoum.

Dennis White was fascinated the first time he saw one of these flying boats landing alongside the ship;

'Dar Es Salaam was the first port we visited which really gave the impression of being truly tropical'.

Palm trees fringed the narrow entrance to the harbour and Dar Es Salaam was a peaceful haven for *Gloucester* where the local citizens had laid on a full programme of events for their visitors from the Royal Navy. Roy Tremaine kept a souvenir programme guide from the visit of the ship, produced by the 'Tanganyika Standard', which outlined sporting and social events.

Rickshaws carried the men around Dar Es Salaam, at a cost of 6d for fifteen minutes running time. Here they could sample the delights of The Railway Hotel, described by the proprietress, Mrs Hardar, as the 'Favourite House for Sailors', and offering fish and chips for 1/-, or eggs and bacon for 1/ 6d. Not to be outdone, the Splendid Hotel went all out and held a dance on Monday 19 June to celebrate the visit of HMS *Gloucester*.

During their visit the ship's company organised a concert which was so well attended that they had to put on a second house. The Royal Marine Band played for their guests and the highlight of the programme was their star performer, Richard Harley, popularly known as, 'The Singing Marine'. Richard had trained as an opera singer before the war and his singing talent was immediately recognised by Royal Marine Band Major H G Rogers, who invited him to accompany the band on such occasions.

Dar Es Salaam – June 1939.

On Thursday 27 June, *Gloucester* sailed north to the island of Zanzibar where the Sultan made an official visit to the ship while she was in port. His ornately decorated barge arrived alongside the ship with the Sultan sitting, on a magnificent gold chair, among sixteen finely dressed oarsmen. Rear Admiral Leatham and Captain Garside, who gave the Sultan a tour of the ship followed by lunch in the wardroom, welcomed him aboard.

A group of boy seamen were subsequently invited to visit the Sultan's palace and a rumour quickly spread around the ship that he kept a magnificent palace containing a harem. Their excited anticipation of meeting the Sultan's concubines was dashed, however, when they arrived outside the palace and were met by some very sedate wives of British settlers. The ladies had organised tea and cakes for the boys on the lawn outside and later, to their dismay, they were given a tour of the exterior of the palace.

> SOUVENIR PROGRAMME AND GUIDE
>
> commemorating the
>
> # NAVAL VISIT
>
> TO DAR ES SALAAM
> OF
>
> **H. M. S. Gloucester**
> JUNE, 1939

BEER IS BEST
AND

The Most Popular Beer in
DAR ES SALAAM
IS

INDIA PALE ALE BREWED BY

EAST AFRICAN BREWERIES LTD.
(Established 1922)

Ask For **I. P. A.**

IT COSTS YOU LESS!

Souvenir Programme.

In these weeks the entire ship's company was having a wonderful adventure in the tropics and the men felt very remote from Europe and rumours of an approaching war.

From Zanzibar, *Gloucester* and her suntanned ship's company sailed east, out into the Indian Ocean to the Seychelles. Here they could buy bottles of rum which had seaweed in them and they saw turtles for the first time. On one of the islands, a local chief made a gift of turtles to the ship. Some were made into soup but three of them were kept to be taken back to the zoo at Colombo.

During the voyage the turtles were kept in the canvas bath which had been used for the 'crossing the line' ceremony. The turtles were

The Sultan of Zanzibar arrives alongside HMS Gloucester.

Read Admiral Leatham welcomes the Sultan aboard.

not popular with many of the men because at night, while the men were trying to sleep on deck, the turtles used to slosh about in the water and keep everyone awake.

The ship sailed on, eventually recrossing the equator, to the Maldive islands. From there *Gloucester* returned to Colombo, the capital of Ceylon and the base for the East Indies station. She had been at sea for five months and was now due for maintenance and repainting. While the ship was manoeuvred into the dry dock of Walker's Yard at Colombo, some of the crew had an exciting journey by train through the hills to the beautiful rest camp at Diyatalawa. Michael Noonan and Alan Hugill were among the boys who travelled over seventy miles through the jungle to Kandy and up into the 6,000ft hills. Michael recalled;

'We went in this old smoke-belching train and the clouds covered the hills above us. Eventually we passed through them and after a spectacular journey, with the clouds now beneath us, we arrived at the camp'.

At the Diyatalawa rest camp the boys and men had a wonderful leave. Walks and picnics were arranged and many tried their hand

Read Admiral Leatham and Captain Garside with the Sultan.

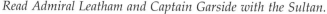

Inquisitive onlookers as a turtle is hauled aboard.

at golf in the idyllic surroundings and cool climate of the hills. Sam Dearie, a stoker who came from Glasgow, had endured many months working hard in the sweltering heat in the engine room on-board *Gloucester*. He never forgot the novelty of being woken up in the mornings, at the rest camp, by a servant who brought him a cup of tea. The idyllic rest at Diyatalawa came to an abrupt end however when everyone was woken up early one morning and instructed to pack their bags to travel back to Colombo. The threat of war had been sensed by many of the ship's company and on reporting back to the ship, they found the duty watch reammunitioning and making ready to put to sea.

On 27 August, *Gloucester* slipped her moorings and headed out into the Indian Ocean, north towards Aden. In a few days she would be engaged in the war against Germany and the skills and courage of her crew tested to the utmost.

Diyatalawa Rest Camp. The Post Box was converted from a WW1 Torpedo.

CHAPTER THREE

Ceylon to South Africa: War Clouds and Weddings

On Saturday 2 September 1939 Vice Admiral Leatham, Commander of the East Indies station,[1] received a signal to prepare for hostilities. The following day Dennis White was on watch in the telegraph office when the message came through from the Admiralty to 'commence hostilities'.

Michael Noonan was on duty at his defence station in the Director Control Tower when the officer in charge, Lt Brooke, sent him down to the boys messdeck to listen to the radio news from London. Michael heard the Prime Minister, Neville Chamberlain, broadcasting the news that a state of war existed;

'There was a roar on the messdeck and everyone seemed pleased that the waiting was over'.

Royal Marine Jan Gardiner remembered that, like most of the men, he had known that war was imminent and he couldn't wait to get started;

'We had been trained for it and to a certain extent we'd been brainwashed to think that we couldn't be beaten'.

Les Thomas summed up the true feelings of many of the men;

'We weren't worried when war broke out. We all believed there was no way that anyone could beat the Royal Navy'.

During the month of September *Gloucester* patrolled around the Red Sea, where the temperatures were constantly high. Once war was declared the ship was closed up at all times, and the heat below decks became almost unbearable.

Commander J R D'Aet

As *Gloucester* was Vice Admiral Leatham's flagship she received news of world events which most other ships were not privy to at this time. From Thursday 7 September until 10 October, 1939, the news was published daily in the ship's own newspaper, *Gloucester's Western Morning News*. Each copy was numbered and in the top right hand corner where the cost would normally be displayed was the word, 'Priceless'. Cyril Pearson managed to save all thirty-four issues of the ship's newspaper and in the 1980s he presented them to the Captain of the current HMS *Gloucester*.

Britain had been at war with Germany for a week when *Gloucester's Western Morning News* reported that no major naval operations had taken place. Optimistically it predicted that the convoy system, which was being put into operation, would counteract the U-boat menace.

On 19 September however, the newspaper reported the sensational sinking of HMS *Courageous* by a German submarine. Of her ship's company of 1,260, a total of 512 men were lost. On 27 September the ship's paper reported that Mr Churchill, First Lord of the Admiralty, had told parliament that he regarded the loss of *Courageous* as a hundred-to-one chance.

The threat of Italy joining the war eased when Mussolini declared a non-belligerency policy and with tension in the Middle East easing, *Gloucester* returned to Colombo on 10 October 1939 for the completion of her mini refit.

Commander in Chief, Vice Admiral Leatham left *Gloucester* and transferred his flag ashore in Colombo. Captain Garside and Commander D'Aeth were reunited with their wives who had travelled out to Ceylon from Britain.

The members of the ship's company who had missed the opportunity during their first visit, now had a chance to spend some time at the rest camp at Diyatalawa but during their stay bad news came from Britain.

The battleship HMS *Royal Oak* had been sunk on 13 October, in Scapa Flow, by a German submarine *U47*, under the command of Lieutenant Gunther Prien. Further reports also came through about the menace of U-boats in the waters around Britain and in the Atlantic.

During early November, with her refit complete, *Gloucester* was deployed in the Bay of Bengal. She made her way north to Burma before steaming up the mighty Irrawaddy River to visit Rangoon. On the journey upstream they passed pagodas and Buddist temples. Almost as soon as the ship arrived at Rangoon, however, Captain Garside received orders to leave and make way to the Indian Ocean where the German raider, *Graf Spee* had begun sinking British merchant ships.

Commander J R D'Aeth. In this photo sent to his daughter Jennifer, he wrote on the back, 'The Commander at Work'.

Michael Noonan recalled an exciting journey back down the Irrawaddy;

> *'The Harbour Master had said that we couldn't go downstream in the dark but Captain Garside decided that he would sail without a pilot and take the responsibility himself. About half an hour after dark we slipped away down river. The current of the river was about thirteen knots and the ship had to be making about ten knots headway to be able to steer her, so we travelled downstream at about twenty-three knots. The lights of the villages on the bank went flashing by and they reminded me of travelling on a train through the darkness'.*

Eventually *Gloucester* reached the open sea and set off on the long voyage through the Bay of Bengal and across the Indian Ocean to the island of Madagascar. On 15 November, the German pocket battleship, *Graf Spee* sunk the 706-ton tanker *Africa Shell*, south of Madagascar and on the following day she stopped a Dutch steamer in the same area. As a result of these actions, Vice Admiral Leatham formed several groups of ships to search for the German raider.

Gloucester and the French sloop, *Rigault de Genouilly* searched the area between Madagascar and the Seychelles. The *Graf Spee*, however, continued to sink British ships until she was eventually engaged in battle off the coast of South America. After the battle, on 13 December, the German ship took temporary refuge in Montevideo for four days. On 17 December she headed for the open sea where she was scuttled, having sunk nine British merchant ships.

The sinking of *Graf Spee* gave renewed optimism to the Allies, including the people of South Africa who turned out to welcome *Gloucester* as she sailed into Durban, only a few hours after the uplifting news had been received. Crowds of people were gathered on the dockside, waving and cheering. Michael Noonan remembered that as soon as the ship docked the ship's company were assembled on the forecastle;

> *'Captain Garside told us that we were ambassadors for Great Britain and must be on our best behaviour at all times. He said that the people of Durban loved the Royal Navy and he was sure that we would have a wonderful time. That was typical of the captain, he was always looking after our welfare as well as the reputation of the Royal Navy'.*

Once ashore the men found that the hospitality which Captain Garside had spoken of had not been exaggerated. Affluent families were waiting in cars to whisk the sailors away to their houses, where they were treated to all the comforts of home life.

Nineteen-year-old Dennis White had come a long way since the days when he delivered telegrams on a bicycle in Salisbury. He and a friend went ashore, where they were met by a married couple;

'They showed us around the area and took us to their home. For the whole time that we were in Durban we didn't have to spend a penny'.

Royal Marine Jack Ivey, from Brixham in Devon, went ashore with his good pal, 'Sharkey' Ward. They were taken to the home of Mr Raymond Paul and entertained by his family. Later he drove the two boys to the Valley of a Thousand Hills. Jack recalled;

'It was the prettiest place I'd ever seen'.

Jan Gardiner, who had celebrated his twentieth birthday only a few months before, went ashore with a pal from Plymouth;

'We were taken to a bungalow, which was built on stilts to prevent insects and wildlife from getting into the premises. The family took us to a plantation and gave us a wonderful time'.

Bandsman Fred Brisley was only nineteen years old when he and fellow musician, Ronnie Fisher, went ashore and were met by a local bank manager, Mr Brown;

'He picked us up at the dockside and took us to his home, which was just outside Durban. Mr Brown's family made a terrific fuss of us and fed us wonderful meals. We enjoyed the luxury of a bath, which was quite a change from having to shower with a crowd of blokes on-board ship. They even gave us clean pyjamas and lovely comfortable beds to sleep in'.

Billy Grindell, the stoker who had left the dole queues in Cardiff to join the Royal Navy, also enjoyed Durban but didn't take up the offers to visit the South African homes;

'I remember seeing the cars lined up by the Lever Brothers building but I was too shy to come forward. I was OK when I was with the lads but in women's company I didn't know what to say'.

Les Thomas, from Abergavenny, was twenty-one at the time and was less inhibited. He went to the home of Mr Bernard Lindsay, a barrister, who

Royal Marines Jackie De Grouche and Jan Gardiner (kneeling) with their hosts in Durban.

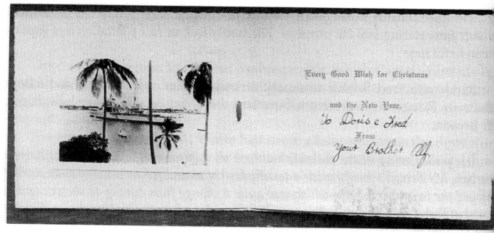

Every Good Wish for Christmas

and the New Year.

to Doris & Fred

From

your Brother Alf.

Christmas Card – 1939.

drove him away in a big American car. Les recalled that the Lindsay family lived in a luxurious home;

> *'They had a butler and because I was an unsophisticated boy I got cold feet and thought about trying to escape through the toilet window. In the end I stayed but I had difficulty enjoying the meal because I was so unsure of what to do. I remember we had plums for dessert and I didn't know what would be the best way to eat them, so with difficulty I tried to chop the flesh off them with my spoon and made a terrible mess'.*

On 20 December, Richard Harley was ashore and met the woman who became his wife. A dance had been organised at the City Hall and the 'Singing Marine', fell in love with a beautiful South African girl. He applied for permission to get married and despite attempts to dissuade him by his Royal Marine commanding officer, he was later married in Capetown.

The hospitality that the ship's company received in Durban was exceptional and despite elaborate plans being made for a huge Christmas party, the celebrations came to an abrupt end on 21 December when the ship was ordered to sail. The wonderful reception at Durban had been arranged by the Mayor, Mr Ellis-Brown and Members of 'The Tin Hat Society' (MOTHS), who were First World War veterans. Mr Ellis-Brown's son was among thirty-one South Africans who were serving on board *Gloucester*.

Once again crowds of people came to the dockside, bringing with them hampers of food for the crew of whom they had taken such good care. *Gloucester* sailed from Durban and the men faced the bleak prospect of having to spend the first Christmas of the war at sea.

Boys' Mess at Christmas 1939.

They soon adjusted to life back on board ship and made the most of the festive season. Dennis White enjoyed a fruitcake that his mother had sent and Nobby Hunt entertained his messmates by dressing up and dancing for them. The Royal Marine band played Christmas carols and the ship's harmonica group, led by Lieutenant Dick Burge, entertained with many popular numbers of the day. The messes were decorated and the boys and men had their own celebrations at sea.

1939 had been an exciting and eventful year with sea trials, the commissioning and a voyage through the Mediterranean to the Indian Ocean and the tropics. They had visited three continents and seen places that many of the ship's young company had never even heard of before they left Devonport. Their future, however, held no such delights.

Note

1. Leatham was promoted from Rear to Vice Admiral on 1 August 1939.

CHAPTER FOUR

Gathering the Fleet:
First Gunfire

In the first week of January 1940, *Gloucester* sailed back to Colombo. It was here that Royal Marine Captain Richard Formby joined the ship, having sailed from Britain on a troop ship.

Captain Formby, a RM boxing champion, showed the sensitive side of his personality in his letters to his wife, Pamela;

It is very hot and sticky and last night I took my mattress on deck and slept well in the open air. I have loathed these weeks without you all, so God knows how I will manage till the end of the war. Now that the Russians and Finns are at it too, it may go on forever.

Before *Gloucester* left Ceylon, Richard Formby went up into the hills at Nuwara Eliya. From here he wrote another letter to his wife;

From the Grosvenor Hotel, Nuwara Eliya, Ceylon.

Yesterday morning we climbed the highest mountain here, 8,200 feet. We went with a man called Harry Greer. We started at 7.15am and made the top by 10am. There wasn't a cloud for miles. The whole of Ceylon was right under us. It was lovely. I wished that when I'd climbed to the top I had found you. I was afraid there was not much hope ... instead there were some people who Greer knew. They had a picnic with them and they gave us some. The path up the mountain was marvellous, you would love it. It twists and turns and at each turn you meet some different flower. Dozens of different rhododendrons on trees, not bushes. Old Man's Beard and all sorts of orchid which have Formby Flower Show 'beat'. The whole path is covered by trees, so it is no too hot. We got down again by noon and had some beer in The Hill Club.

At the beginning of the New Year it had become apparent that the cruiser strength of the Royal Navy was inadequate. The Admiralty acknowledged this and by February 1940 they had converted forty-six liners into armed merchant cruisers for use on convoys. *Gloucester* was later engaged in the defence of convoys on both the east and west coasts of Africa and on trade protection duties in the Indian Ocean. Captain Formby's letters describe the arduous nature of these duties;

HMS Gloucester, *East Indies Station. 3rd March 1940*
We've been at sea for 14 days, except for a few hours to refuel. Up until yesterday the weather has been bloody, wet, cold and rough. Cold enough to wear the thick blue golf sweater on watch at night. The sea is calm now and last night, when I came off watch, the only ripple on the water was made by the ship. The moon was full and it looked as if you could see down miles and miles into the water. The sea out here is so clean, so blue and so deep. There are millions of flying fish and little porpoise.

Tomorrow we get back where we started but I'm damned if I know for how long we stay, or where we will go. It is bound to be a long way for there is nowhere under 2,000 miles. We never go straight and always fairly fast. Except when the weather is decent, it is unutterably boring and very often I just long to get on to a rackets court or somewhere, for any sort of exercise. We play bridge all the time, there is literally nothing else to do, no point in letter writing, for it may be 14 days before it is posted.

HMS Gloucester, *East Indies Station. 29 March 1940*
Don't worry if you don't hear from me for at least a month from now, perhaps longer. I have only had one letter from you this month, God knows what they do with the rest. I did get the parcel from George Henry Lee, but it reminded me so much of Ma, I hardly liked to open it. How I hate to think of Firwood without mother there. I wonder how you are all getting along and if cook and Nellie have made up their argument. How is Jennifer getting along at school, and how are Richard and Cha Cha. I hate everything so much and the thought of the war going on and on for years simply appalls me. It can't go on for three years – I'll be 35.

I feel terribly depressed today, I don't know why. We must never let another war ruin the children's lives. It would be too awful to think of Richard fighting in a war. I am determined he will never have anything do with the Services, for it brings the worst kind of misery. We must really get going to make Formby a real financial success, so we have something to give them all later on. I'm sure Richard should go into your Pa's business after Cambridge.

'It is getting very hot here. We had a very calm trip and saw some whales. I had no idea they were so big and moved so fast'.

'I wonder why you fall in love with someone so much that life without them becomes a blank. There are dozens of other people in the world but no one like you. I am dying to get home and help with the awful time you are having'.

Captain Richard Formby. Royal Marine

By April the phoney war in Britain was coming to an end as Germany began the invasion of Denmark and Norway. The situation in Western European deteriorated and ominous rumblings from Italy suggested that the war would spread to the Mediterranean.

Despite a demand for ships in home waters, arrangements where made to gather a fleet based in the Eastern Mediterranean. *Gloucester* was among the ships detailed to form part of the 7th Cruiser Squadron and on 13 May she set sail from Simonstown. Her time in the Indian Ocean had come to an end and in a few weeks her ship's company would be facing the onslaught of war in the confined waters of the Mediterranean.

On 22 May 1940 *Gloucester* reached Aden, where she was joined by the aircraft carrier *Eagle* and Royal Australian Navy cruiser *Sydney*. The three ships escorted a convoy of ANZAC troops through the Red Sea and on 26 May, safely reached Port Said, before sailing on to Alexandria.

The ancient port of Alexandria was now the base for the Eastern Mediterranean Fleet where, Commander in Chief, Sir Andrew B. Cunningham had gathered together ships from the Far East, the East Indies and Home Fleets to defend the vital seaway through the Mediterranean to the Suez Canal.

The fleet, which he had assembled was an imposing one. Together with the battleship *Warspite*, the Commander in Chief's flagship, were the battleships *Malaya*, *Ramillies* and *Royal Sovereign*. In the 7th Cruiser Squadron with *Gloucester*, were *Orion*, *Neptune*, *Sydney* and *Liverpool*, while the 3rd Cruiser Squadron was made up of *Capetown*, *Caledon*, *Calypso* and *Delhi*.

In addition there were twenty-five destroyers, as well as HMAS *Stuart* and four destroyers from the Royal Australian Navy, a dozen submarines from the China Station and the aircraft carrier *Eagle*. To service the fleet, the repair ship *Resource* and the submarine depot ship *Medway* were also at Alexandria.

Despite the impressive assembly of his fleet, Cunningham had a number of concerns about the back-up services available to him. Many of the ships were old and with only one floating dock, the scant repair facilities of a shipping line, and the workshops of the Alexandria tramways, it was clear to the Commander in Chief that the fighting efficiency of his force could be seriously reduced through the lack of adequate maintenance.

The need to protect Alexandria against air attacks was another problem facing Cunningham and with low reserves of ammunition, the defence

Sir Andrew Browne Cunningham. (By courtesy of the National Portrait Gallery, London)

of the city was limited to twenty-four anti-aircraft guns and an inadequate number of searchlights.

Cunningham had already identified lack of air cover as a potential problem as early as December 1939. He had stressed that not only would aircraft be needed for reconnaissance to locate enemy naval forces but they would also be essential for providing protection to the fleet from aerial attack. It was a problem, which was to persist, and one which *Gloucester* and all other ships in the Mediterranean would eventually pay for.

Conscription into the armed forces was now well established and soon some of the ship's company would be drafted to other ships. The experience they had gained was vital to the efficiency of the Navy, especially in view of the large numbers of inexperienced HOs, ('Hostilities Only' ratings) who were passing through their training and coming onto the ships. The men who had commissioned *Gloucester*, before the outbreak of war and now justifiably regarded themselves as professional sailors often resented the recruitment of 'amateurs'.

Richard Garner was an 'HO' rating who joined *Gloucester* soon after she arrived in Alexandria. He was eighteen years old and had been a bank clerk before enlisting into the navy. Standing on the dockside with all his kit, he looked across the harbour to where *Gloucester* was moored and eagerly awaited a boat to ferry him out to his new home;

'As I stood on the jetty, HMS *Diamond* was berthed nearby and a big bearded matelot was working near the bows. He shouted to ask if I was going out to the *Gloucester* and had I just come from England? I happily replied yes to both questions. His attitude changed when he realised that I was an 'HO' rating and he yelled back me, "Well you might as well 'eff off back. We can win this effing war without you lot". It was my first introduction to the 'real' navy and when I eventually got on board *Gloucester* I took more stick, especially when they found out that I had previously been working in a bank. They nicknamed me "The Bank Damager"'.

Richard recalled how terrified he was the first time the ship put to sea and his feeling of claustrophobia when air raids were taking place. At times his action station was an auxiliary wireless station in the bowels of the ship, which was manned in case the main station was put out of action;

'I had to sit there with nothing to do, as the wireless sets would only be brought into use if the main wireless office was hit. I preferred to be busy at action stations because that took your mind off things, but sitting down there with nothing to do was terrifying, especially when you could hear the shrapnel hitting the sides of the ship'.

The situation in the Mediterranean came to a head on 10 June when the Italian Foreign Ministry sent for Sir Percy Loraine, the British Ambassador in Rome. Count Ciano, Mussolini's son-in-law,

Gloucester *in the Suez Canal.*

saw him and delivered 'a declaration of war' to the British Ambassador. Cunningham immediately ordered the fleet at Alexandria to two hours notice to make steam.

Michael Noonan clearly remembered hearing the news;

'I was on the boats crew when the captain announced that we were at war with Italy and that all leave was cancelled. All liberty men were immediately recalled'.

The following day, *Gloucester* and the 7th Cruiser Squadron put to sea and with *Warspite, Malaya, Eagle* and nine destroyers sailed north-west towards Crete. The cruisers *Caledon* and *Calypso* joined them before the whole force headed west to carry out a search for Italian ships heading towards Libya.

That night *Gloucester, Liverpool* and four destroyers were deployed south, to attack patrols off Benghazi and to bombard Tobruk. As they sailed towards the North African coast the Italian navy scored their first hit on a Royal Navy ship. The submarine *Bagnolini,* commanded by Cdr. Tosoni-Pittoni, torpedoed the cruiser *Calypso,* commanded by Captain Henry Rowley, south-west of Crete. One officer and thirty-eight ratings on *Calypso* were killed and the rest of the ship's company were picked up and taken back to Alexandria. *Gloucester's* guns were fired in action for the first time as dawn broke on 12 June and an Italian minesweeper, *Giovanni Berta,* was sunk off the Libyan coast. *Gloucester* and *Liverpool* also bombarded Tobruk and the shore defences returned fire, however both ships managed to evade the enemy shells which fell some distance from the ships. This was the first experience of action against the enemy.

Ossie Lang, the cook, was at his action station in the forward magazine and he remembered the dreadful feeling of claustrophobia that swept over him as the compartment was sealed from the outside;

'I had to load 6 inch shells on to the lift ready to be taken up to the guns of 'A' and 'B' turrets. I was always frightened of having my fingers crushed when I did this but the most frightening thing to us was that

if the ship caught fire the first thing they would do would be to flood the compartment and we would all drown'.

On 14 June, *Gloucester* and the rest of the fleet made a cautious re-entry into Alexandria which, in their absence, had been heavily mined by Italian submarines.

During the remainder of the month the allied fleet was involved in operations in the eastern Mediterranean, particularly against Italian submarines. Intelligence reports estimated that there were about fifty submarines operating in the area. Allied ships succeeded in sinking five Italian submarines but three of the ten British submarines operating in the same area were also lost.

Towards the end of June, *Gloucester* and the rest of 7th Squadron were covering two convoys on passage from Alexandria to Malta. Flying boats on reconnaissance reported three Italian destroyers heading for Italy. The 7th Cruiser Squadron altered course and at 1830 on 28 June, sighted the Italian ships about seventy-five miles west-south-west of Cape Matapan. *Gloucester* and the other cruisers immediately opened fire at extreme range. Commander Baroni, aboard *Espero* and in command of the three Italian ships, turned to face the British force, giving the other two Italian destroyers the chance to escape. *Espero* was hit and sunk whilst the other two sailed to safety.

The importance of good aerial reconnaissance, which Cunningham had constantly stressed, had been highlighted in this engagement. Cunningham was also concerned about the high expenditure of ammunition, which had been used by 'Southampton' class cruisers. Older cruisers were fitted with 8 inch guns, two abreast, but the newer ships, such as *Gloucester* and *Liverpool*, had 6 inch guns triple mounted. Ammunition was soon expended from these ships firing salvoes from twelve guns. The expenditure of ammunition from the high angle guns was also a concern and became a principal factor in *Gloucester* being sunk the following year.

Despite these concerns, Cunningham summed up the situation in the Eastern Mediterranean in optimistic terms. At the end of June, he reported to the First Sea Lord that Italian communications with

Gloucester's guns open fire on Tobruk at dawn, two days after Italy had declared war.

the Dodecanese Islands had been cut; the enemy's communications with Libya had been threatened; Italian submarines had been relentlessly hunted and attacked and surface ships of the Italian Navy given a taste of the Royal Navy's efficient gunnery skills.

The Commander in Chief was also heartened by the quality of men under his command and described their enthusiasm and devotion as being beyond all praise and said that no Commander in Chief had better subordinates;

> *'It was their outstanding spirit of invincibility in any emergency that enabled them to rise over all our difficulties'.*[1]

At home the war was going badly for Britain, despite the successful evacuation of over a third of a million troops from Dunkirk. On 13 June, the Channel Islands had fallen to Germany and two days later, as almost 100,000 troops were being evacuated from Cherbourg and St Malo, it became evident that France would soon capitulate.

Although part of the French fleet had sailed to Casablanca and Oran, some French ships had been operating from Alexandria under the command of Vice Admiral R E Godfroy. With the imminent fall of France, the operational availability of the French navy was in doubt.

The French fleet had given valuable assistance to Admiral Cunningham. During the first sortie by the British fleet in the Eastern Mediterranean, on 11 June, four French cruisers and three destroyers had sailed into the Dodecanese islands to attack Italian airfields. Three days later, other French ships shelled the Ligurian coast of Italy. The French navy had proved a valuable force to have operating alongside the British fleet in the Mediterranean.

The British government was now concerned that the Royal Navy might be deprived of the co-operation of the French. Even worse, the French ships might be taken over by the German or Italian navies, to be used against the British fleet. So long as there was uncertainty as to the future of the French navy it was impossible for the British fleet, at Alexandria, to put to sea.

The Admiralty, under the direction of Winston Churchill, recently appointed Prime Minister, gave their urgent attention to this problem. They arranged operation 'Catapult', a plan to seize the French fleet should they refuse to fight with the British forces. It was of concern that the French fleet might try to sail back to France, which was now in the hands of Germany. A tense situation arose in the congested harbour at Alexandria where the French fleet was uncertain of their future.

In Mers-el-Kebir, at the opposite end of the Mediterranean, a similar situation occurred. The British exchanged gunfire with the French, which resulted in the sinking of two French battleships and

Gloucester's *4 inch guns in action.*

one cruiser with the loss of over 1,250 French sailors. These were men who had been fighting alongside the British only two weeks earlier.

Cunningham was anxious to avoid creating a similar situation in Alexandria. Not only was there a possibility that British ships would be damaged but there was a real danger that the harbour's entrance would become blocked if ships were sunk. Cunningham set about negotiating with the French Admiral, Godfroy, either to have the French ships handed over to him or for Godfroy to de-militarize his fleet. At first Godfroy appeared ready to co-operate but when news of the action at Mers-el-Kebir reached him he broke off negotiations and decided to take his fleet to sea.

Cunningham was desperate to avoid a catastrophe and rather than engage the French fleet he flashed a message, several times, to the French ships explaining the hopelessness of their situation. At the same time he despatched a number of boats to sail around the French ships and hold up message boards which implored the French crews to see sense and stay in harbour. Godfroy eventually came under pressure from his own officers and agreed to demilita-rize his fleet. The whole affair had taken three days to resolve during which time the Admiralty had signalled to Cunningham that they were unhappy with the prolonged nature of the negotiations.

Royal Marine Jack Ivey remembered the French confrontation;

'I was detailed with other marines to patrol the harbour in one of the ship's whalers. We had a machine gun aboard. It was a tense affair'.

Les Thomas recalled that *Gloucester* had received a signal ordering her to open fire on the leading ship if the French fleet attempted to sail. Les was delegated to one of *Gloucester's* boats to standby as a boarding party;

'I remember I had a pair of flags, a signalling lamp and a revolver. It was nasty affair and I confess that I was frightened'.

With the situation eventually resolved and Cunningham's prolonged negotiations vindicated, he could now turn his attentions back to the threat from Italy and was able to put to sea once again.

Note
1. Cunningham of Hyndhope, Admiral of the Fleet, Lord. *A Sailor's Odyssey*, Hutchinson, 1951, p.240.

CHAPTER FIVE

Direct Hit: Our Captain is Dead

On 7 July 1940, *Gloucester* and the rest of the fleet sailed from Alexandria for Malta, on convoy escort duty. During the night two enemy submarines were encountered and attacked. The following day however, the Italian aircraft that Cunningham described as delivering 'fairly heavy bombing' attacked the convoy.[1] Aircraft attacks, by 126 Italian planes persisted throughout the day and Cunningham gave credit to the efficiency of the Italian Air Force;

'*Their reconnaissance was highly efficient and seldom failed to find and report our ships at sea. The bombers invariably arrived within an hour or two. They carried out high level attacks from about 12,000 feet, pressed home in formation, in the face of the heavy anti-aircraft fire of the fleet and for this type of attack their accuracy was very good*'.[2]

Michael Noonan remembered that the formation of Italian aircraft held a curious sense of beauty, despite their deadly mission;

'*Captain Garside was very clever at avoiding bombs by training his telescope on the aircraft and on the occasions when he could actually see the bombs dropping he was able to give instructions for evasive action to be taken*'.

Perspiring under the heat of the

Tot time.

sun, the gun crews kept up a continuous barrage throughout the afternoon but just before 1600 on 8 July, the bridge of *Gloucester* received a direct hit. She was the first ship of the Royal Navy to be hit by enemy aircraft in the Mediterranean and Admiral Cunningham's worst fears over the lack of air cover had been tragically realised. Captain Garside, Commander D'Aeth and sixteen other men on the bridge were killed instantly by the explosion of the bomb. Also killed in the raid were; Lt Commanders Churchill and Lindsay; Sub-Lieutenants, Murray and Layard; Midshipman Atkins; Chief Yeoman Frazer and Leading Signalman Hyde; Leading Seaman Hensby; Able Seaman Ward; Ordinary Seamen Owens, Foster, Knight, Allison and Nolan; Boy Seaman Rodda and Boy Bugler Godliman.

In an instant the men of *Gloucester* had lost their greatly respected captain: the man who had looked after their welfare and moulded them into the efficient and happy ship's company which they had become during the previous sixteen months.

Michael Noonan was on watch in the Transmitting Station and remembered that *Gloucester* and the rest of the fleet had been under attack all day;

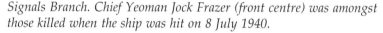

Signals Branch. Chief Yeoman Jock Frazer (front centre) was amongst those killed when the ship was hit on 8 July 1940.

'At about 1545, as the watches were about to change over, I heard the bugler sound 'alarm to arms', which signalled that an air attack was imminent. The boy bugler Godliman never finished the call; he was killed instantly when the bomb hit the bridge. His bugle was later found over 100 feet away from the bridge'.

The Transmitting Station, deep down in the ship, was connected electronically to the Director Control Tower above the bridge. The connecting cables passed down through a steel trunk, which ran from the keel of the ship to the Tower and a piece of red hot metal from the bridge came down through the trunking hitting a petty officer on the shoulder.

Stoker Sam Dearie was in the engine room when the ship was hit and saw another stoker with blood on the back of his head. Sam thought that the stoker must be wounded but soon discovered that the blood had come onto him through the air intakes from the upper deck.

Marine Richard Harley was on the P2 High Angle gun, situated on the port side aft of the bridge, and he was also covered in blood from the bridge. Later an officer's cap badge was found near the gun.

Other ratings working close to the bridge were fortunate to escape serious injury. Roy Tremaine and Les Thomas were on the flag deck, just below the bridge. Roy remembered debris being blown onto the flag deck and that he was knocked over by the blast. Les recalled that the sound of the bomb was;

'like an express train rushing through'.

Cyril Pearson also had a very narrow escape at his action station, which was in the Cypher Room, adjoining the bridge. It was his practice to turn up five minutes early to relieve his opposite number on watch but when it was Cyril's turn to be relieved, the rating usually turned up at the exact time that the watches changed over. Cyril had spoken to his opposite number about this and he had agreed to change over five minutes before the watch ended. As Cyril made his way down the ladder from the bridge the bomb fell, killing the rating who, on that day, had turned up five minutes early to relieve him of his watch.

Immediately after the explosion, damage control and first aid parties were sent to the bridge. As a result of the direct hit from the Italian bomb, the ship could not be steered from the bridge. For a time she was uncontrolled until Lt Cdr Reginald P Tanner took charge from the aft steering position. Commander D'Aeth had been at this position, but just before the attack action stations had been stood down and he had made his way back to the bridge to report to the captain. Bill Howe was a member of the damage control party and witnessed the carnage on the bridge;

'Most of the men appeared to have been killed outright by the blast, although we did find one young sailor, lying in a pool of blood, who was still registering a faint pulse'.

The seriously injured sailor was Fred Farlow. He was carried down to the sick bay on a 'Neil Robertson' cane stretcher where senior doctor, Surgeon Lt Cdr R E Dingwell, examined him. Fred had sustained 138 separate wounds and he was later issued with a certificate to confirm his injuries. It read;

'AB Farlow, being on port side No 3 air lookout, on 8/7/40 and injured from splinters from a bomb during action against enemy aircraft. Sustained burns to the abdomen and face. Splinter wounds to both buttocks, back, right thigh and right leg involving severe lacerations of the tissues extending inward from the sights of insertion. He also sustained perforation to the tympanic membrane of both ears. Aged 19. Dated 9/7. Signed R P Tanner Lt Cdr RN. Captain R Formby RM and RG Dingwell Surgeon Lt Cdr RN'.

Fred recalled the incident;

'When it happened I was on the bridge and heard what sounded like a steam train going through a railway station at high speed. After the explosion a young lad from South Africa, Lloyd Nolan looked up and said to me that he was all right, then he died almost immediately'.

One of Fred's first visitors in the sick bay was Regulating Petty Officer Lofty May. May was noted for being a strict disciplinarian but nevertheless he brought Fred a packet of twenty Players cigarettes and a box of matches. Fred told him that he had never smoked a cigarette before but the RPO insisted that it would make him feel better. Unable to light the cigarette by himself May lit one up and put it in Fred's mouth. Fred was left strapped on the stretcher and sedated with morphine until *Gloucester* arrived back in Alexandria, a few days later. Over 50 years later Fred was still smoking.

Ossie Lang, the cook from south Wales, was in the sick bay suffering from yellow

Commander Reggie Tanner DSC. He took charge of the ship after the Captain and Commander were killed.

jaundice at the time of the bombing, but was quickly turned out of his bed to make room for the casualties and instructed to help with carrying the stretchers;

'Some of the bodies smelled of burned flesh and due to the motion of the ship, some kept sliding off the stretchers. I was very frightened at the time and remember that, as we were going back to the bridge, an officer stopped us and said that there was nothing else we could do for the people up there and that we should get below and take cover'.

Michael Noonan was also shocked by what he saw on the bridge and recalled that the bodies were carried off to the hangar where the sailmaker sewed them into canvas bags.

In the early evening Captain Garside and seventeen of his men were buried at sea. The service was short and Michael Noonan said that an officer called down to the padre;

'Please hurry up with the service, we are in dangerous waters'.

After committing their comrades to the sea, the ship's company returned to their duties in sombre mood.

Stoker Billy Grindell described it as an unbelievably sad time and Frank Teasdale recalled;

'We suddenly realised that this was the start of the war for us'.

Richard Harley had helped to clear the bridge and was sitting in the Royal Marines mess later that evening;

'The mood was heavy and nobody was speaking. I looked up and saw Harry Freeman. At the same time he looked up and saw me. We both burst into tears'.

The sad news later reached the families of those who had been killed. Peggy Garside, the Captain's wife, was living in Alnmouth, Northumberland with her son Roger and three year old daughter, Rosie;

'I was at a W.I. meeting when they brought the telegram to me. I knew at once what the news would be, even before I opened the telegram'.

The following obituary later appeared in *The Times*;

'A man of wholehearted charms and tireless energy, young for his rank he was regarded by his contemporaries as destined for the highest rank. "Freddie", as he was known to his friends, lived life with a happy nature and a great gift for friendship. Whatever his hand found to do he did with all his might whether at work or play. The death of a man of such ability with such a zest for life is a tragedy'.

Of the twenty-three officers and men on or near the bridge, only five survived the explosion.

Following this incident, *The London Gazette*, on 11 September 1940 announced the following awards for members of *Gloucester's* company;

Cdr R P Tanner	DSC
Lt Cdr J Brett	DSC
CPO J C E Horn	DSM
Lt Cdr A S Webb	Mentioned in dispatches
CPO(SBA) H T Hicks	Mentioned in dispatches[3]

Gloucester stayed with the fleet even though her bridge was out of use, but her crew was given little opportunity to reflect on the tragic events of the previous day. The Italian fleet, made up of two battleships, six cruisers and seven destroyers, had been sighted by reconnaissance planes heading towards Calabria. Cunningham saw the opportunity to engage them and by noon the following day, 9 July, Cunningham's fleet had closed on the Italians. *Gloucester* was ordered to join *Eagle* and give the aircraft carrier protection with her 6-inch guns. Soon after 1500, the Italian ships were sighted and both fleets opened fire. With shells falling all around them and the British cruisers outgunned, *Warspite*, with her 15-inch guns, engaged and hit the Italian battle-ship *Cesare*, at a range of thirteen miles.

Admiral Ricardi immediately ordered his fleet to turn about under cover of a smoke screen. The British cruisers and destroyers chased after them, causing considerable confusion. To add to the Italian's troubles, their own bombers attacked them as they headed back towards Italy. The Italian air force did however also attack the British Fleet with large bomber formations, from which *Eagle* and *Warspite* received special attention. *Gloucester* kept up a constant barrage to protect *Eagle*.

Admiral Cunningham described the attacks as most frightening and said that at times a ship would disappear behind great splashes and then emerge as though from a dark, thick wood of trees.

The Italian fleet returned to their home bases despite their superiority in firepower. Cunningham said that never again did the Italians stand up to the British battleships despite, on several occasions, having stronger forces.

Cunningham's fleet followed the Italian ships to within twenty-five miles of Calabria before turning south towards Malta. The allied convoys from Malta, which his force had originally set out to cover on their passage to Alexandria, were undamaged despite air attacks by the Italians. On 13 July all the ships sailed safely into Alexandria.

The battle of Calabria, though causing little significant damage to the Italian Fleet, did establish the Royal Navy as the dominant sea force in the Mediterranean. *Gloucester* won the first of her five battle honours during this action.

In Alexandria, dockyard workers immediately set about repairing *Gloucester's* damaged bridge. Meanwhile Reverend W T Bonsey, who had replaced Reverend Payton as ship's padre, held a memorial service for Captain Garside and the seventeen men who had fallen alongside him on 8 July. It was a sad ship's company, most of whom had commissioned the ship in Plymouth, as they remembered their respected captain and colleagues.

While the ship was in Alexandria, Royal Marine Captain Richard Formby seized a long awaited opportunity to write home;

> HMS *Gloucester. 15 July 1940*
>
> *Yesterday at lunch, there were three letters from you. I had Dick Kirby on-board ship, in fact the Wardroom was crowded. I had your letters in my hand, but was unable to read them. I was nearly demented, but reading them later made up for it. I do love your letters. They are so wonderful and make me want to get back to you. The letters go airmail via Mombassa, Durban, Cape Town and by sea from there.*
>
> *We have had a terrible time and I am the luckiest person alive. I cannot tell you much but we have been in action for the last fourteen days. There were bombs falling everywhere. We caught it pretty hot and had a hell of a lot of people killed. God alone knows why I wasn't killed. The Captain, the Commander, the First Lieut., the Navigator, the Sub Lieut., and thirteen others were all killed within yards of me. They were blown to bits. Behold, I was not touched. I damn well thought I was dead I can tell you. I remember thinking, 'What will happen to Pam and the children?' I thanked God we had been so happy.*
>
> *I never want to see sights like that again. The poor Captain was just alive when I got to him. I was deaf and nearly blind but quite OK. Seeing the Captain in such a state was awful. He was a marvellous man, everyone loved him. He was excessively kind to me. The Commander was blown to bits too, and Churchill, our First Lieutenant had only just been married a few weeks. How awful it all is.*
>
> *The ship is alright and we sail on. Don't worry, I can assure you that by the time you get this the Italian Navy will be finished. We dusted them down good and proper. Things will be much better now and we, I hope, safer ... draw your own conclusions. I promise I am quite alright again, not deaf, blind nor shocked, not that I was much anyway. We got into Port the day before yesterday. I was exhausted from lack of*

sleep. None, literally for a week, perhaps an hour or two at odd times. The reaction from the strain was terrific. Everyone went ashore and some of us played tennis in the afternoon, others played golf. I needed violent exercise badly. In the evening we went to the Union Club and met all the boys. There were dozens I knew and many you do too. They all sent you loving messages. Later that night I was given a cable from you to tell me that Mother had died. What dreadful news on top of everything else.

Poor old Mother, everyone took from her, but you were about the only person who gave her anything in return. Mother loved you a lot. If ever there was a good woman she was one. She was always seeing if she could help us in any way. I blame myself now that I let you take up the whole of me. I would hate anyone to take Jennifer, Richard or Cha Cha away from me. I suppose I would be happy if they found the right person. That means everything.

I feel very much older these days. The last months have been so awful. Leaving you nearly killed me with grief. Mother dying is an added blow. The terrible mess in France and Italy that we hear about, all my friends dying, it has shaken me a lot. Tell Daddy how ashamed I am to feel like this. Life will never be the same again.

Notes

1. *A Sailor's Odyssey* p.258.
2. Ibid.
3. All these men were killed on 22 May 1941, with the exception of Lt Cdr Webb who had been drafted from *Gloucester* prior to her sinking.

CHAPTER SIX

The Mediterranean: Convoys and Criticism

The war in the Mediterranean was intensifying and an increasing number of air raids were directed at Alexandria. The men on *Gloucester* were in no doubt by now that they could expect plenty of action in the months ahead and it was with this in mind that they met their new captain, Henry Aubrey Rowley.

Born in Bristol in 1896, Captain Rowley had an already distinguished career behind him. In his thirty years of service he had seen action at the Battle of Jutland and had served on a number of ships around the world. Rowley had been in command of HMS *Calypso* when she was the first ship in the Mediterranean to be torpedoed and now he was joining *Gloucester*, the first ship in the Mediterranean to be hit by aerial attack.

Lt Cdr Tanner, who had taken charge of *Gloucester* after the bombing, was promoted to Commander and stayed aboard to replace Commander D'Aeth. Lieutenant John Brett was promoted to Lieutenant Commander and became the First Lieutenant and Fred Otter, a native of Robin Hood's Bay, Yorkshire, who by then lived in the East Devon village of Otterton, replaced Chief Yeoman Frazer. Petty Officer Bob Wainwright, also a yeoman, was drafted from the cruiser *Liverpool*, a sister ship of *Gloucester*.

Midshipman Derek Napper joined the ship on 22 July, where he met Captain Rowley and soon came to admire and respect him. Derek described him as;

'A marvellous man who was imperturbable, very calm and during bombing raids on the ship, gave his orders quietly'.

When the repairs to the ship were completed in Alexandria, *Gloucester* sailed to Port Said where a new Director Control Tower was brought alongside by a floating crane and fitted by the Ordinance Officer and his team. Before long the Control Tower was painted and *Gloucester*, now fully operational, sailed back to Alexandria. Cunningham was still concerned about the inadequacies of Alexandria, both because of its poor repair facilities and the difficulty of protecting the fleet from the continuous problem of air raids.

Indicative of the dangers was a raid, described by Cunningham, when an enemy aircraft flew low over the breakwater and discharged two heavy objects which made a great splash close to *Gloucester*. It was later discovered that the objects were torpedoes and that they had embedded themselves in mud, without exploding. No damage was sustained but nevertheless it was a narrow escape for *Gloucester*. There were no barrage balloons over Alexandria and, following their attack, masts were erected on the breakwater and every ship in harbour was instructed to fly kites with explosive charges attached to them whenever there was sufficient wind.

On 4 August, *Gloucester* became the flagship of the 4th Cruiser Squadron (soon to become the 3rd Cruiser Squadron). As flagship, she now carried Rear Admiral E de F Renouf who stayed with the ship until April 1941, when his health failed and he was replaced.

During August the need to strengthen the Eastern Mediterranean fleet was again emphasised by Cunningham and a decision was taken to dispatch the battleship *Valiant*, the aircraft carrier *Illustrious* and two anti-aircraft cruisers *Coventry* and *Calcutta* from Gibraltar to Alexandria.

The objective of the operation, codenamed 'Hats', was to deliver the reinforcements east, to the Sicilian Narrows, where they would be met by a force from Alexandria. On 30 August, Force H sailed from Gibraltar with *Renown*, *Ark Royal*, *Sheffield* and seven destroyers as escorts for the principal ships bound for Alexandria.

In the eastern Mediterranean the 3rd Cruiser Squadron led by *Gloucester* and consisting of *Kent*, *Liverpool* and three destroyers was already at sea in the south Aegean when, also on 30 August, Cunningham's force of *Warspite*, *Malaya*, *Eagle*, *Orion*, HMAS *Sydney* and nine destroyers, left Alexandria. The following day *Gloucester* and her accompanying ships met up with Cunningham's force south-west of Cape Matapan and headed west to meet Force H from Gibraltar.

No air attacks were made on the warships but Italian bombers attacked a convoy of three

Captain Henry Aubrey Rowley, DSO RN.

Chief Yeoman Fred Otter. He replaced Jock Frazer (The photo was taken in 1936).

merchant ships bound for Malta, which had also sailed with Cunningham's force, and the SS *Cornwall* was hit. Despite her magazine blowing up, the steering and wireless being put out of action and being holed below the waterline, her captain steered the ship with the propellers and she safely reached Malta.

Strategically the Italian navy and air force were ideally placed to attack allied shipping sailing through the Mediterranean, particularly when the ships passed through the Sicilian Narrows. It was therefore perhaps surprising that despite the Italian fleet being sighted only ninety miles to the north of Cunningham's force, they disappeared overnight. The next day they were seen in the Gulf of Taranto, returning to port.

At 0900 on 1 September, *Gloucester* and the ships of the 3rd Cruiser Squadron met Force H. While the destroyers took it in turn to refuel in Malta and the battleship *Valiant* and cruisers *Calcutta* and *Coventry* discharged stores and munitions, Cunningham's force waited south of Malta, fending off bombing attacks.

As the force reunited to sail back to Alexandria two Italian planes shadowed them. To the delight of the Allied ships however, two Fulmars from *Illustrious* brought the Italian planes down, '*to the loud cheers of the ships' companies who had had just about as much as they could stand of being bombed without retaliation*'.[1]

On the return leg to Alexandria the fleet was split into two divisions, passing north and south of Crete. On 4 September, *Eagle* and *Illustrious* sent their aircraft to attack Italian airfields on the island of Rhodes, the bases from which enemy Italian aircraft had been attacking Alexandria. Scarpanto was also shelled by HMAS *Sydney* but despite losing four Swordfish aircraft from *Eagle*, and being attacked by Italian MTBs, two E boats were sunk by allied destroyers.

Operation 'Hats' had successfully delivered the reinforcements to Alexandria and the value of having radar on both *Valiant* and *Illustrious* was to be of particular importance in the fight against air attacks. Until then the Eastern Mediterranean Fleet had had to rely on visual sightings of aircraft but with the advantage of radar, enemy planes could be plotted when they were about fifty miles away. A further significant advantage was that the aircraft, which

Near misses from Italian bombers.

Illustrious carried, could give some cover to the fleet when at sea.

Gloucester, Liverpool and *Kent* together with the destroyers *Mohawk* and *Nubian* had been dispatched to the Gulf of Nauplia to meet a convoy of five steamers. Despite three air attacks on their voyage south they made it back safely to Alexandria on 5 September.

Naval historian, Captain S W Roskill, summed up the operation as a success since it not only strengthened the naval forces in the eastern Mediterranean but at the same time safely delivered much needed stores to Malta. He added that despite the Royal Navy attacking Italian air bases, the Italian fleet had shown disinclination, yet again, to engage the Royal Navy.

Following the entry of Italy into the war and the fall of France, troopship convoys bound for Egypt had been sent on the long voyage around the Cape of Good Hope and through the Suez Canal. Although Churchill welcomed the success of Operation 'Hats', he still regarded Cunningham as irritatingly over cautious in the use of the Mediterranean fleet. Churchill sent a message to Sir Dudley Pound, the First Sea Lord;

'It would have been quite easy to have transported the armoured brigade through the Malta channel and it would now be in Egypt instead of more than three weeks away'.

The Prime Minister's frustration with Cunningham was also apparent when he added;

'I am not impressed by the fact that Admiral Cunningham reiterates his views. Naturally they all stand together like doctors in a case which has gone wrong. The fact remains that an exaggerated fear of Italian

Walrus aircraft touching down close to Gloucester.

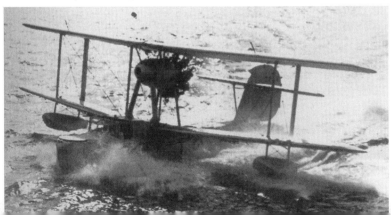

Gloucester's *Walrus being hoisted on board.*

aircraft has been allowed to hamper operations'.[2]

History has shown that Cunningham had every reason to be cautious about the use of his fleet with inadequate air cover and that with the scant repair facilities in Malta and Alexandria, he could ill afford to underestimate the Italian's air strength.

Gloucester was busy during the month of September on patrols in the eastern Mediterranean. During this time she used Alexandria to refuel and reammunition. On 11 September, she was again in port and Royal Marine Captain Formby wrote a letter to his sister;

HMS Gloucester. *11 Sept. 1940*

Dearest Kit

I have had three letters from you in the mail, and very welcome they were I can tell you. I love all the news, except the often recurring news that Colin and Derek are on leave. I got a day's leave a month ago and went up to Cairo.

At the moment I am doing the morning watch, and it is just dawn. It is very beautiful, and the French ships are sounding off their elaborate calls. They have a pretty slack time I think, but they are good chaps, and I feel sorry for them. Since we started paying them, they can go ashore a lot, and the married men have all gone home. It shows, women may win the war yet.

We have been up to several tricks but the Italian fleet won't fight. Possibly they can't risk a fight with all their troops in Africa. If they got a good hiding at sea then the boys in the desert would not be too pleased.

On 28 September, *Gloucester* and *Liverpool* left Alexandria on Operation MB5. Aboard the two ships were almost 2,000 troops from the Cheshire and Gloucestershire regiments who were to be taken to Malta as reinforcements. *Gloucester* and *Liverpool* were escorted, for the hazardous voyage, by *Warspite*, *Valiant* and *Illustrious*, the

Liverpool *under attack – Picture taken from* Gloucester.

cruisers *Orion*, *Sydney* and *York*, plus eleven destroyers.

On the following day Italian air reconnaissance located the force and, as a result, the Italian fleet put to sea with five battleships, seven heavy cruisers, four light cruisers and twenty-three destroyers, from their bases at Taranto and Messina. The Italian force was therefore considerably stronger than the British fleet and, during the afternoon of 29 September, twenty eight Savoia SM79s made many air attacks on the fleet, which escaped undamaged.

Illustrious had only nine Swordfish available and, with the Italians dominating the air, the British planes were unable to attack the Italian ships. By 30 September however, the convoy had reached Malta. *Gloucester* and *Liverpool* sailed into the Grand Harbour, whilst the escorting ships patrolled to the south of the island.

Derek Napper remembered the excitement he felt as *Gloucester* and *Liverpool* sailed into Malta.

'*The cliffs overlooking the harbour were crowded with people cheering the arrival of the two ships. The Maltese were magnificent: I remember the bravery they displayed despite persistent and intensive Italian air raids*'.

The following day *Gloucester* and *Liverpool* rejoined the fleet for the voyage back to Alexandria. The Italian fleet once again returned to their bases and on 3 October *Gloucester* arrived safely in Alexandria.

A few days earlier an important breakthrough had been made by allied intelligence when the Italian Alfa code, the equivalent of the German Enigma code, was decyphered. As a result of this, the Royal Navy now knew Italian naval deployments and the submarine *Gordar*, which had been sent to make human torpedo attack on Alexandria, was sunk on 30 September.

On 8 October, *Gloucester* was at sea again and had met up with convoy MB6, which consisted of four steamers, en route from Alexandria to Malta. The steamers were escorted by the a/a cruisers *Calcutta* and *Coventry* and four destroyers, whilst the fleet under Admiral Cunningham gave cover. In view of the heavy aerial attacks of the previous convoy, and the presence of the Italian navy, the four merchantmen were well protected but the enemy was not sighted which was probably due to the stormy weather at the time.

After escorting the merchantmen to Malta, the fleet set out on 11 October with a small convoy from Malta to Alexandria. En route they came across a flotilla of Italian destroyers; two enemy destroyers were sunk and another *Artigliere*, was damaged and later sunk by *York*. The sinking of *Artigliere*, and Cunningham's subsequent report to the Admiralty, led to further friction between him and their Lordships in London.

In his report, Cunningham gave credit to the Italians for their spirited efforts and also stated that rafts had been dropped for the crew of *Artigliere* and a signal sent to the Italian Admiralty, giving the position of the rafts (Cunningham had deemed it unwise to stop and pick up the survivors after *Havock* had been bombed whilst picking up 545 survivors from *Bartolomeo Colleoni*, which had been sunk on 19 July.) Cunningham's humane action however was not accepted in London and he was told;

> '*In view of feelings of public here, suffering under intensive and ruthless attacks, it might be well to exclude from future communiqués references to gallantry of the enemy or to compromising our fleet's position for benefit of the enemy*'.[3]

The fleet's position was, of course, well known to the Italians and the tenor of the message to Cunningham was yet another example of London misreading the situation in the Mediterranean.

As the fleet headed back to Alexandria, *Gloucester* and the other cruisers gave cover for *Eagle* and *Illustrious* while they flew off aircraft to bomb Italian airfields on the island of Leros. The planes dropped almost 100 bombs during the raid and hit the airfield's hangars and fuel tanks. The Italians, in retaliation, attacked the fleet with torpedo planes and *Liverpool*, *Gloucester's* sister ship, was hit in the bows, causing a fire and an explosion in the foremost magazine.

Air mechanic John Stevens remembered watching *Gloucester's* shipwrights helping to cut away the bows from the damaged *Liverpool*. *Orion* towed *Liverpool*, stern first, with *Gloucester* escorting them on the slow passage back to Alexandria. Despite moonlit skies, no attacks were made on the ships but the calm was not to last for long.

They arrived at Alexandria at 0100, in the midst of an air attack which was being carried out over the harbour. Low flying aircraft, thought to be carrying torpedoes, made their approaches as the ships sailed in through the Great Pass, the shallow entrance to the harbour. Cunningham described the scene;

> '*most spectacular ... firing a blind barrage on both sides with our guns flashing and the sparkle of bursting shells all over the horizon*'.[4]

Once again *Gloucester* had survived to fight another day.

On 28 October 1940, Italy presented an ultimatum to Greece: unless Italian troops were allowed to be stationed at certain strategic points on Greek territory, Italy would no longer regard Greece as neutral. This was clearly unacceptable to the Greek government and as a result the invasion of Greece began.

Suda Bay, strategically placed on the western end of Crete, could now be used as an important refuelling base for the fleet. Although quickly established as a significant base, Suda Bay still lacked proper defence against air attacks and its security was seriously impaired. In the weeks and months ahead, *Gloucester* came to experience the dangers of refuelling in Suda Bay as well as the increasingly hazardous operations involving transporting troops to, and later from, Greece.

On 28 October, the day the Italians invaded Greece, *Gloucester* was at sea with *Orion, Sydney* and *York*; the following day they met Admiral Cunningham's fleet south of Crete. Cunningham's objective was to cover the passage of a convoy of ships into Suda Bay on 31 October and to attack the Italian fleet should they appear. Italian reconnaissance planes did shadow the British fleet but no attacks were made on the ships, although Suda Bay and Canea received heavy raids.

November was to be an eventful month for the fleet's cruisers and destroyers as they covered convoys both to Suda Bay and to the Greek mainland port of Piraeus. Cunningham described it as a time in which;

'*They had no rest*'.[5]

Within a week of the invasion of Greece reinforcements were sent to Malta in five supply ships on convoy MW3. *Gloucester* sailed as one of the escort ships for the convoy, which despite air attacks reached Malta safely.

Immediately after the convoy reached Malta, *Gloucester* took part in Operation 'Coat'. This operation escorted the battleship *Barham*, and cruisers *Berwick* and *Glasgow*, together with four destroyers from Gibraltar, as additional forces to Cunningham's fleet. The welcome additions had been met in the treacherous Sicilian Narrows and despite a number of aerial attacks, the convoy passed safely on to Alexandria.

Notes

1. *A Sailor's Odyssey* p.272.
2. Gilbert, Martin, *Finest Hour*. Heineman. 1983. p.772.
3. *A Sailor's Odyssey* p.279.
4. Ibid p.279.
5. Ibid p.283.

CHAPTER SEVEN

Operations and Honours: The Last Christmas

Gloucester was immediately prepared for her next deployment which was to accompany *Illustrious*, together with the cruisers, *Berwick*, *Glasgow* and *York*, plus four destroyers, for an aerial attack on the Italian fleet which was lying in the harbour at Taranto. The attack, code-named Operation 'Judgement', had long been the idea of Rear Admiral A L St G Lyster. He was responsible for the Fleet Air Arm and had spoken to Admiral Cunningham earlier in the year about the possibility of such an attack. Despite Sir Dudley Pound's antipathy towards the idea, Cunningham gave it his full backing and Lyster went ahead with his plans and training of his air crews.

An accurate disposition of Italian ships in the harbour was obtained with the assistance of Royal Air Force reconnaissance aircraft operating from Malta. Reconnaissance photographs showed that five battleships were in Taranto, with a sixth entering the harbour. A number of cruisers and destroyers were also seen in the harbour. Cunningham remarked;

'So all the pheasants had gone home to roost'.[1]

It was no coincidence that the Italian fleet was in Taranto as their naval chief of staff, Don Amico Cavagnari, had ordered that whenever possible confrontation with the Royal Navy was to be avoided.

Having the bulk of the Italian fleet concentrated in one place, the Fleet Air Arm was now presented with an excellent opportunity to mount a raid. The operation required not only meticulous planning but also incredible courage from the pilots, and an element of luck. The scene was now set for one of the most daring operations of the war.

Operation 'Judgement' was originally planned to take place on 21 October, an apposite date since it was the anniversary of Nelson's great victory at Trafalgar. However, a fire in the hangar on *Illustrious* had destroyed two Swordfish aircraft and damaged a number of others. The date for the operation was therefore re-arranged to 11 November, when there would be a full moon.

The Swordfish aircraft carried by *Illustrious* were outdated, even in 1940; they were fabric covered biplanes with open cockpits and could only fly at 139 mph flat out. Fully laden, this speed was reduced to 100 mph. The good points of the Swordfish however were that they were easy to fly and maintain and they could operate when seas were rough and the aircraft carrier was heaving in the water.

Their lack of speed was a significant problem and determined that Operation 'Judgement' would have to take place at night, which added to the difficulties of navigation for the pilots. Furthermore, reconnaissance photographs had revealed that the harbour at Taranto was protected by barrage balloons, making low flying particularly hazardous. A further difficulty was that anti-torpedo nets protected the Italian ships.

In order to overcome these difficulties, it was decided that the first planes over Taranto would drop flares to illuminate the barrage balloons' hawsers, enabling the torpedo carrying aircraft to fly low over the harbour and release their torpedoes. The pilots faced enormous odds; they knew they would be flying slow planes, at low altitude, between barrage balloon hawsers and into a hail of gunfire from ships and anti-aircraft batteries surrounding the harbour.[2]

Gloucester, Berwick, York, Glasgow and the destroyers were detailed to screen *Illustrious* from attacks by Italian aircraft. 21 Swordfish aircraft flying in two waves carried out the raid and at 2035 Lieutenant Commander K Williamson led the first wave of 12 Swordfish, flying off *Illustrious*.

Soon after take-off, one of the Swordfish developed engine trouble and had to return to ship. Another plane became detached from the flight and arrived over Taranto twenty minutes ahead of the main group and in doing so alerted the Italian defences. By the time Lt Cdr Williamson arrived with the remaining 10 Swordfish, the Italians were waiting for them.

Williamson was the first to fly over the harbour, which was illuminated by parachute flares. Diving from 7,000 feet to 700 feet, he levelled out, then going down to sea level, flew between the barrage balloon hawsers and over the breakwater across the harbour.

The battleship *Conte di Cavour* was ahead of Williamson as he flew through a hail of fire before releasing his torpedo and ascending over the battleship's superstructure. The intensive barrage of fire, put up by the Italian ships and shore batteries, was too much and Williamson's Swordfish was hit and crashed into the sea. Other Swordfish then attacked. The battleship *Duilo* was hit and four of the six attacking aircraft managed to make direct hits on Italian ships, despite overwhelming gunfire at close range. The remaining Swordfish of Williamson's flight, each with eight 60-pound bombs, successfully dropped them on shore depots and on ships in the inner harbour.

Ten more Swordfish, under the command of Lt Cdr J W Hale, took off for Taranto an hour after Williamson's aircraft had left *Illustrious*. They could see the fires and a barrage of gunfire directed towards them as they approached the harbour. Hale was the first to attack. He faced the intensity of battleship guns at point blank range as he released his torpedo and flew over the *Littono* and away to safety. Despite the firepower of the Italian defences only one plane of the second wave was hit; the pilot and his observer perished. The surviving Swordfish aircraft made it back to *Illustrious* despite being riddled with holes from the enemy attacks.

The Fleet Air Arm had lost two aircraft in the operation but the bravery of the pilots and observers had brought about the sinking

The devestation in Taranto after the Fleet Air Arm raid.

or serious damaging of three Italian battleships, *Littono, Duilo* and *Conte di Cavour*, two cruisers and a number of destroyers. Furthermore, damage had been caused to oil tanks and shore installations and the effect of the raid was so devastating that the Italian High Command ordered their surviving ships to sail north to Naples.

Derek Napper watched from *Gloucester* as the Swordfish took off. The entry recorded in his Midshipman's Journal on 11 November 1940 reads;

> *'When it grew dark and the moon came out,* Illustrious *flew off her aircraft on Operation 'Judgement'. There were 22 in all, 12 carrying heavy bombs and 10 carrying torpedoes. At 2230,* Valiant *picked up an aircraft on RDF and broke W/T silence.* Glasgow *and* Berwick *set up a pom-pom barrage. Soon the aircraft was identified as one of those that had left* Illustrious *but had developed engine trouble and couldn't get to Taranto. By 0130, the first of the attacking aircraft had returned and by 0300 the last had returned to the carrier. Rear Admiral Lyster made a signal that the raid had been a great success with one Vittorio class battleship hit and left burning, two Cavour class battleships hit many times and fires started by bombs. Later the Italians admitted the loss of one battleship. Two torpedo-carrying aircraft failed to return'.*

Williamson and his observer, who were shot down on the first wave survived and were taken prisoners by the Italians. *Glasgow* and *Berwick* fired in error at the Swordfish that had been forced to return because of engine problems. With radar in its infancy such attacks were not unknown and Derek Napper recalled that on another occasion, *Gloucester* fired on some Blenheim aircraft by mistake.

The raid on Taranto was heralded as a great success and Cunningham described it as;

> *'Admirably planned and most gallantly executed in the face of intense anti-aircraft fire...the zeal and enthusiasm with which these deliberate and accurate attacks were carried out, in comparatively slow aircraft, in the face of intense fire cannot sufficiently be praised'.*[3]

The success of the raid on Taranto was internationally acknowledged, especially by the Japanese Military authorities who used this raid as their inspiration for the subsequent attack on Pearl Harbor.

The effect of Operation 'Judgement' on the strategy of naval operations in the Mediterranean was such that the Italian fleet, now operating further north from Naples, needed to spend more time at sea if they were to be effective against the Royal Navy. Now they could easily be observed by reconnaissance aircraft operating from Malta, Cunningham's assessment of the value of air support was vindicated and in the months ahead the control of the seas would be dictated from the air. On 14 November, fighters from *Illustrious* shot down three Italian reconnaissance planes as *Gloucester* and the rest of the fleet returned to Alexandria.

Back in Britain, Churchill, badly in need of some good news to compensate for the air raids on British cities, told the House of Commons of the raid on Taranto and described it as;

'*this glorious episode*'.[4]

The Prime Minister's news was cheered loudly by the MPs in the house.

Following Operation 'Judgement', Alexandria received an increasing number of raids from Italian aircraft, possibly in retaliation for the Taranto raid. With poor anti-aircraft defences covering Alexandria, the Italian air force flew over the city virtually unmolested whilst the fleet was at sea.

The air raids placed even more strain on the already weary ships' companies. Not only were the repair facilities being damaged but the ships' crews, who had little rest whilst at sea, were denied rest ashore since they were often at action stations whilst in harbour. There was to be no respite for the men in the months ahead.

Within two days of returning from Operation 'Judgement', *Gloucester* was at sea again, bound for Piraeus, the port of Athens, in company with the cruisers *York*, *Ajax*, *Orion* and *Sydney*. Around 4,000 troops and supplies of stores were taken to the port following the escalation of the Italian offensive against Greece. It was the first of many such convoys carrying troops to Greece and the already cramped conditions on the messdecks made it impossible for the sailors to find space to rest between watches.

Gloucester carried men of the Leicestershire Regiment and Fred Brisley recalled the soldiers playing cards on the upper deck;

'*They put on brave faces but when the air attacks came they ran for cover. After the squaddies left the ship there was always a lot of mess to clear up, especially as many of them were seasick*'.

Although the Taranto raid had seriously eroded the effectiveness of the Italian navy, the Italian air force was still operating from its bases in the Dodecanese islands and in particular on Rhodes. The convoys to Piraeus were therefore subject to frequent air attacks by Italian bombers.

The convoy to Piraeus did however give the *Gloucester* men an opportunity for a quick run ashore. Michael Noonan had a few beers in the 'Kit Kat' bar, went to see the Parthenon and bought souvenirs to take home to Ireland.

By 20 November, *Gloucester*, having disembarked the troops at Piraeus, had returned to Alexandria. Royal Marine Albert Tubby took shore leave in Alexandria but was in trouble when he returned to the ship after he had met up with a couple of soldiers. The three men had had a good drink and at the end of the evening, Tubby invited his new pals back on-board *Gloucester*. The trio was fast asleep when the ship was ordered to sea and the next morning Tubby was taken before Commander Tanner, as a defaulter. He complained to the Commander that there had recently been 1200 soldiers on the ship when it sailed to Greece and nobody had said a word about that. Needless to say Commander Tanner was singularly unimpressed with Tubby's line of defence. Bandsman Ken Macdonald had fond memories of Marine Albert Tubby;

'He was one of the best known and most popular characters on the lower deck. A rotund, 'Three Badge' Marine with twinkling eyes and a remarkable sense of humour, he was renowned throughout the ship for his droll and witty attitude.'

Three days after *Gloucester* returned to Alexandria she was ordered to sea again as part of Force E, to escort convoy MW4 to Malta. The cruisers *York* and *Glasgow* accompanied *Gloucester*, and as the slow moving convoy headed due west they knew full well what to expect from the Italian aircraft. As they approached Malta, Force H from Gibraltar was escorting a convoy east, to Malta. Italian battleships, cruisers and destroyers were also at sea in an attempt to intercept Force H.

As the two forces closed, south of Cape Spartivento, *Gloucester* was ordered to leave Force E and join the battleship *Ramillies* and a force heading north-west through the Sicilian Narrows. Here they would strengthen Force H against the anticipated Italian attack.

Ken Macdonald with his wife.

The Italians once again showed a disinclination to fight, despite their faster ships, and turned about and made off for Sardinia at full speed. Force H with its convoy of three merchant ships and four corvettes continued on to Malta unscathed but the encounter did have further repercussions.

A Board of Enquiry was set up to examine the wisdom of Force H having placed the safety of the convoy first rather than chasing and attacking the Italian fleet. Admiral Cunningham was in no doubt that this was yet another example of those in power in Britain failing to understand the complexities which the Royal Navy faced whilst operating in the confined waters of the Mediterranean.

Mussolini was also unhappy with his forces and replaced his Chief of the Naval Staff, Admiral Cavagnari, with Admiral Riccardi.

On 3 December *Gloucester*, now safely returned east from Malta, was refuelling in Suda Bay alongside the cruiser *Glasgow*. The monitor HMS *Terror* was based in the bay as the mainstay of the a/a defences and a boom defence had been constructed across the bay to protect ships against submarine attack. However, Suda Bay still lacked a suitable net defence against torpedo attacks and as a result of this, low flying Italian aircraft hit *Glasgow*.

Derek Napper recorded the attack in his Midshipman's journal;

'At about 1540 a red flag was hoisted by ships in the bay indicating an air raid and very shortly afterwards two Italian aircraft appeared over the hill on our starboard side. Pom-poms and 4-inch guns opened fire and short barrage was ordered on the 4-inch guns. But at the critical moment, as the cutter was being hoisted inboard, the aircraft dropped two torpedoes and dived over the low-lying hills on the opposite side of the harbour. One torpedo struck Glasgow *on the starboard side forward of the cable locker at about 14 bulkhead and the other in Y flat aft. The so-called netting across the harbour had no effect in stopping the torpedoes. The next hour following the explosions I was standing by with a fire-fighting party but the need for our help never arose. The only apparent damage was a crinkling of the stern. Two people were killed, or died of their injuries and about ten were wounded. We were ordered to sea at 2030'.*

Although the young midshipman's journal recorded that *Glasgow* did not appear to be badly damaged, she could in fact only make sixteen knots on the subsequent journey to Alexandria, accompanied by *Gloucester*. Admiral Cunningham later wrote that *Glasgow* was badly damaged and after being temporarily repaired, she left the station for more permanent repairs.

Royal Marine Jan Gardiner was at his action station, on the 4-inch guns on the starboard side, when the attack took place;

'I saw two Italian planes coming over the headland and the cutter, which was in the process of being hoisted aboard, was left dangling over the side. The .5 machine guns weren't manned, so being a machine gunner I got to the gun and opened fire. I can see it to this day as they tried to torpedo us. Both aircraft disappeared but two torpedoes hit Glasgow. They were so close to us as they flew over that I sprayed them with machine gun fire and got one of them'.

Gloucester had been moored next to *Glasgow* throughout the attack and yet remarkably, she had escaped undamaged.

After escorting *Glasgow* back to Alexandria, *Gloucester* was back in action a few days later off the coast of North Africa. On 8 December, General O'Connor launched an assault on the Italian position in Libya, following three months of allied forces being built up. In support of the allied army offensive, Cunningham organised the Naval forces to carry supplies for the land forces and to shell enemy positions ashore.

The Naval force sent to assist the army was made up of four groups, *Gloucester* being in Force D. With aircraft acting as reconnaissance for the ship's guns, *Gloucester* formed part of the considerable firepower from the sea which shelled enemy positions at Halfayan and Sollum, on the Libyan coast. The action on land was a great success and the allies took Sidi Birani. On 16 December, Sollum and Fort Capuzzo were also captured. *Gloucester* returned to Alexandria to refuel but was soon in action again.

At 0100 on 16 December, in a force made up of the battleships *Valiant* and *Warspite*, the carrier *Illustrious*, cruiser *York* and eleven destroyers, *Gloucester* put to sea. The fleet sailed into the Aegean and aircraft from *Illustrious* carried out attacks on Italian airfields on the islands of Rhodes and Stampalia. Later that day the rest of the fleet put into Suda Bay to refuel, while *Gloucester* and *York* were detached to make a sweep for Italian supply convoys.

Cunningham's intention was to take his force to Albania to shell the port of Valona, the main supply depot for the Italian army in Albania. On 18 December the weather was particularly bad with heavy rain and high winds and, as aircraft from *Illustrious* could not fly, the carrier was left behind at Suda Bay. The rest of the Commander in Chief's force sailed for Albania and later that day, *Gloucester* and *York* rejoined them.

Derek Napper's journal records;

'18/12/40. Met Vice Admiral Light Forces and C in C and steamed up the west coast to bombard Valona being, with Duratzo, Italy's chief port on Albania. The weather made it doubtful that the operation could

be carried out but by 1600, when the island of Zante was on our
starboard beam, conditions had improved. It was still bitterly cold and
the mountains of Zante were snow capped'.

Derek was not the only one feeling the cold: his Commander in
Chief, Admiral Cunningham, was wearing a balaclava which his
wife had knitted for him. The contrast could not have been more
extreme for the men of *Gloucester*, who exactly twelve months
earlier had been wined and dined in the warm sun at Durban.

The battleships *Warspite* and *Valiant* who, with their 15-inch guns,
fired 100 rounds on the Italian base led the shelling of Valona. By
the time the Italian defences had organised themselves the whole
fleet was sailing away south. It was yet another example of the
dominance of the Royal Navy who, having carried out a successful
operation on the Albanian coast, were less than fifty miles from the
Italian coastline.

Cunningham sailed back to Malta and *Warspite* entered the
Grand Harbour to loud cheering from the Maltese people, who
were standing on the barracas overlooking the harbour.
Meanwhile, *Gloucester* and *York*, after fuelling at Suda Bay resumed
their sweep for Italian convoys in the Aegean Sea.

Christmas Day 1940 was spent at sea and Derek Napper
remembered that everyone did their best to enjoy the day, despite
the limited facilities, and recalled that on board *Gloucester*, the day
was renamed 'Gloucesmas Day'.

Chief ERA Charles Jope sent what was to be his last Christmas
card to his family in England. The card shows *Gloucester* at anchor,
with the words, 'Hearty greetings for Christmas and every good
wish for the New Year'. On the card he wrote, 'From Char to Mum
and Eve with love'.

Telegraphist Richard Garner managed to keep a rare copy of a
special ship's newspaper which was produced for that Christmas,
the 'Gloucester Sunday Express'. It displays the ship's crest above
a sketch of the ship and the message, 'A Happy Xmas', is
surrounded by holly and mistletoe. The newspaper included
statistics of *Gloucester's* travels and records that, on 22 December

The last christmas card sent home by ERA Charles Jope.

1940, the ship had completed 100,000 miles at sea since the beginning of the war and a total of 118,000 miles since she was commissioned.

On 28 December, *Gloucester* put into Piraeus before sailing back to Alexandria. 1940 had been an eventful year in which *Gloucester* had sailed from the warmth, and relative peace and freedom of the Indian Ocean into the dangerously confined waters of the Mediterranean. The men had seen their Captain, Commander and several other comrades killed when the ship had been the first of the fleet to be hit by Italian aircraft. The bombardment of Italian positions in North Africa; convoys to Malta and Piraeus; the

ERA Charles Jope.

battle of Calabria; the raid on Taranto and the shelling of Rhodes and other Dodecanese bases used by the Italian air force, as well as the recent attack or the coast of Albania, had hardened the ship's company into an experienced force. *Gloucester* and her ship's company had become a valuable asset to Cunningham's fleet. They had come through numerous attacks from Italian bombers, both at sea and in Alexandria, and had witnessed ships around them being

Signalman Roy Tremaine (third from left) with friends in Athens.

hit. The men, from the Captain to the youngest boy seaman, were fully aware that the Mediterranean was a dangerous theatre of war. Yet their spirit remained high as they entered 1941 and, to their delight, Surgeon Lieutenant Commander R G Dingwell was awarded the OBE in the New Year Honour List.

Notes
1. *A Sailor's Odyssey* p.285.
2. There were 21 4-inch guns, plus 200 smaller ones including pom-poms around the harbour. (Pearce, Frank, *Sea War*, Robert Hale 1990 p.63.
3. *A Sailor's Odyssey* p.286.
4. Hansard 13.11.40 Col.1713.

CHAPTER EIGHT

Bombarding Bardia: Incredible Bravery

On 2 January 1941, *Gloucester* led the 3rd Cruiser Squadron from Alexandria, accompanied by the battleships *Warspite*, *Barham* and *Valiant*, between a screen of destroyers. The battle fleet was joined at sea by *Illustrious* and at 0800 the next day the force had reached a position from which they could bombard Bardia, in North Africa.

The enemy garrison at Bardia, which was particularly well fortified, had proved a stumbling block for the allied army's advance and Cunningham agreed to attack the stronghold from the sea.

The accuracy of the shelling was crucial since the garrison was surrounded on three sides by the allied army. Fighter aircraft from *Illustrious* protected the fleet, whilst reconnaissance planes, catapulted from *Gloucester* and the other cruisers, relayed the fall of shot back to the fleet. The intense firepower of the fleet lasted from 0810 to 0855 and as a result the Australians captured Bardia and took 25,000 Italian prisoners. With the port of Bardia now reopened, the army was able to receive stores and ammunition from the sea to reinforce their stronghold.

The next day, *Gloucester* was back in Alexandria preparing to take part in a complicated operation, codenamed 'Excess'. The majority of the fleet at Alexandria was to cover a convoy of merchant ships sailing to Malta, with munitions. Force H from Gibraltar had the responsibility of escorting a convoy of supplies for the Greek Army, east as far as the Sicilian Narrows where it would be met by the fleet coming from Alexandria. While these convoys were in transit, Cunningham ordered eight empty ships to be sent from Malta to Alexandria.

Gloucester, Southampton and the destroyers, *Ilex* and *Janus* (Force B), under the command of Rear Admiral E de F Renouf aboard *Gloucester*, left Alexandria on 6 January ahead of the main fleet, to carry troops to Malta. Once the troops were landed, the orders for *Gloucester* were to take up escort duties for the convoy coming from Gibraltar.

The complexity of the timings meant that the two fleets had to meet in the Sicilian Narrows for the handover of escort duties for the eastbound convoys. All went well for the first two days and, on 8 January, after safely landing the troops at Malta, *Gloucester*, *Southampton* and the destroyers sailed on to meet the oncoming convoy.

Cunningham later wrote of *Gloucester's* dangerous voyage through the Sicilian Narrows;

'They were lucky to get through safely. During their passage west, in bright moonlight, they were sighted and challenged by a signal Station (Italian) in Pantellaria'.[1]

Leading signalman Les Thomas was on watch at the time and remembered the intense activity on the bridge;

'Rear Admiral Renouf became excited and wanted the signal from the enemy acknowledged. Captain Rowley told him that if we acknowledged the signal the Italians would realise that we were a British ship and they would open fire on us. The Admiral insisted that we acknowledge the signal. The Captain didn't answer him, but remained as cool as a cacumber and ordered the ship to be turned at 90 degrees. The agitated Rear Admiral shouted at the Captain and asked him what he was doing. Captain Rowley replied, in a quiet voice, "Putting as much distance as we can between us and the enemy, Sir." Renouf said nothing'.

This altercation between Captain Rowley and Rear Admiral Renouf was perhaps an early indication of the extreme strain, which eventually led to Renouf being removed from his command.

After altering course, *Gloucester* and *Southampton* both cut mines with their paravanes. The mines exploded close to the ships but fortunately they caused no damage. The rest of Force H came under heavy attacks from Italian aircraft and from the torpedo boats *Circe* and *Vega*, the latter being sunk by *Bonaventure* and *Hereward*. An Italian submarine, *Settimo*, was also in the vicinity but missed the British ships with a salvo of torpedoes.

The destroyer *Gallant* however was not so fortunate when a mine blew off her bows and she had to be towed back to Malta by the destroyer *Mohawk*. *Gloucester*, *Southampton* and *Bonaventure* escorted her safely into harbour. Gallant reached Malta on 10

Royal Marine R 'Champ' Whitely, killed 11-1-41.

January 1941, the day on which the Luftwaffe made their debut in the Mediterranean.

JU87s, the German Stuka dive-bomber planes, under the command of Captain Hoggel and Major Enneccerus, together with JU88s, the German bomber planes, and Italian bombers, attacked the fleet. Six of their bombs hit *Illustrious* and the battleship *Warspite* was also hit. The terrifying dive bombing of the Stukas was a form of attack that the fleet had never seen before but it was to become a feature of life at sea in the months ahead.

Admiral Cunningham recorded that he was too intrigued by this new form of bombing to be frightened: he admired the skill of the pilots as they circled above the fleet and then peeled off to dive at the ships before releasing their bombs at point blank range. He also recorded that the Stukas, which attacked *Illustrious*, were so low that they flew along the flight deck, below the level of the ship's funnel.

The skill of the German pilots, which had been developed during the Spanish Civil War and in the German advance across Europe, was now directed at the ships of the Mediterranean fleet. Cunningham's demands for more air cover for the allied ships, which he had repeatedly made to the First Sea Lord, was now further vindicated.

Illustrious was badly damaged and escorted back to Malta but then attacked by another twenty-five dive-bombers on the journey. She eventually slid into the Grand Harbour where she remained until 23 January, constantly under attack from enemy aircraft who caused further damage. Dockyard workers carried out sufficient repairs to eventually get the carrier away to Alexandria.

Royal Marine W Burgoyne, killed 11-1-41.

At 0500 on 11 January, *Gloucester* and *Southampton*, having escorted *Gallant* into harbour, steamed out to join the rest of the fleet. By early afternoon both ships were nearing the fleet, which by now was heading east away from Malta. During the afternoon the two cruisers came under attack from twelve JU87s under the command of Major Enneccerus. A bomb hit *Gloucester* on the roof of the Director Tower, incredibly it did not explode, despite penetrating through five decks.

In the same attack however, a large bomb exploded so close to the starboard side that a hole was blown through the Royal Marine's forward mess deck. The attack had been delivered so quickly that Captain Rowley, still without the advantage of radar, did not have time to call the ship's company to action stations.

The off duty marines were resting in their mess and received the full blast of the bomb. Eight Royal Marines and a leading seaman were killed by the blast and a further fourteen men were injured. The messdeck was in a state of devastation.

Ernie Evans, who had watched the ship being launched when he was still a schoolboy, had recently joined *Gloucester* as a young Royal Marine. When the ship was hit, he had just finished washing his clothes;

> 'At about 1530 I was going to get some tea, after doing my dhobying,[2] when I heard an explosion from the messdeck. The bosun's mate, who usually spoke with authority, called out, in a small shaky voice, "alarm to arms, alarm to arms". Then I saw 'Sticks' O'Leary[3] disappear in front of my eyes when a bomb hit him. That bomb went down through the decks and landed on the deckhead of the galley without exploding'.

Volunteers were called for to go to the marine's mess deck, where Ernie witnessed the carnage;

> 'Most of them had been killed by shrapnel. Frank Wills was badly injured in the back and about eight bodies were floating around in water and a number of men were injured. The water was pumped out and we filled the hole with hammocks before the shipwrights made repairs. The bodies were got out and put into the sick bay before their burial at sea. I was

Royal Marine Ernie Evans. He joined the ship in January 1941 and had seen her launched in 1937 when he was a schoolboy.

only eighteen years old at the time and I'd never really thought about being killed. It shook me to see men I knew lying dead or injured.'
Derek Napper was also eighteen years old at the time and recorded in his midshipman's journal;
'11/1/41. Everyone thought we had left the danger zone. Several mines were sighted and the .5s were firing intermittently throughout the day. At about 1520, I went to have a wash before tea. The machine guns started firing and I imagined another mine was being dealt with, till the pom-poms opened fire. I rushed through the mess decks to get to the air defence position, only to find the marine's mess full of smoke and with blood all over the deck. The First Lieutenant told me to go to the sick bay but there was an enormous crowd of people outside and I saw that stretchers were being fetched so I carried on to the air defence position. When I arrived there the high level bombers were active, although the dive bombers had disappeared. We continued firing for some time, both with pom-pom and 4-inch, and I fancied they would never leave us alone. One bomb struck the Director Tower and passed through, close to the range taker, wounding him in the head. It killed a marine drummer inside the Director support and finished up in the Met office, from where it was thrown over the side by some officers.'
An act of incredible bravery was undertaken by young NAAFI assistant, William Black, who sat on the 500lb bomb to prevent it from rolling around the deck until it could be thrown overboard.[4]
Marine, Richard Harley helped to take men to the sick bay;
'I saw two of my friends in there, unconscious and dying. I wanted to stay with them but I made myself go out. I felt cold-blooded but I knew I couldn't afford to get too upset as that was what we were trained to be like. All the same, I never got used to losing friends, just like I never got used to the smell of death which used to pervade the ship at such times.'
The following men lost their lives in this action;

Ldg Sea	J Phelan
Marine Cpl	H Walker
Marine	M O'Leary
"	W Burgoyne
"	R Whitely
"	E Green
"	A Lewis
"	R Basset-Burr
"	A Jesson.

Following the action on 11 January 1941, these awards were subsequently announced;

Lt E O Daniel	DSC
L/Seaman R S Smith	DSM
Cdr (Eng) S St G Griffin	Mentioned in despatches
Lt Cdr J Brett	Mentioned in despatches
Lt J E B Mattei	Mentioned in despatches
NAAFI Asst W Black	Mentioned in despatches

During the raid on *Gloucester*, *Southampton* was hit in the wardroom and the Petty Officer's mess. The ship was soon ablaze from stem to stern with men trapped below decks. *Gloucester*, assisted by the destroyer *Diamond*, came to the rescue of the crew of *Southampton*, many of whom were badly burnt. By 1900 all hope was given up of saving *Southampton* and she was sunk. *Gloucester* and *Diamond* picked up survivors and took them back to Alexandria.

Richard Garner never forgot the awful scenes he witnessed;

'*It was one of my worst experiences in the Royal Navy. I shall never, never forget seeing* Southampton, *a mass of flames. We were trying to get alongside her to take off survivors when I heard the screams of men trapped down below, banging on the ship's hull.*'

The injured men were taken aboard *Gloucester* and many were laid on the upper deck. Maurice Conquest, a telegraphist who had joined the navy as an 'HO' rating, said;

'*I was very distressed by the sight of so many men lying around with their faces blackened from the horrendous burns which they had sustained.*'

A week later, Cunningham wrote a private letter to Sir Dudley Pound, the First Sea Lord. In this he expressed his concerns about the vulnerability of *Southampton* class cruisers, of which *Gloucester* was one;

'*18/1/41. I don't like these 'Southampton'class. They are fine ships but that great hangar structure seems to provide a good point of aim, they are always being hit there.*'[5]

Notes

1. *A Sailor's Odyssey* p.301.
2. 'dhobi' is a term for washing clothes.
3. "Sticks" O'Leary", nicknamed because he was a marine drummer. He was the nephew of Leading Seaman Maurice O'Leary and had specially asked to be drafted to *Gloucester* to be on the same ship as his uncle. Maurice forever felt guilty that his nephew had been killed because of joining his ship. Maurice himself survived the sinking on 22 May 1941.
4. NAAFI Asst. William Black lost his life in the sinking on 22 May 1941.
5. ref. B.Lib MSS 52561.

CHAPTER NINE

Fiasco and Breakdown: Incredible Stress

G *loucester* sailed back to Alexandria where the injured men were put ashore before the ship was sent to Port Said for repairs. *Illustrious* arrived later at Port Said, and after being further repaired she sailed to the United States for more extensive repairs. A decision was made at Port Said to transfer the invaluable radar system from *Illustrious* to *Gloucester*. Leading seaman Douglas Hall, from Edinburgh, a radar technician, was also transferred from the aircraft carrier to *Gloucester* where his substantial experience of operating the radar system was required.

When *Illustrious* sailed for America, the fleet was left without an aircraft carrier. *Eagle* had been deployed to the Indian Ocean and South Atlantic and although *Formidable* had been deployed as a replacement, she had been unable to get through the Suez Canal, which had been mined by German aircraft.

Gloucester now fitted with radar and being less than two years old, was an even more valuable asset to Cunningham's fleet. Captain Rowley and the ship's company could therefore expect to continue to play an important operational role with little respite from the Luftwaffe in the months ahead.

Alexandria was now equipped with barrage balloons and provided better protection for the fleet. Shore leave for the men became more tolerable but at sea they had insufficient rest. When divided into watches the most sleep they could get was three and a half hours but when at action stations, which they were for much of the time, the men got no sleep.

Leading Signalman Roy Tremaine recalled that men slept wherever they could find a space, such as on or under the mess tables. They snatched sleep as often as possible, always in their clothes. Telegraphist Richard Garner recalled that they often tried to sleep around ladders leading to the upper deck so that they could make a quick getaway if the ship was hit.

Apart from a lack of sleep at sea, the men were also deprived of adequate meals when at action stations. Ossie Lang and the rest of the cooks had to be at their own action stations and so were unable to prepare meals for the men. The only sustenance the men received at such times was soup or a corned beef sandwich and a cup of 'Ki'; a chocolate drink made with condensed milk and a favourite with sailors throughout the fleet. The lack of sleep and food was not restricted to the lower decks, even Admiral Cunningham said that at sea he never undressed when snatching a few hours sleep.

When the ship put into Alexandria, the main thing the men wanted to do was to eat, drink and sleep before they put to sea again. For Captain Rowley however, there was little time for relaxation, even when the ship was in harbour. He had to make reports and run checks to ensure that the ship was fully ready for her next deployment.

Ernie Evans recalled being on sentry duty by the ship's keyboard which was located outside the captain's cabin;

'As a keyboard sentry I was often on duty outside the captain's cabin and used to have to take the book to him to be signed. In harbour I saw him a lot but when we were at sea he stayed on the bridge. When we were in harbour he left the cabin door open and on a number of occasions I saw him asleep with his head on the desk'.

It was under such arduous conditions that the training which the men had been subjected to earlier, either as ratings at HMS *Ganges* or as officers at Dartmouth Naval College, undoubtedly stood them

in good stead. The ship's company had been welded together, first by Captain Garside, and then by Captain Rowley. It was now that the efficiency and esprit de corps of the Royal Navy would prove invaluable.

Gloucester rejoined the fleet at Suda Bay to carry out convoy defence work and attacks on Italian supplies to Libya. Such operations

Midshipman Derek Napper. He later rose to the rank of Captain.

were by now becoming routine, with most of their time being spent at sea and only returning to Suda Bay in order to refuel. After carrying more troops to Malta, *Gloucester* took part in a commando operation, on 23 February, against the Greek Island of Castellerizzo. The island lies east of Rhodes, close to the Turkish mainland and in 1941 was one of the many Dodecanese islands held by the Italians. The British needed a base for motor torpedo boats to operate effectively against enemy shipping and the island of Castellerizzo was earmarked as an ideal location.

The strategy for the capture of Castellerizzo was for *Gloucester* and a small force of ships to land commandos on the island by night. Aboard *Gloucester*, the commandos armed with machine guns, knuckledusters and knives, kept to themselves as the ship made its way to the island. Few, if any of the men on the lower deck knew the purpose of the exercise. Richard Garner said;

'Nobody knew what was happening, but that was not uncommon. When we left harbour the captain would come on the tannoy and tell us briefly where we were off to but no further information would be given'.

The operation went well at first and the island was captured without too much difficulty. To the surprise of the allied troops, however, the Italians responded with bombing raids from Rhodes and later they bombarded and landed troops from destroyers onto the island.

The British force experienced problems with their radio communications and also found that their arms were quite insufficient to prevent the Italians retaking Castellerizzo. The commandos were soon back on board *Gloucester* and heading for Alexandria, much to the mystification of the ship's company.

Cunningham described the taking and abandonment of Castellerizzo as;

'A rotten business which reflected little credit on anyone'.

In a despatch to the First Sea Lord he went on to say;

'we have learned a lot from it and won't repeat the mistakes.'[1]

Churchill, at a meeting of the War Cabinet, went further and described the landings as; *'a fiasco.'*[2]

Rear Admiral Renouf had been aboard *Gloucester* for five months at this time. The intense pressure, which the ship had been under, had also placed a great strain on Renouf. His erratic behaviour had been brought to the attention of the First Sea Lord, Sir Dudley Pound, by Cunningham. In a letter dated 8/2/41 Pound replied to Cunningham;

'As regards Renouf. I feel that this must be left to you. We can't afford to employ an officer if there is a better one available, and if you are not in every way satisfied I do hope you will suggest somebody being sent to relieve him'.[3]

After the unsuccessful raid on Castellerizzo it was decided to replace Renouf with Rear Admiral Glennie. On 11 March Cunningham again wrote to Pound regarding the abandonment of Castellerizzo;

'I put Renouf in charge and he, poor man, cracked in the middle of it...Renouf just cracked up through anxiety but he also has some stomach trouble. I'm sure Glennie will be excellent'.[4]

On 28 March, Pound replied;

'I was very sorry to hear about Renouf's breakdown...As a matter of fact, I expect he is a bit too highly strung to stand the racket...'[5]

The strain of being constantly in action was taking its toll on the officers and men of *Gloucester*. Rear Admiral I G Glennie replaced Renouf although the men on board were never told the reason for Renouf's departure.

Notes
1. *A Sailor's Odyssey* p.316.
2. *Finest Hour* p.1025.
3. B.Lib. MSS 52561.
4. Ibid.
5. Ibid (Renouf never returned to duty and was placed on the retired list on 3 April 1943.)

CHAPTER TEN

Battle of Matapan: Engaging the Italians

At the eastern end of the Mediterranean the pressures of war were intensifying. The Greek army was struggling to hold out against the Axis powers; the Luftwaffe, operating from Italian bases held dominance in the air; the Eastern Mediterranean Fleet had responsibility for escorting convoys to Greece and Malta in addition to providing support for the army in North Africa. These multiple demands brought the fleet almost to breaking point. To further exacerbate the problem, the aircraft carrier *Formidable* still hadn't arrived to replace *Illustrious*. Cunningham again appealed to the First Sea Lord for more fighter planes and in particular, those that could operate at long range.

Operation 'Lustre', the codename for the movement of allied troops to Greece, began on 4 March 1941. Cunningham was in no doubt about the dangers which faced the convoys and the additional burden of heavy commitments which the fleet would be expected to undertake in the next two months. In a letter to the Admiralty he described his resources as being;

'taxed to the limit and by normal security standards my commitments exceed available resources.'[1]

Despite the concerns felt about sending troops to Greece, Churchill was in favour of the operation and believed it to be necessary to preserve British prestige in France, Spain and particularly the United States. To Churchill's delight, on 7 March, the War Cabinet unanimously confirmed the decision to give military assistance to Greece.

Gloucester was in the first convoy to sail to Piraeus; it was the first of many journeys that she would make during March. The convoys frequently came under attack from enemy aircraft and the ship's company was at action stations for long periods. The barrels of the 4.2-inch guns on *Gloucester* had become so worn that the ordinance branch had to change them in Alexandria.

Nobby Hunt was part of the team that carried out the work;

'We changed the barrels ourselves before the ship put to sea again because the dockyard facilities in Alexandria were so overstretched'.

The convoys to Greece carried no less than 58,000 British and Dominion troops, plus their stores and military equipment. Of the total number of troops carried, *Gloucester* and other cruisers took 11,000, before the convoys ceased on 21 April.

On 24 March, *Gloucester*, in company with *Ajax*, *Orion* and the Australian ships, *Perth* and *Vendetta*, escorted convoy AG9 to Piraeus. After seeing the troopships safely into harbour, *Gloucester* returned to Suda Bay for fuelling. The Bay was well established now as a depot for the British fleet and defences had been improved since *Glasgow* was torpedoed. Anti-submarine nets stretched across the entrance to the Bay but they were still not adequate enough to prevent a brave attack by the Italians on the cruiser *York*.

In the early hours of 26 March, six Italian motor boats manned by frogmen were dispatched from two Italian destroyers, *Crispi* and *Sella*, who remained outside the bay. The motor boats, loaded with explosives, managed to get into Suda Bay and raced towards *York* and a Norwegian tanker, *Pericles*. The frogmen, under the command of Lt Cdr Faggioni, showed considerable courage and

Soldiers resting on board Gloucester.

enterprise as they dived from the boats just seconds before their craft hit *York* and *Pericles*. The tanker was holed amidships, though most of her cargo remained intact. *York* however was severely damaged and with her boiler and engine rooms flooded she had to be beached. It was a severe blow to the Eastern Mediterranean Fleet since *York* was the only cruiser with 8-inch guns on the station. She later became an a/a battery, but was eventually destroyed by German bombers. The six Italian frogmen who took part in the raid were all picked up, some by Royal Marines from *Gloucester*.

Royal Marine Ernie Evans immediately went to P2 gun when the 'alarm to arms' was sounded';

'It was just before dawn when I heard the explosions. I got to the gun and began looking for aircraft. Then we noticed York *had been bottomed by the stern. Some Royal Marines from* Gloucester *took the Italians as prisoners and put them ashore. As soon as the marines got back on board we put to sea'.*

Bill Howe, the farmer's boy from Manaton on Dartmoor, was a member of the boat's crew that was sent to capture the Italian frogmen. Bill recalled the incident;

'I was on the ship's motor boat and we picked up two Italian frogmen who were trying to swim ashore. They were taken back to Gloucester *by the Royal Marines and then put ashore before we put to sea'.*

The actions of the Italian frogmen were most courageous and in complete contrast to the reluctance of the senior officers of the Italian Navy to engage the Royal Navy at sea. Admiral Cunningham admired such acts and praised the Italians for their gallantry when carrying out such raids.

Gloucester put to sea, leaving the stricken *York*. Les Thomas recalled the men of the *York* waving, and shouting out, *'you can have it all now'*, as they anticipated a rest from action and possible drafts

Roy Tremaine searches the horizon for the Italian fleet while Chief Yeoman Fred Otter looks on.

back to the United Kingdom. In fact many of *York's* company went to Greece, in other ships, a few weeks later where they assisted in the beach evacuations of the British and Dominion troops from Greece.

Orion, under the command of Vice Admiral Pridham-Wippell, had now replaced *Gloucester* as flagship. In addition to *Gloucester* and *Orion*, Pridham-Wippell's force also consisted of the cruisers *Perth* and *Ajax* and the destroyers *Ilex*, *Hasty*, *Hereward* and *Vendetta*. On the day after they left Suda Bay, 27 March, reconnaissance aircraft from Malta reported three Italian cruisers and a destroyer, heading south-east towards Crete. Cunningham deduced that if the small Italian force was travelling away from Italy, they were probably intending to join up with the rest of the Italian fleet in order to attack the convoys to Greece. Pridham-Wippell's force was ordered to be in a position south-west of Crete by daylight on 28 March.

Back in Alexandria, Cunningham was most anxious that the Italians should not realise that the British fleet knew their position. He therefore ordered a convoy, on way to Piraeus, to continue until dark and then to turn about and return to the safety of Alexandria. The Admiral was also aware that the Japanese Consul in Alexandria was passing information to the Italians about the movements of Allied shipping in and out of Alexandria. Cunningham devised an ingenious deception to mislead the Japanese informers. Packing a suitcase and his golf clubs, the Admiral made a great show of leaving *Warspite*, as if intending to spend the night ashore. Later that night however, he returned to *Warspite*, in secret, and the fleet put to sea to join up with Pridham-Wippell's force, which included *Gloucester*. The aircraft carrier *Formidable* had, by now, joined the fleet and early on the morning of 28 March her aircraft reported four Italian cruisers and some destroyers close to *Gloucester*. Cunningham's force was still about ninety miles astern of Pridham-Wippell's ships. The latter, realising that he was outranged by the Italian firepower and the speed of the newer Italian ships, decided to turn his force round and lead the Italians into Cunningham's advancing battleships.

Nineteen year old Michael Noonan vividly recalled the words of Captain Rowley as he spoke to the men over the tannoy;

> *'We expect to be going into action against the Italian fleet in about one hour. The ship's company will take breakfast in two watches and whilst at breakfast, change into clean clothing and clean underwear. Good Luck'.*

Gloucester *under attack during the Battle of Matapan.*

The instruction to wear clean clothing was a precaution against wounds becoming infected, should the men sustain injuries.

At 0812, the Italians opened fire at a range of thirteen miles and the battle of Matapan began.

Cunningham wrote about the Italian attack;

'It was accurate to start with and seemed to be concentrated on Gloucester, *which, 'snaked the line', to avoid being hit. At 0829 when the range had dropped by about a mile, Gloucester opened fire with three salvoes from her 6-inch guns, all of which fell short. The enemy altered course to the westward and at 0855 ceased firing. Pridham-Wippell swung round to keep in touch'.*[2]

Gloucester and the rest of Pridham-Wippell's force followed the Italians until 1100, when an Italian battleship, *Vittorio Veneto*, was spotted at a range of sixteen miles. The 15-inch guns of the enemy ships clearly outranged the 6-inch guns of the British cruisers and as Pridham-Wippell ordered his force to turn away 180 degrees from the Italians, the battleship opened fire. Under the cover of a smoke screen from *Gloucester*, the rest of Pridham-Wippell's force attempted to escape at full speed.

Gloucester narrowly escaped being hit by the Italian battleship but did sustain damage to one of the brackets holding a prop shaft. Captain Rowley reported to Pridham-Wippell that *Gloucester* was only capable of making twenty-four knots and with *Vittorio Veneto* bearing down and straddling her with 15-inch shells, the situation looked hopeless. Just when it seemed that *Gloucester* must be hit, the ERAs and stokers in the engine room somehow managed to increase the ship's speed to thirty knots.

Signalman Les Thomas recalled how close the shells were;

'Once the shells started coming over, I ducked beneath a canvas screen for protection. It was daft really but somehow it made me feel safer.'

Gloucester *laying a smoke screen at Matapan as shells explode around her.*

Most of the men in the signal branch were on the signal deck, just below the main bridge from which the captain controlled the ship. On the bridge, alongside the captain, was Chief Yeoman Fred Otter, whose duty was to receive and send signals on the captain's behalf.

Bob Wainwright, a Petty Officer Yeoman, was also on the bridge and could see the Italian ships in the distance;

'I had a grandstand view as they started to send the shells over us. When they came over the top of us it was like the sound of a tube train approaching'.

Cunningham ordered the battleship *Valiant* to assist *Gloucester* and the rest of Pridham-Wippell's ships. Swordfish aircraft from *Formidable* were also flown off to attack *Vittorio Veneto*, which then turned away.

During the afternoon more Italian cruisers were sighted, but by now Cunningham's force had joined Pridham-Wippell's and the

Near miss, 28 March 1941

British fleet set off in pursuit of the Italians, who were some sixty-five miles ahead of them. At 1500 aircraft from *Formidable* again attacked *Vittorio Veneto*, hitting her three times and slowing her down, although not enough to allow the British fleet to get to her before dark. Fleet Air Arm aircraft from Crete and RAF bombers from Greece also supported the British fleet. It was one of the rare occasions in the eastern Mediterranean theatre that the Royal Navy received so much support from the air. At 1644 Cunningham signalled to Pridham-Wippell to take his cruisers, including *Gloucester*, ahead of the main battle fleet in an attempt to make contact with the enemy. By 1830 reconnaissance aircraft reported that *Vittorio Veneto* was surrounded by the Italian fleet and making fifteen knots westward towards Taranto and that they were about forty-five miles ahead of the British ships. At 1930, as darkness fell, *Gloucester* reported that the enemy ships were only about nine miles away from them. Swordfish aircraft again attacked the enemy fleet.

Cunningham now had to decide whether to risk his ships in a night action against the heavy guns of the Italians. He was particularly concerned about the safety of his only aircraft carrier *Formidable*. Furthermore, he knew that because his ships were close to the Italian mainland, they could expect heavy aerial attack by enemy aircraft as soon as daylight came. It was a difficult decision but he sent his destroyers ahead to attack the Italian ships.

At 2111, *Gloucester's* radar picked up an unknown ship, which was stopped about five miles from *Gloucester's* port beam. At 2210, the battleship *Valiant* had reached the area and also picked up a ship on her radar which she reported to be over six hundred feet in length. At 2225, three enemy cruisers were seen silhouetted against the sky, two of which were identified as the modern *Zara* class, which carried 8-inch guns.

Cunningham's battleships closed to within one and a half miles of the Italian cruisers. Because the range of the British battleship's 15-inch guns was around sixteen miles, this made sitting ducks of the targets ahead.

The Italians were completely taken by surprise when the searchlights of *Greyhound* and *Warspite* were switched on. They were so unprepared that their guns were pointing fore and aft. *Valiant* and *Barham* opened fire with 15-inch broadsides and within minutes the Italian cruisers were a mass of flames and twisted metal. *Gloucester* and the rest of Pridham Whippell's force, meanwhile, were still pursuing *Vittorio Veneto*, but following a signal from Cunningham at 2300, they withdrew to the north-east where the fleet was to regroup.

At 0300 the destroyer *Havock*, having earlier sunk an Italian destroyer, reported the Italian cruiser *Pola*, stopped nearby. *Pola* had been hit by a torpedo from one of *Formidable*'s aircraft and turned out to be the ship that had earlier been picked up on the radar by *Gloucester*. The ratings of *Pola*, most of whom were drunk, were completely out of the control of their officers. The quarter deck was littered with bottles and clothing and the ship was a shambles, despite the fact that she had neither been fired on nor had she fired any of her guns in the surface action. After taking the crew from *Pola*, she was sunk at 0410. The sinking of *Pola* was the last action of the battle of Matapan.

Next morning Cunningham took the fleet back into the area where the Italian ships had been routed. The sea was covered with oil, debris and hundreds of bodies, as well as survivors clinging to wreckage.

Eighteen year old Ernie Evans went to the upper deck and was amazed at the sight he witnessed;

> *'There were hundreds of bodies and also some survivors in the water. I looked down and saw the bodies bumping against the ship's side. As we watched, we couldn't believe what we were seeing and I remember somebody saying that it looked like a sea of the dead'.*

Ted Mort, just eighteen years old at the time, also remembered seeing the bodies being pushed aside by the ship's bows.

Ken Hooper, a twenty-one year old 5th class electrical artificer, had been on one of the work parties standing by to carry out repairs in the event of *Gloucester* being hit during the action. Following the long period at action stations he recalled the morning after the battle;

> *'It was a beautiful day and as the fleet went back in formation we must have been a formidable sight. There were hundreds of white bodies floating in the sea and I think most of them must have been killed by blast because they didn't appear to have any injuries. Many of the survivors were on chairs, doors, or messdeck tables although some were in carley floats. They waved to us to be rescued. It was an awesome sight for a youngster like me'.*

Richard Garner was on the bridge with fellow telegraphist, 'Lofty' Patterson. As the pair were looking at the Italians in the sea, Richard remembered them shouting out, 'English very good, English very good', obviously hoping that they would be rescued. Richard remarked to Lofty;

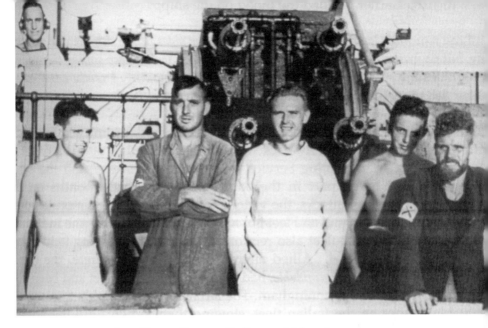

A pom-pom crew: Lee, Flynn, Happer, Keeling and Morraine.

    'Makes you think, doesn't it. We were responsible for all that. Christ what a mess'.
Before Patterson could respond, a voice from behind them said;
'If it wasn't them it could have been you, now get on with your work'.
The two young ratings turned around and saw Captain Rowley standing behind them. He went on;
'I don't like it either, but remember, it could have been you'.
German aircraft soon arrived on the scene, forcing the fleet to abandon rescue attempts. As the fleet withdrew, Cunningham ordered a message to be sent to the Italian Admiralty, giving the position of the survivors. A total of nine hundred Italian sailors were saved by British ships and as a result of Cunningham's signal to the Italian Admiralty, the Italian hospital ship, *Gradisca*, arrived and picked up a further one hundred and sixty men. The British fleet had secured a long sought after victory and one that effectively kept the Italian fleet in port for the rest of the war.
    Three Italian cruisers, *Zara*, *Pola* and *Fiume* together with two destroyers, *Alferi* and *Carducci*, had been destroyed against the loss of one British aircraft.
    Cunningham thought that *Gloucester* had been singled out by the Italians, whether because she was the most up to date cruiser, now with radar, or because she had made smoke to cover the other ships and therefore was more exposed to the enemy, is not clear. Whatever the reason, *Gloucester* was most fortunate not to have been hit and her survival reinforced recognition of the skill with which Captain Rowley had navigated the ship out of danger.

The ship's company had been at action stations for a total of thirty-six hours. Richard Garner recalled the mood on the ship;

'I can remember hearing the shrapnel hitting the sides of the ship. It was a funny thing, but no matter how much danger we were in men would keep saying things like, "What about the poor bastards back in London or Plymouth". I really admired the humour that many of the men maintained under the most difficult conditions'.

On the voyage back to Alexandria the fleet came under some heavy attacks from the air, but arrived safely back in harbour on Sunday, 30 March. The following day a Thanksgiving Service was held on *Gloucester* and the other ships which had taken part in the battle. After so many months on the receiving end of enemy attacks, the victory was a much needed morale boost, not only for the Mediterranean Fleet but also for the people at home in Britain. The success of the battle fleet also reinforced Cunningham's long held views that air support was vital. Allied aircraft operating from Crete, the Greek mainland and the carrier *Formidable*, had located the Italian Fleet and been able to give their position to Cunningham. The aircraft were also able to carry out invaluable attacks on the Italian fleet, slowing them down until the surface ships could get to them. In contrast the Italians had no air support. Two months later however, at the battle of Crete, the positions would be reversed and the enemy would dominate the air once again.

The following awards were made to officers and men from HMS *Gloucester* following the battle of Matapan.

Captain H A Rowley	DSO
Cdr (E) H C Brown	DSO
Lt Cdr R A F Heap	DSC
Lt Cdr R J Robertson	DSC
Wrt Eng J W Costelloe	DSC
Ch ERA W H Waldron	DSM
PO (Tel) P A M Welch	DSM
Ldg Seaman F A Bowgen	DSM
Mid J E Lewis	Mentioned in Despatches
A/B N F Bradley	Mentioned in Despatches
ERA 2 B G Horwell	Mentioned in Despatches
T Sig Bsn E G Middlecote	Mentioned in Despatches

Notes
1. *A Sailor's Odyssey* p.318.
2. Ibid p.327.

CHAPTER ELEVEN

Tobruk and Tripoli: 'Churchill is difficult'

O n the day the British fleet arrived back in Alexandria, Italian and German troops attacked the Allied army in Libya and by 3 April Benghazi had fallen. Three days later Germany declared war on Greece and the German 12th Army invaded from Bulgaria. The enemy offensives placed an additional burden on Cunningham's already overstretched fleet.

In North Africa the immediate priority was both to defend and supply Tobruk, whilst at the same time attacking enemy positions, especially airfields along the coast. Attempts also had to be made to intercept Italian sea convoys to Libya. Malta was of vital strategic importance to the Royal Navy in this plan.

In Greece things were no better and on 7 April the port of Piraeus was heavily bombed and the SS *Clan Fraser*, loaded with ammunition, had exploded causing severe disruption to the port facilities. The raids however were merely a curtain raiser to the bombing and mine laying of the port by the Luftwaffe.

The role of the Royal Navy in the Eastern Mediterranean, in early April, continued to have three main objectives; the supply and support of the allied army in North Africa; the maintenance of Malta as a base to disrupt Italian convoys; to provide support for the army in Greece.

Priority was given to the first of these objectives by the government in London, who still appeared to have underestimated the dangers and difficulties that the fleet was facing. Churchill's exasperation with Admiral Cunningham is evident from a message that the Prime Minister sent to the Admiralty and which was passed on verbatim to Cunningham. The message was that HM Government had given instructions that;

> *'every possible step must be taken by the Navy to prevent supplies reaching Libya from Italy and by coastal traffic, even if this results in serious loss or damage to HM ships'.*

It went on to deal with the difficulties being faced by the army in Libya and concluded;

> *'Failure by the Navy to concentrate on prevention of such movements to the exclusion of everything not absolutely vital will be considered as having let the side down'.*[1]

Churchill's unhelpful attitude was part of a long standing feud with the First Sea Lord, Sir Dudley Pound, who had written, as early as 1 December 1940, in a letter to Cunningham;

> *'The PM is very difficult these days, not that he has not always been so ...one just has to put up with his childishness, as long as it isn't vital or dangerous.'*[2]

The Royal Navy in the Mediterranean was dealing with an increasing number of commitments and had been subjected to many dangerous tasks since Italy had entered the war. For the Prime Minister and his government to suggest that Cunningham's forces would shirk from their duties at this time and; *'let the side*

Boys' Mess. Divisional Officer Lt R S Brooke, centre, holding 'Minnie', the ship's cat.

down', was not only unhelpful but displayed a lack of appreciation for Cunningham's personal attributes and the commitment of the officers and men under his command.

Yet another example of a lack of understanding by the government was evident in a message sent to Cunningham instructing him to sink the battleship *Barham* and the cruiser *Caledon* at the entrance to the harbour at Tripoli. Cunningham realised that this plan was unwise since the enemy would still have been able to get supplies in by using small craft to negotiate the sunken ships. More importantly he knew that not only would two vital ships be lost, but that attacks on the ships from enemy aircraft and shore batteries would result in a considerable loss of life. The plan angered the Commander in Chief, particularly as the ships' companies would be unaware of the mission they were being sent on since secrecy demanded that the men could not be told of the plan to scuttle their ships. Cunningham conveyed his arguments against the operation and received a reply saying that the operation had been cancelled. These pressures from HM Government illustrate the frustration that Cunningham had to deal with, in addition to his already excessive workload.

By the second week in April, Cunningham's ships were working flat out to keep the army supplied and, at the same time, mounting attacks on enemy convoys and supply ports. At sea the ships' companies were either at defence stations, which meant eight hours on watch and four hours off, or at action stations which meant that they were on watch all the time. Either way the outcome was that sleep and food remained in short supply. Even in port these necessities could rarely be satisfied as the ships were constantly needed at sea and could only spend enough time in harbour to refuel and take on ammunition. It was against this arduous background that the ship's company of *Gloucester*, in common with the rest of the fleet, carried out their operations.

On 15 April, *Gloucester*, in company with the destroyer *Hasty*, bombarded enemy transport that had concentrated on the coast road near Capuzzo. The bombardment, which was successful in disrupting the enemy transport lines, was by no means one way. Although neither *Gloucester* or *Hasty* was hit, an indication of the dangers faced during such attacks close to enemy lines can be gauged from the damage sustained to the gunboat *Gnat*, which had been hit eight times on the previous day in a similar bombardment.

After the bombardment of Capuzzo, *Gloucester* did not return to Alexandria but was ordered to join up with the gunboat *Ladybird* and, on 18 April both ships carried out further bombardments on enemy targets between Bardia and Sollum. Immediately after the action, *Gloucester* sailed north-east towards Malta to join up with the battleships *Warspite*, *Barham* and *Valiant*, who had escorted a convoy to Malta on 20 April.

Under cover of darkness the three battleships and *Gloucester*, sailed south to attack Tripoli, the major port of supply for the enemy armies. The codename given to the attack on Tripoli was Operation 'Tripe': the objective was to cause as much disruption as possible to the port. The dangers of operating some eight hundred miles from Alexandria, close to enemy airfields, in mined waters and at night made Operation 'Tripe' a particularly dangerous mission.

The strategy for the operation was to take the sea force close enough to Tripoli to carry out the bombardment and it was ingenious, to say the least. Lieutenant Commander Haggard, the commanding officer of the submarine *Truant*, had been instructed to wait four miles out and guide the force towards the entrance to the harbour. *Gloucester* and the three battleships were approaching the rendezvous point when they saw a navigation light pointing seaward from *Truant's* periscope. After rounding the submarine, the four ships silently steamed in close to the harbour before opening fire. The barrage continued from 0500 until 0545. Admiral Cunningham, aboard *Warspite*, later wrote that *Gloucester's* four triple mounted 6-inch guns must have been particularly effective.

Petty Officer Yeoman Bob Wainwright was on the bridge of *Gloucester* during the action;

'As the 6-inch guns opened fire they were first at 45 degrees but when we got closer in they levelled out. The blast from our guns was such that I was knocked sideways and my tin hat blew off. I thought for a minute that my head had been blown off but then as I recovered I realised that I couldn't hear anything. I tried to shout down the voicepipe but I couldn't speak either'.

Bob Wainwright's hearing was permanently damaged from the blast.

The intensity of the barrage caused considerable disruption to oil installations ashore and seven ships in the harbour were sunk. Incredibly the shore batteries did not open up for some twenty minutes and even then their fire was haphazard. When the bombardment was over the force steamed away at full speed without sustaining any damage, much to the surprise of Cunningham who had expected to lose at least one ship or sustain some damage from aerial attacks.

After the action the battleships sailed back to Alexandria but *Gloucester* was deployed, by Cunningham, to Malta to support a flotilla of destroyers who were engaged in disrupting enemy convoys to Libya. Between 26 and 30 April, *Gloucester* covered the 5th Destroyer Flotilla, which had just arrived from Britain and was under the command of Lord Louis Mountbatten. Events in the eastern Mediterranean were now coming to a head and the already overstretched fleet could expect little respite. On 17 April, General Wavell, realising the position in Greece was hopeless, had made plans to withdraw the army and by the 22 April, the Greek government, under King George, had withdrawn to Crete. On 25 April, Hitler issued 'Directive 28', which was an operation to capture the island of Crete and use it for an air base against British positions in the eastern Mediterranean.

The arrival of *Gloucester* at Malta coincided with frequent enemy mine laying attacks from the air. This meant that, either the ship could not put to sea until the mines were cleared, or she could not get back into harbour because mines were blocking the entrance. When she was in harbour those members of the ship's company who were not engaged on the guns were sent ashore but the enemy attacks were so intense that they had little rest.

Royal Marine Fred Brisley recalled that, despite the siege of Malta, life somehow went on and many of the bars managed to remain open. By now the Maltese however had developed a sixth sense about air attacks and Fred remembered how the civilians would suddenly scatter to take cover. He said that it was then that you knew an air raid was about to begin even though no sirens had sounded.

Petty Officer EA Ken Hooper had good reason to remember *Gloucester's* last visit to Malta. At sea he had been suffering from an abscess on his lower back and was being treated in the ship's sick bay. On arrival in Malta he was sent to Carfa Military Hospital where an operation was carried out. Ken was informed that he would have to remain in hospital for three weeks. He never saw *Gloucester* again and probably owes his life to the abscess that had to be removed from his back.

On 30 April, *Gloucester* was returning to Malta with Mountbatten's 5th Destroyer Flotilla, following an operation against enemy shipping. *Kelly*, *Jackal* and *Kelvin* safely entered the harbour but just as *Jersey* reached the harbour she hit a mine and sunk, blocking the entrance. *Gloucester* and the destroyers *Kashmir* and *Kipling*, unable to get into Malta, were instructed to proceed west to Gibraltar and meet up with Force H, to bring a convoy back through the Mediterranean.

Passing through the Sicilian Narrows that night, *Gloucester* exploded a mine in her paravanes that caused a huge explosion close to the ship damaging the hull. Ernie Evans recalled that the pumps were manned all night in the flooded compartment. Later that day *Gloucester* was repeatedly attacked by enemy aircraft and during one of these attacks she was hit again. The bomb passed through the stern of the ship without exploding. Incredibly there were no fatalities and the ship fought off the enemy aircraft before making way without further incident, to Gibraltar.

With the ship again damaged, and considering the length of her commission, the rumour soon spread that they would be on their way home. Sadly, the men were hoping for something that was not to be and the ship was put into dry dock for emergency repairs. Gibraltar was the nearest place that *Gloucester* had been to her homeport of Devonport, since her commissioning over two years earlier. Because of her invaluable radar and experienced ship's company *Gloucester* was too much of an asset to the Mediterranean Fleet to be sent back to Devonport for decommissioning.

Whilst the ship was being repaired in Gibraltar, the ship's company did have a brief respite from the intense pressure which they had been subjected to in the eastern Mediterranean and Malta. Ernie Evans remembered *Gloucester's* last visit to Gibraltar;

'We were in the Fleet Club and somebody passed a remark about how scruffy Gloucester *looked and what an untidy state she was in. Considering that we had just had a bomb pass right through the ship and that we had been bombed nearly all the way to Gibraltar, it was not surprising that she looked a bit dishevelled. The lads, however, resented the remarks and voices were raised. The next thing I heard was, 'Up the* Gloucester' *and a huge fight broke out between* Gloucester *and the rest of Force H'.*

The incident in Gibraltar proved that the men of HMS *Gloucester*, which was aptly known as 'The Fighting G', were prepared to fight on land, as well as at sea, to defend the proud name of their ship.

Notes
1. *A Sailor's Odyssey* p.343.
2. ref: B.Lib MSS 52561.

CHAPTER TWELVE

Last Trip Ashore: Expectation and Exhaustion

O n the evening of 5 May, Force H set out from Gibraltar under the command of Admiral Sir John Somerville. The operation, codenamed 'Tiger', was intended to escort a convoy of transport ships east, with much needed supplies; in particular, tanks for the Army. The Admiralty had raised considerable doubts about passing this convoy through the Mediterranean, knowing how strong the Luftwaffe's position was in Sicily, but at the Prime Minister's insistence the convoy went ahead. At the same time, the opportunity was taken to transfer the battleship, *Queen Elizabeth*, and the cruisers *Naiad* and *Fiji* to Alexandria in order to strengthen Cunningham's overstretched fleet.

As Force H proceeded east and neared the Sicilian Narrows, it came under heavy attacks from the air by Messerschmitts and Stukas. Although the strong naval force ensured that bombs hit none of the merchant ships, SS *Empire Song* sank after hitting two mines and SS *New Zealand Star* was also damaged. A torpedo attack by an Italian submarine narrowly missed the battleship *Queen Elizabeth*, but by 9 May Force H met up with Cunningham's force, which had sailed west from Alexandria.

The two fleets met in thick fog and when the leading ship of Force H came into view, Cunningham's Chief Yeoman received the signal, '*Doctor Livingstone, I presume*'. Cunningham signalled back, '*On Stanley, on*'. Force H turned about to return to Gibraltar and Cunningham took over the convoy to Alexandria.[1]

Gloucester and the rest of the convoy had some respite from the Luftwaffe's attacks the following morning, due to bad visibility. Later in the day the weather cleared and the men were called back to their action stations when the attacks resumed. The destroyer *Fortune* received a heavy hit, but the rest of the convoy escaped under cover of gunfire from *Gloucester* and the rest of the escorting ships.

The convoy arrived safely at Alexandria on 12 May and the transports unloaded their invaluable cargo of 238 tanks and forty-three Hurricane aircraft. It had been yet another exhausting operation, particularly for the men on *Gloucester*. They had been bombed and hit on their passage to Gibraltar and attacked almost constantly on the return voyage east. Furthermore, while the rest of Force H had returned to Gibraltar after the convoy had been met by Cunningham's fleet off Malta, *Gloucester* had had to continue escorting the convoy and thereby endure further attacks from the air on the second leg of the journey.

News of the safe arrival of Operation 'Tiger' was received in Britain with great relief, especially as it came at a time when good news was in short supply. On 10 May the worst attack of the Blitz had taken place over London and in one night 1,400 people had been killed, 5,000 homes destroyed and 12,000 people had been made homeless.

The King and Queen wrote to Churchill expressing their relief that Operation 'Tiger' had arrived safely. Reference was made in the letter to the loss of one transport ship and damage to another and went on to say, about 'Tiger';

> *'Even though he lacks a claw or two it is to be hoped that he will still be able to chew up a few enemies'*. The letter also opined, *'Any risk was worth taking'*.[2]

In Alexandria, however, there was little time for the *Gloucester* men to celebrate the success of 'Tiger'. The day before the convoy had reached Alexandria, Rudolph Hess had parachuted into Scotland. His mission was to persuade the British government that Britain could not

Rear Admiral H B Rawlings. (By Kind permission of the National Portrait Gallery)

win the war; he believed that he would then be sent back to Berlin with an offer of peace terms. Hess's misguided appraisal of the situation may well have been determined by the efficiency with which the German army had swept through Yugoslavia and Greece, and it appeared to many observers that the allied position in the eastern Mediterranean was tenuous to say the least.

While *Gloucester* had been sailing the length of the Mediterranean, the bulk of the evacuation of the Allied army from Greece was completed. In all, a total of 50,672 troops were evacuated, though the loss in ammunition, guns, transport and stores was heavy. With the fall of Greece on 27 April, Major General Bernard Freyberg VC was put in charge of the defence of Crete and it was to this island that Admiral Cunningham now turned his attentions.

Cunningham's concerns over the lack of air cover were exacerbated not only by aircraft losses in the defence of Malta but also by a shortage of anti-aircraft ammunition for the fleet. On 18 May, he wrote to the First Sea Lord about the enemy superiority in numbers of fighter planes, reconnaissance aircraft and his concerns about the shortage of anti-aircraft ammunition for his ships His fears would be realised in the day ahead as the Germans prepared for the invasion of Crete.

The arrival of Rear Admirals E L S King and I G Glennie also meant the reorganisation of Cunningham's command structure. King, in *Naiad*, took over command of the 15th Cruiser Squadron and Glennie, in *Dido*, took over command of the destroyers. Rear Admiral Rawlings took command of the 7th Cruiser Squadron, to which *Gloucester* was attached.

After the safe arrival of Operation 'Tiger' at Alexandria, *Gloucester* sailed to Port Said for urgent repairs to be carried out to her heightfinder. As soon as these repairs were complete, Captain Rowley was ordered to embark a battalion of the Leicestershire Regiment for passage to Crete. With *Fiji*, also carrying soldiers, the two cruisers sailed north into the dangerous waters around Crete.

On the night of 15 May and into the early hours of the 16 May, the troops and their equipment were safely landed at Crete's

Rear Admiral E L S King. (By kind permission of the National Portrait Gallery)

capital, Heraklion. The landing had to take place during the hours of darkness because throughout the day the Luftwaffe had carried out heavy bombing raids on Crete. Having the advantage of being able to read the enemy's messages through the Enigma code, Freyberg knew that a German airborne invasion of Crete was planned, followed by a seaborne supply of troops and equipment.

After disembarking the troops, *Gloucester* and *Fiji* carried out sweeps for enemy shipping heading towards Crete. They found none and, being short of fuel, were ordered back to Alexandria. On Sunday 18 May, *Gloucester* returned to Alexandria to refuel and the visit was to be her last in the ancient harbour.

Marine Jack Ivey, who joined the ship when she was commissioned, had been put ashore earlier with injuries to his head and knee. He recalled what had happened to him;

'The ship had altered course and as she tilted I fell and hit my head. I was taken to see Doc Singer and he found that I had also smashed my patella in three places. I spent the next eighteen months in and out of hospital'.

While Jack lay in hospital he received a letter from his good pal, 'Sharkey' Ward:

Tuesday 13th 39 Mess. HMS *Gloucester*
Dear Jack,

I was going to send these letters up by McDermid but there was no leave. I can't tell you what is happening but I expect we are going to sea some time tonight. So cheerio and I will see you when I come back. If you like, you can collect those films I left at that chemist, the name of the chemist is Webb. Excuse me for opening one of your letters, it was the only way I could send this note. So far there is no registered letter for you.

Yours Sharkey.

PS. Enclose £1, it will do you more good than me.[3]

Peter Everest joined *Gloucester*, his first ship, on Sunday 18 May. He was just sixteen years old and had arrived

Royal Marines Mawby and Ward (behind), Martin and Ivey (front). Only Jack Ivey survived the war.

in Alexandria earlier, after sailing from Britain on board the SS *Empress of Britain* in a convoy of about twenty-five ships. After disembarking from the troopship, Peter had to wait about a week before being taken by lorry, with other men bound for their new ships. He was the only boy present and remembered seeing *Gloucester* for the first time;

'The ship was camouflaged and looked enormous. I was very impressed when I first saw her. When we got on board we were met by a Regulating Petty Officer who told the new arrivals, 'The things you must keep with you at all times are your identity card and your Mae West'.

Peter remembered how the hairs on the back of his neck stood up when the RPO impressed on them the dangers of being at sea. His introduction to life aboard *Gloucester* was harsh and on the first night he was unable to find a space in the boys' mess for his hammock so he settled down on the canteen flat. During the night, some of the ship's company was returning from leave. Peter got battered and bumped about as the men stumbled across the place where he was trying to sleep. Captain Rowley, all too well aware of the strains on his crew, had arranged for shore leave for a handful of men and their last time ashore in Alexandria remained a special memory for those who were fortunate enough to be granted leave. Leading Signalman Les Thomas was one of the few who were selected for extended shore leave at the rest and recuperation centre at Sidi Bish, about ten miles outside of Alexandria;

Boy Seaman Peter Everest.

> '*I was told that my name had been drawn out of a hat, along with some others, to go to Sidi Bish. It had been a school at the outbreak of war and was converted into a sort of rest camp, run by a padre. Strangely enough, I wasn't all that pleased to have been chosen to go to the camp and that night I went back into 'Alex' and met some of the boys in Rameses Square. We had a good drink in the George IV and at the end of the night they went back on board and I went back to the camp. When I arrived, the padre was waiting with a message from Captain Rowley that leave had been cancelled and we were all to report back to the ship. The padre had been told that if we didn't get back by midnight it would be too late, as she had to sail at that hour. By the time I got back to the camp* Gloucester *had already sailed, although the padre did say that one of the men had managed to get back in time. I can't imagine how the padre must have felt when he heard that* Gloucester *had gone down four days later and that the man he had managed to get back to the ship could well have lost his life*'.

Leading Stoker George Cock was also ashore on Sunday 18 May. George, whose nicknames were 'Rosie', because of his red cheeks and 'Whistling Rufus', because of his cheerful disposition, had three brothers also serving in the navy. Albert Cock, George's younger brother by two years remembered the last time they met up;

> '*I was on the Commander in Chief's staff in Alexandria when I met George for a drink in the Fleet Club. He had only just joined* Gloucester *before her final voyage and that was the last time I ever saw him*'.

George Cock.

John Marshall was a fifteen-year old Royal Marine bugler who had been on board HMS *Bonaventure* when she was torpedoed and sunk on 31 March 1941. He was picked out of the sea and taken to Alexandria by HMS *Hereward* but he suffered such bad nightmares that he was sent to Sidi Bish for a spell of rest and recuperation, where he stayed until Sunday 18 May. By then, John had recovered sufficiently to be drafted to *Gloucester*, which was coming into Alexandria for refuelling. John was pleased with the draft because many of the boys, including seventeen-year old boy seaman Harry Coxell, had earlier been drafted from *Bonaventure* to *Gloucester*. John recalled what happened to him next;

'I was waiting in the shore base when the ship arrived back in port. I packed my bags and jumped aboard a lorry that was going to the jetty. On the journey the lorry broke down and by the time I reached the jetty Gloucester *had sailed'.*

Ken Macdonald had gone ashore with Fred Brisley on their last night in Alexandria. The pair had been together from the day the ship was commissioned and had forged a friendship, which had grown since the idyllic days in the Indian Ocean. Fred recalled;

'I was determined to spend all the money I had before I went back on board'.

They both had a good time but became separated before the end of the evening. Exhaustion and the effects of the alcohol they had consumed caused them both to fall asleep and they overstayed their leave. Ken Macdonald woke some time later and, horrified to find himself still ashore, raced back to the harbour just in time to see *Gloucester* beginning to move out of Alexandria. A felucca was nearby and Ken managed to persuade the boatman to take him out to the ship. As they neared the harbour's outer limits, Ken was pulled aboard.

Fred Brisley slept on until the following morning, by which time the ship had gone. He was put under close arrest and although his indiscretion probably saved his life he never absolved himself of guilt;

'It was a rotten feeling. I felt that I had let other people down and I have had that feeling ever since'.

Fred was not the only one to miss the ship's sailing, and all those who failed to get on board were put on a charge of being absent without leave, a serious offence under King's Regulations. When the fate of *Gloucester* became known however, the matter was regarded as, 'An Act of God', and all the charges were dropped.

On the evening of Sunday 18 May, as *Gloucester* was preparing to leave Alexandria, Admiral Cunningham came alongside in his barge and spoke to Captain Rowley. The Captain, ever mindful of the welfare of his men, told Cunningham that the crew was just about worn out after so much time at sea, most of which they had been at action stations. Cunningham told Captain Rowley that when *Gloucester* returned to harbour he would go on board and speak to the men. The same evening, Cunningham wrote, in a letter to Sir Dudley Pound;

'...I am a little unhappy about Gloucester's *ships company. They have been a long time from home and taken more bombs and mines than any other ship out here. However, I am going on board as they get a day in and I don't doubt I can cheer them up'.*[4]

At this time, Royal Marine Captain Richard Formby managed to write a brief letter to his wife, Pamela, who had taken the family to Wales after a bomb had hit their house in Formby, Lancashire. This was the last time she heard from him.

From HMS *Gloucester 20 May 1941*
To Abersoch

We have been at sea for five weeks with only a day in port and I'd love a game of golf or any form of exercise.

I suppose you have been driven away from Formby by those damned raids. I wondered when you would go and I'm not surprised. I just pray that you get a few quiet nights at Abersoch. I hold out hope for some leave, but Philip Renfold was so rushed when I asked him, he made no sense.

Notes

1. *A Sailors Odyssey*, p.146.
2. The Admiralty, who acknowledged the extreme danger that the first operation had encountered, two months later refused Churchill's proposed repeat of Operation 'Tiger'. The second convoy was routed around the Cape of Good Hope.
3. Sharkey Ward was killed nine days later when *Gloucester* was destroyed.
4. B.Lib MSS 52561.

CHAPTER THIRTEEN

Battle of Crete: 'Revenge in the Making'

Peter Everest, the sixteen-year old boy seaman who had just joined *Gloucester*, awoke early on the morning of Monday 19 May to discover the the ship had left harbour in the night and they were at sea. Peter was perplexed in his new home. He knew nobody else on board and had difficulty finding his way around the ship. When he was given his action station on a machine gun on the aft starboard side he was unsure of exactly what he was supposed to do.

At 0800 on Tuesday 20 May, Operation'Mercury', the German codename for the invasion of Crete began when the Luftwaffe discharged parachute troops in the Canea area. It was the first airborne invasion in history. The Germans planned to drop 23,000 troops, from 500 troop carriers, during the first three days. The Luftwaffe's principal strike force, Fliegerkorps VIII, was under the command of General Wolfram von Richthofen and was made up of bombers, dive bombers, fighters and reconnaissance aircraft, totalling 710 planes.

It was an awesome force, much of which would be directed against the British navy in the days ahead. Many of Richthofen Fliegerkorps pilots had gained experience in the Condor Legion during the Spanish civil war, over Poland and France and later in the campaigns in the Balkans. The ships of the Eastern Mediterranean Fleet therefore were about to encounter a large air force, with experienced pilots, but with no support from the handful of British aircraft, which by now had been withdrawn to Egypt.

During the afternoon of 20 May, allied reconnaissance aircraft had located a flotilla of twenty-five enemy caiques travelling from Piraeus towards their advance base of Milos. By late evening the caiques had overcome strong headwinds and heavy seas to reach Milos, from where they would sail to Maleme on the north-west coast of Crete.

Cunningham's strategy for the prevention of a seaborne invasion on Crete was to divide the fleet into separate forces, each with its own part to play in the seas to the north of Crete. Force B, made up of *Gloucester* and *Fiji* and the destroyers *Greyhound* and *Griffin* were ordered to carry out a sweep, during the night of Tuesday 20 May, between Cape Elephonsi and Cape Matapan. At 0700 on Wednesday 21 May, having sighted nothing, they joined Force A1 which was then in a position fifty miles west of Crete.

Rear Admiral Rawlings, commanding Force A1 from the battleship *Warspite*, also had *Valiant* and the destroyers *Napier*, *Kimberley*, *Janus*, *Isis*, *Imperial* and *Griffin* under his command. With the fleet now covering the seaways to Crete, the Eastern Mediterranean Fleet awaited the anticipated invasion flotilla.

As Cunningham was taking steps to intercept the flotilla between Milos and Maleme, reports were received that dive bombing raids and machine gunning had taken place at Suda Bay, throughout the afternoon and evening. At Heraklion, the Naval Officer in charge reported more attacks in the late afternoon and estimated that in three hours no less than four hundred German aircraft had taken part in the raids. In addition to the earlier parachute drops around Maleme, more drops were made at Heraklion and Retimo. The German assault on Crete was an indication of the force of the Luftwaffe and an ominous indication to Cunningham of the precarious position of his fleet.

Rear Admiral Rawlings' A1 Force was sixty miles west of the Anti Kythira channel by dawn on Wednesday 21 May and proceeding south-east to join up with Rear Admiral Glennie's Force D, made up of the cruisers *Dido*, *Orion* and *Ajax* and the destroyers *Hasty*, *Hero* and *Hereward*. With the Luftwaffe enjoying supremacy of the air, Cunningham's directions were that the British fleet should retire south of Crete by day, thereby reducing the threat from the air. Furthermore, with the naval forces joined together better protection could be given by a concentrated anti-aircraft barrage.

During the forenoon and afternoon of Wednesday 21 May, the fleet suffered many intensive attacks from the Luftwaffe. *Gloucester* and the rest of the ships under Rawlings' command were attacked in the morning and for two and a half hours in the afternoon. Although there were no casualties, the intense barrage put up by the ships had expended a considerable amount of ammunition. The question of ammunition supplies for the ships was giving so much concern to Rawlings that he sent a signal to the ships under his command, warning them of the need to conserve their supplies of high-angle ammunition.

The other forces at sea around Crete also suffered intense attacks by the Luftwaffe, but with the policy of concentrating the ships to throw up an intense barrage, the bombers and dive-bombers were held at bay. The cruiser *Ajax*, in Force D, suffered some damage during the morning but by afternoon Force D had joined with Force A1 in order to concentrate the anti-aircraft defences.

At 1300, Force C, patrolling east of Kythira and under the command of Rear Admiral King, lost the destroyer *Juno*, after enduring three hours of heavy attacks. *Juno*, was the first casualty in the sea battle for Crete and after being hit by three bombs, she sank in only two minutes. Considering the number of ships at sea and the intensity of the air attacks, the loss of only one ship was indicative of the effectiveness of the strategy of concentrating the ships to give mutual support against air attacks. Force A1, Force B, which included *Gloucester*, and Force D, destroyed at least three enemy aircraft and damaged another two on 21 May.

Force A1, and Glennie's Force D, had assembled in an area to the south-west of the island of Kythira. The strength of this force was considerable: it was made up of the battleships *Warspite* and *Valiant*, the cruisers, *Gloucester*, *Fiji*, *Ajax*, *Orion* and *Dido* plus eight destroyers. The group offered considerable mutual protection whilst at the same time being in a position to intercept any attempts by the Italian fleet to defend the seaborne invasion of Crete. The Germans had tried to get the Italian fleet to put to sea in order to draw the British ships away from the seaborne routes to Crete. It would have been a logical strategy for the axis powers to put further pressure on the British, yet the Italian fleet did not put to sea.

Several reasons have been put forward by Commander Bragadin, the Italian naval historian, for the failure of the Italians to put to sea; the strained relationships between the axis powers; a shortage of fuel for the ships; the Luftwaffe's belief in its own invincibility. Whatever the reasons, it is probable that the crushing defeat at Matapan, only a few weeks earlier, had made the Italians very reluctant to meet the Royal Navy in a further encounter.

Whilst the British forces at sea were enduring relentless attacks from the air, the Germans had captured the airport at Maleme. To reinforce their foothold on Crete, they had organised two flotillas of commandeered Greek caiques and small coastal steamers to transport arms and supplies to their troops on the island. Each vessel carried about 100 German Mountain Troops and a few Italian marines in addition to the equipment aboard. The first of the two convoys which had made its way from Piraeus to Milos, set off on the final seventy mile journey to Crete in the early hours of 21 May.

The Italian battle fleet remained in harbour, although a few small ship were released for escort duty to the seaborne invasion of Crete. The destroyer *Lupo* was in charge of the Milos to Crete flotilla. Commander Mimbelli, the ship's captain, had the unenviable task of escorting the flotilla: *Lupo* was armed with only three 3.9 inch guns and four 18-inch torpedo tubes, and the flotilla could sail at a speed of only four knots to Crete. The Royal Navy dominated the approaches by night, therefore it was imperative that the convoy should arrive at Canea Bay before nightfall.

At 1000, Commander Mimbelli received instructions to turn the flotilla and return to Milos. These instructions were based on German reconnaissance reports that British warships were operating in the flotilla's direct line of approach to Crete. After returning to Milos, further reconnaissance from the Luftwaffe reported the seas to be clear of Royal Navy ships to the north of Crete and so the flotilla left Milos once again.

The slow speed of the heavily laden caiques meant that they would take over seventeen hours to travel the seventy miles to Crete and it was therefore impossible to reach their destination before dark. Allied reconnaissance soon reported the flotilla's slow progress and Cunningham ordered the ships of Forces B, C and D to close in and intercept the invasion flotilla, under cover of darkness.

At 2330, Admiral Glennie's Force D found the luckless convoy when it was just eighteen miles north of Crete. The flotilla, defended only by *Lupo*, was hopelessly outgunned against the cruisers *Dido*, *Orion* and *Ajax* and the destroyers *Janus*, *Kimberley*, *Hasty* and *Hereward*.

As soon as the searchlights picked out the caiques, Commander Mimbelli laid a smoke screen to hide his charges and then engaged the British ships with gunfire and torpedoes. Despite his bravery, and the fact that *Lupo* was hit by eighteen 6-inch shells during the next two hours, Commander Mimbelli was unable to prevent the routing of the convoy and only a few of the original twenty-five ships in the convoy escaped destruction. Greek crews who had been pressed into service by the Germans manned the caiques, which were carrying German Mountain Troops. Despite waving white sheets, the caiques were blown apart by Glennie's ships and many of their passengers drowned.

Admiral Glennie found the sinking of the Greek caiques unpleasant and in his report on the destruction of the flotilla he later wrote;

> 'When illuminated they were seen to be crowded with German troops and to be flying Greek colours. The crews, obviously pressed men, were standing on deck waving white flags and it was distasteful having to destroy them in company with their callous masters'.[1]

At the time it was believed that some 4,000 German troops had been killed when the convoy was destroyed. On Friday 23 May, the *Evening Herald*, Plymouth's local newspaper, carried the headline;

'Captain Tells How Cruisers Smashed Nazi Crete Sea Convoy'.

followed by a sub-heading;

'Ships Rammed: Water Full of Thousands of Germans'.

A Press Association Special Correspondent who had interviewed the captain of one of the cruisers in Alexandria wrote the report. The unnamed officer described to the Press Correspondent how Glennie's ships had destroyed the invasion force and the report said;

> 'Large numbers of caiques were sunk by ramming'.

The news of the destruction of the invasion flotilla was also given to the nation in a radio broadcast given by Commander Anthony Kimmins in which he described how the enemy vessels had been sunk by torpedoes and gunfire. *The Daily Express* later printed the story;

> 'Hun soldiers came tumbling up from between decks and leaping overboard. They were all in their full heavy equipment. In several cases these caiques were rammed. There's many a ship in the Mediterranean Fleet with a proud dent in her stem, and so the whole of that first German landing force was sent to the bottom while our ships came away unscathed'.[2]

The destruction of the invasion convoy did not, in fact, account for as much loss of life as was first thought. Research has since shown that the actual number of troops being transported was 2,331 and the final casualty list, issued by the German 12th Army, amounted to 311 officers and men. Whatever the numbers of casualties, those who were fortunate enough to have been picked up by the badly damaged *Lupo*, or by an air-sea search, told stories of being rammed and run down in the sea. The accounts of German soldiers who were aboard the small boats in the flotilla are of crucial importance in understanding events that took place later in the day. These accounts were fed back to the Luftwaffe pilots who then sought revenge.

A German Officer who was aboard one of the vessels said that morale on all the ships was good and the men were singing the, 'England Song', accompanied by men playing concertinas. Suddenly his caique was hit, followed by another broadside; it then sank in a huge tongue of flame. Some of his men had jumped overboard and some had been blown into the sea by the explosion before they managed to get to a dinghy.[3]

Joseph Wuerz, a paratrooper, recalled how the Greek crew had sabotaged the engine of the caique shortly before the British ships attacked the convoy. His caique had therefore become detached from the convoy and he saw the destruction of the other invasion vessels;

'We could neither shoot nor help; we just stood by, looking on in helpless rage. One of my dearest friends was found dead after sixteen hours, floating in the sea. Sixty of my company drowned. The survivors were brought back to Athens'.[4]

Following the decimation of the invasion flotilla, the Germans held an enquiry and evidence was heard from men who had survived the ordeal.

Lieutenant Walter Henglen said that the crew of the caique he was on had attempted to surrender by waving a white towel and signalling with white handkerchiefs. He added that as the British ships were only two hundred metres away they must have seen them through their binoculars, but the next thing he knew was that between ten and fifteen shells hit the craft. Once in the sea, Lieutenant Henglen said;

'Machine gun bullets splashed in a semi-circle around me'.[5]

Ernst Stribny, also a survivor, said that a British cruiser had repeatedly passed through the wreckage, firing at the soldiers in the sea and many men had drowned by being sucked under by the ship's propellers.[6]

Corporal Grimm also gave evidence of being machine gunned in the sea and of seeing at least ten men die in this way. He added, ominously, that the revenge for this act was then already in the making.[7]

Notes

1. Letter of Proceedings: Crete, 19-23 May 1941, Rear Admiral Glennie, June 4th 1941 PRO ADM 199/810 110319.
2. *Daily Express* 30.6.41.
3. Hadjipateras C N and Fafalios M S, *Crete 1941 Eyewitnessed*, Efstathiadis (Athens) 1989. p.123.
4. Ibid p.125.
5. *The Lost Battle of Crete* p.240.
6. Ibid.
7. Ibid.

CHAPTER FOURTEEN

Indecision and Lack of Ammunition

The objectives of the British Fleet and the Luftwaffe were both clear and unequivocal. For the navy the objective was to prevent a seaborne invasion on Crete whilst the Luftwaffe's aim was to clear the British Fleet from around the seas of Crete.

The lack of air support for the Royal Navy was now a crucial factor since the fleet was operating in the waters north of Crete, dangerously close to enemy airfields. Cunningham's pleas and arguments for more air support in the preceding months had been unanswered in London. For the first time in history the might of a sea force was about to be pitted against the strength of an air force.

While the German convoy was being decimated by Glennie's Force D Captain Rowley, aboard *Gloucester* and in command of Force B, consisting of *Fiji* and the destroyers *Greyhound* and *Griffin*, had spent a watchful but uneventful night in the Aegean. As daylight broke on 22 May 1941, the small force was sailing west to rejoin Rawlings' A1 Force and the morning sun rose to reveal a beautiful clear sky.

At 0630, two waves of enemy aircraft, each consisting of twenty-five Stukas, attacked the cruisers. *Gloucester* and *Fiji* were the first British ships to come under attack from the pilots of Fliegerkorps Vlll. For an hour and a half countless attacks took place and both *Gloucester* and *Fiji* were damaged by near misses. The superstructure of *Gloucester* was peppered by fragmentation bombs and more serious damage was avoided through a combination of Captain Rowley's skill in manoeuvring the ship, the untiring work of her gun crews and a certain amount of good fortune. At about 0800 the last of the enemy planes left and Force B reached the relative safety of Rawlings' battle fleet half an hour later.

Glennie had already taken his ships west to rejoin Rawlings' A1 force following the destruction of the German invasion force from Milos. The encounters with the Luftwaffe and the destruction of the convoy during the previous day had once again raised the problem of ammunition shortages on Glennie's ships.

Gloucester and the other three ships in Force B rejoined Rawlings' A1 force south-west of Kythira. Force B had been under attack from 0630, apart from a brief respite between 0800 and 0900. Admiral Rawlings' A1 Force, which now included *Gloucester*, came under attack at varying intervals from 0900 and throughout the morning. Rawlings said that the expenditure of high angle ammunition; 'gave cause for anxiety'.[1]

The ammunition returns provided good reason for his concern. At 0931, battleships *Warspite* and *Valiant* had 66% and 80% respectively but it was the cruiser deficiencies that caused most concern. *Ajax* had 40%, *Orion* 38%, *Fiji* 30%, *Dido* 25%, but alarmingly, *Gloucester* reported that she had only 18% of her ammunition left.

At 1045, Admiral Glennie's Force D, which included *Ajax*, *Orion* and *Dido*, departed to Alexandria to reammunition. Why *Gloucester* didn't leave with them is a mystery. Bearing in mind that her ammunition returns at 0931 showed that she had only 18% of her high angle ammunition left, and with the air attacks continuing, it was clear that this meagre supply would soon be used up, no matter how prudent her gun crews were.

Force D's return to Alexandria had been ordered by Cunningham, who at the time was unaware of *Gloucester's* depleted ammunition. Nevertheless it is difficult to understand why Rawlings, who did know, did not detach *Gloucester* to Alexandria with Glennie's force, all of whom had more ammunition than *Gloucester*.

Admiral King's Force C meanwhile, was steaming north towards the island of Milos, in an attempt to intercept any further Crete-bound invasion convoys. From 0700 the force came under attack from the air but at 0830 a caique was sighted, with German troops aboard. The Australian cruiser, *Perth*, was detached from Force C, to sink the luckless caique, which was a survivor from the flotilla that Glennie's force had routed in the early hours of the previous night.

J K E Nelson was a sailor aboard *Perth* who recalled seeing the caique flying a swastika but then they ran up a white flag. He said that after some Germans had abandoned the caique, *Perth* opened up with her pom-poms and more German troops came up onto the deck and dived over the side. *Perth* finished off the caique with a salvo from her 4-inch guns, while a German soldier was still desperately clinging to the rigging.[2]

King's force then sank a small merchant ship and at 1000, saw an enemy torpedo boat escorting some caiques about twenty-five miles south of Milos. The convoy which they came across was a second invasion flotilla bound for Crete and larger than the one that had been devastated during the previous night. King deployed his destroyers to give chase to the enemy convoy. The cruisers *Perth* and *Naiad* engaged the Italian destroyer *Sagittario*, the principal escort ship of the convoy, which by now was making smoke to hide the caiques.

King's force had become divided during this action and was therefore vulnerable. With mounting air attacks from Stukas and JU88 bombers, King now had to make a crucial decision: whether to pursue and destroy the enemy convoy or turn about and head west to link up with Admiral Rawlings' force, to the west of Kythira.

In King's force, *Carlisle*'s speed had been reduced to twenty-one knots, and because of the continuous air attacks, Force C's high angle ammunition was being used up at an alarming rate. King decided to call off the chase. With his ships now regrouped, he had to fight his way west to meet up with Rawlings A1 Force.

For over three hours, after turning about, King's force repulsed attacks by Stukas and bombers during which *Naiad* and *Carlisle* were both hit. Captain L T C Hampton, the commanding officer on *Carlisle*, was killed.

Rawlings, meanwhile, was aware of Admiral King's plight and signalled to him that Force A1 would be situated between twenty and thirty miles west of the Anti Kythira channel during the morning, awaiting King's force.

At 1225, Rawlings received a signal from King saying that *Naiad* was badly damaged and in need of support. Rawlings then made the decision to go east into the Aegean and ordered his force to increase their speed to twenty-three knots. *Gloucester* was ordered to prepare to take *Naiad* in tow. The air attacks were now at their most intense and King's ships were fighting for survival. At 1241, Rawlings received a further signal from King that *Carlisle* had been hit. *Fiji* was ordered to make preparations to take her in tow.

As Rawlings' force raced towards King's beleaguered ships it was apparent that ·they would again attract the attention of the Luftwaffe. At 1312, anti-aircraft shells were seen bursting in the sky above King's force and *Fiji* was ordered ahead at full speed to take *Carlisle* in tow. However, at 1330, King signalled to Rawlings that *Carlisle* was not badly damaged, so *Fiji* was hastily recalled.

Cunningham later made adverse comments about some of King's decisions. Although little has been said regarding the misunderstanding of the extent to which *Carlisle* was damaged, it is apparent that *Fiji* was unnecessary exposed for some time because of the mix up.

At 1332, Rawlings' force had reached the middle of the Kythira channel when his flagship, *Warspite*, was dive bombed by three Bf109s coming directly down the fore and aft line of the great ship. The leading plane dropped its bombs, hitting the starboard 4-inch guns. The starboard 4-inch and 6-inch batteries were put out of action and damage caused to the No 3 boiler room intakes reduced the ship's speed.

King's westbound force had, by now, joined with Rawlings' ships, which had been steaming east to support them. Rawlings turned his ships about and the fleet made their escape to the west. Dense smoke from *Warspite's* boiler meant that the turn about had to be carried out away from King's force and as a consequence, a distance of four miles opened up between the two forces.

Rear Admiral King, who was senior to Rawlings, took overall command and from then on he had the responsibility of ensuring the safety of both forces.

Almost immediately he had to deal with an attack on the destroyer *Greyhound*.

Greyhound had been despatched at 1320, to sink a large caique that was travelling south between the islands of Pori and Anti Kythira. Having succeeded in sinking the caique, *Greyhound* rejoined the wing of King's force but was immediately attacked by dive-bombers and hit twice. At 1358, King

Gloucester *ablaze and out of control.*

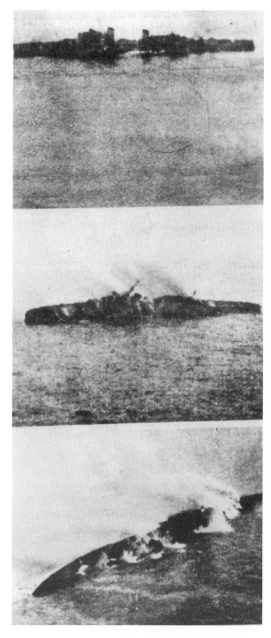

Gloucester's *final moments. Photographs taken by a German Pilot.*

signalled Rawlings to take his force to *Greyhound* to give her support. Incredibly however, only two minutes later at 1400, King changed his mind and ordered Rawlings to give close support to his own force, instead of to *Greyhound*. King then ordered *Gloucester* and *Fiji* to give cover to the destroyers *Kingston* and *Kandahar*, who were already on their way to *Greyhound*.

At 1413, with air attacks continuing, King repeated his call to Rawlings for close support, adding that his ships had practically no high angle ammunition left. Rawlings, by now, was extremely anxious about King's orders to *Gloucester* and *Fiji*. He signalled his anxiety to King informing him of the desperate shortage of ammunition on both ships, especially *Gloucester*. King then changed his orders again and instructed *Gloucester* and *Fiji* to withdraw, at Captain Rowley's discretion.

At 1530, Rawlings' A1 Force and King's Force C, could see *Gloucester* and *Fiji* steaming at full speed in a desperate attempt to rejoin the safety of the battle fleet. However, the two cruisers were by then engaging enemy dive-bombers and because *Gloucester* had used up her few remaining rounds of high angle ammunition, the attacks came in lower and lower.

At 1530, the inevitable happened and *Gloucester* was hit. *Fiji*, herself out of 4-inch ammunition, signalled that *Gloucester* was out of control. Rawlings received the signals from *Fiji* and relayed them to King. King replied that he would order *Gloucester* to be sunk.

King then became uncertain about his decision and at 1555, signalled to Rawlings, saying that if the battle fleet went back to support *Gloucester*, they ran the risk of more ships being damaged or even lost. He then asked for Rawlings' views.

King's signal to Rawlings clearly indicates that he was finding it impossible to decide on the best course of action. In the end, it was left to Rawlings to advise King that in view of the state of Force C, *Gloucester* would have to be left. King then ordered *Fiji* to sink *Gloucester* and withdraw.

Notes
1. Letter of Proceedings PRO ADM 199/810 110319
2. *Crete 1941 Eyewitnessed* p.135.

CHAPTER FIFTEEN

The Sinking: Abandoned and Alone

Rawlings' and King's battle fleet steamed away to safety while *Gloucester's* gunners were reduced to firing star shells at the Stukas, who by now were diving at the ship at mast height before releasing their bombs. Only *Fiji*, herself desperately short of ammunition and still being attacked, remained with *Gloucester*. At this point, *Fiji* decided to leave *Gloucester* and presumably to ignore the instruction to sink her when it became apparent that she would soon go down anyway.[1]

As *Fiji* steamed by the ravaged ship, Captain P R B W William-Powlett ordered carley floats to be thrown overboard for the men of *Gloucester*. It was a generous and courageous act and one that undoubtedly helped to save some lives.

Ernie Witcher, from East Wittering in Sussex, was on board the destroyer *Kingston*, within four hundred yards of *Gloucester* when she was attacked;

'I saw a Stuka diving and as I followed its progress I saw a bomb leave the aircraft and hit Gloucester's main mast, which came down with a shudder and then fell over the side of the ship. Gloucester didn't stand a chance'.

Albert Howden, a Royal Marine aboard *Fiji*, also witnessed *Gloucester's* plight;

'Gloucester was on fire when Captain Powlett came on the tannoy and told us, "We dare not stop. We will go around her at full speed and drop carley floats".

John Wells was a young telegraphist, standing on the compass platform on board *Fiji*. He had a grandstand view of the bombs being dropped and recalled how skilfully the ship was manoeuvred in her attempts to avoid them. He saw the carley floats being dropped and recalled that the Gloucestermen, who were now in the sea, were cheering as *Fiji* steamed by.

On board *Gloucester* the situation was desperate. She had received a number of direct hits, which had immobilised the steering and caused a number of fires to break out. Unable to control the ship any longer and with no high angle ammunition left, the only thing the men could do was to assist the wounded and fight the fires before they were eventually ordered to abandon ship.

John Stevens, a young air mechanic who had joined *Gloucester* in November 1939, was at his action station with the ammunition party to a 4-inch anti-aircraft gun, on the port side of the ship;

'*I remember how* Gloucester *had steamed east into the Kythira channel to relieve King's force and was later sent back to cover the rescue of* Greyhound's *survivors. The attacks by JU87s and JU88s were intense and as they increased, Regulating Petty Officer Harold Allen telephoned from the ammunitions room to ask for help down below as his men were finding it difficult to keep the supplies coming. RPO Allen, a strict disciplinarian, was told in no uncertain terms that the two parties supplying the guns were also desperately in need of help. Within minutes the irate RPO came running up on deck to assess the situation for himself. As soon as he saw the devastation and the strained faces of the gun crews and their assistants, his attitude changed. Allen returned below and shortly afterwards sent up an issue of cigarettes, chocolate and a small rum ration for the gun crews. He must have seen that the fight was hopeless and that we were facing death, or at least serious injury, from the enemy attacks*'.

John's party was later sent forward to the torpedomen's messdeck, which had been hit;

Air mechanic Ebenezer Voakes, Ldg Air mechanic Colin Foster (standing), Air Mechanic John Stevens, A/B Dickie Eaketts, and Marine Abrahams leaning on Air mechanic Lihou. (Lihou left the ship 17-5-41 to go on a course.)

'There were four of us in the party and we ran down a ladder from the after galley flat, along to the sick bay and on to the torpedomen's messdeck. We realised how badly the ship had been hit when we saw so many marines lying dead. Fear took hold of me. The bombs fell continuously and then the ship shuddered and I knew we had been hit yet again. Our leading hand, 'Happy' Day, shouted to us to get up top and away from the messdeck. I was the last one up the ladder and desperately pushing the lad in front of me when I heard a crash, then lumps of hot metal came through the side of the ship. If I'd still been on the deck my legs would have been blown off. We got to the sick bed flat where other men had started to gather amongst the dead and dying. For a time there was no lighting but eventually the ancillary lights came on and we saw more badly injured men being brought in. It was a gruesome sight. Then we were told to go aft. We made our way through the ship, I was about twelfth from the front. Suddenly the hangar deck was hit and the adjacent canteen was blown apart. I still have this vivid memory of cigarettes, chocolates and other things, which the NAAFI sold, flying through the air. Immediately, about eight of the men in front of me dropped dead from the blast. We pressed on and I remember shouting to the men behind me to mind the lads on the deck. It wasn't a stampede but we were all desperate to get to the open part of the ship. Eventually we got to the waist deck and I saw a pal of mine lying by the torpedo tubes, face down. I turned him over and saw that he had been killed by shrapnel. When I reached the hangar deck I realised that I'd left my life jacket near the action station. I raced back along the port side and to my horror I saw that P2 gun had been hit and was hanging over the side with all the gun crew lying dead. I could also see that the after director tower had been hit and had toppled into the sea with the men inside it. The carnage and destruction was terrible. Two other men joined me and we ran to take cover. Then a bomb hit the port side of the ship, causing the pom-pom guns, which were still set on automatic firing, to swing around and spray bullets along the deck. The two men either side of me were killed outright. Just after that Lieutenant Setten called out to me, "Come over here son and help me throw these beams overboard". We pitched about six overboard, then the officer said, "I've got the order to abandon ship. You can go now lad. Best of luck". Within a few minutes the ship was hit again and Lieutenant Setten was killed.

'I went to the side to get off the ship but I took my money belt off first and counted the money in it, then I took my boots off and put the belt beside them. I don't know why I did that. At the time I thought that somehow I would get them back later. I must have been in shock.[2]

'I was about to jump when I looked over the side of the ship. She was listing heavily to port. A Stuka dived at us so low that I could see the pilot's face. He dropped a 500 lb bomb with incendiaries attached to it, and it hit the forward end of the ship. Gloucester was in flames from stem to stern and I knew I had to get away from her before she sank. One of the cutters had been lowered into the sea and I grabbed a rope which was hanging from one of the davits, but the rope had been cut and I plummeted in to the sea, falling between the ship's side and the cutter. I went under the water but as I came up to the surface, someone hauled me into the cutter. There were seven of us in there, with Petty Officer John Mayer sitting in the bow. Gloucester was still being bombed as the Petty Officer told us to pull away. I could see men, still on the ship, trying to get in to the sea, but some were just walking up and down the deck as if unable to comprehend what was happening. There were fires all over the ship'.

Sam Dearie, the stoker from Glasgow, had celebrated his twenty-fifth birthday only nine days before *Gloucester* was sunk. His action station was in a damage control party and when the ship was first hit he said it felt as though she had been lifted out of the sea;

'We got the order to abandon ship. I picked up a wooden form to throw over the side, so that I would have something to hold on to in the water. Just then I saw Toby, the ship's dog, cowering in a corner. He was shaking and terrified. I picked him up and took him to the side of the ship. The dog seemed pleased and started wagging his tail. That dog

Toby – The ship's dog, lost at sea 22-5-41.

*was really spoiled by all of us and I wanted
to try and give him his chance along with
the rest of us so I put him over the side,
into the sea'.*

Toby was seen by some of the
survivors later that evening. He was
clinging to a piece of timber, which was
floating in the sea.

Sixteen year old Peter Everest was
also terrified. The gun where he was
stationed was blown overboard;

> *'I was sheltered from the blast but got
> hit on my head and leg. I remember a
> rating putting his arm around my neck
> and he half carried me to the sick bay flat.
> There were a lot of injured men there and
> I could hear that the ship was still being
> bombed. I heard, "Abandon ship", and
> someone picked me up, took me to the side*

Telegraphist Richard Garner.

> *of the ship and shouted, "Now jump". Luckily, I landed right in the
> middle of a carley float. The float soon filled up with other men: I
> remember that one man had lost an arm'.*

Harry Coxell, a boy seaman who had survived the sinking of
HMS *Bonaventure* just seven weeks earlier, was at his action station
in the cordite handling room;

> *'In the handling room, we didn't hear the order to abandon ship until
> someone shouted down to us that it had been given half an hour ago. I
> went up on deck with Tom Dunne, another boy seaman. We could see
> a dive bomber coming towards the ship and Tom said that we should
> hurry and get in the sea. I said that we would be safer getting under
> the gun turret and I went and hid there. Tom dived into the sea. The
> dive bomber dropped its bomb just on the spot where Tom had gone in
> and I never saw him again. When I got into the water I could see that
> the men who were in groups were being machine-gunned by low flying
> planes, so I stayed on my own until it got dark and there were no more
> planes. I held onto a plank with about fourteen other men but by
> morning there were only two of us left'.*

Ernie Evans, just eighteen years old, was at his action station in
the early morning;

> *'I was on P2 gun, one of the two 4-inch anti-aircraft guns on the port
> side of the ship. We were all tired and hadn't slept for about two days.
> It wasn't long before the JU87s and 88s started to attack us. One bomb*

landed so close to the port side that it bent one of the shields on our gun.

'After the early morning attacks we were again called to action stations, but this time I was sent down to the magazine. I could hear the guns firing and the bombs dropping in the sea. Then there was a terrific explosion in the compressor room, just above us. All the lights went out and I will never forget how claustrophobic I felt at that point. Colour Sergeant Richards told me to get an emergency lamp but when I switched it on the fumes from the explosion were so thick that I still couldn't see anything. I was expecting the magazine to be flooded at any moment but we were lucky that the bomb had damaged the flooding arrangements.

Ldg Stoker Michael Antonucci, killed 22-5-41

'We all got out except for one man who went mad and jumped on my back. I got him off me and then he refused to leave the magazine so we had to leave him behind. We got into the handling room and closed the magazine doors. In the confined space there was just one ladder up to the hatch, which although jammed, was forced open by two other marines. When we got up to the compressor room there was a number of men dead or wounded. After that I never saw any more of the men who had been in the magazine with me.

'The bomb had made a hole down through the ship and I saw a rope hanging down from the quarterdeck, which was three decks above me. I got part way up a ladder, grabbed the rope and went up it like a monkey. How I did it I don't know. As I reached the waist, by the torpedo tubes, the upper deck was in an awful state. X turret, one of the two 6-inch turrets manned by Royal Marines and located at the after end of the ship, was turned over and there were piles of shell cases and bodies everywhere. I decided that the safest place for me would be under the bridge so I made my way forward, through the NAAFI, canteen flat and the sick bay.

'By now, Gloucester was stopped and she was listing heavily. Corporal Plumb was standing beneath the catapult for the planes. He was directing men, either up to the flight deck or to the waist, trying to prevent panic and keep some order. In fact, he was acting like a policeman directing traffic and he did manage to stop the panic. I've often thought that he should have been decorated for his actions.

'Eventually I got to the flight deck where I met Cdr Tanner. His face was black from the smoke. He told me to help him throw some beams over the side. There were lots of men in the sea by now. The Commander said, "It looks like the end of the 'Fighting G' lad. Now over the side you go". I jumped in and swam about two hundred yards away from the ship, just as Fiji was dropping carley floats. The lads on Fiji were cheering and waving to us as they went by. Petty Officer Alfred Hutton was near me in the water.

We lashed three carley floats together and manoeuvred them back to the ship. Men who were already in the sea made their way over to the floats, in a desperate attempt to save their lives'.

Billy Grindell, the stoker from Cardiff, was in a fire and repair party amidships;

'One of our duties was to seal off compartments before opening up the valves on the 12-inch pipes and flooding them. As the lads inside couldn't get out it was a hard task to carry out but it had to be done'.

As soon as the order was given to abandon ship, Billy made his way to the upper deck;

Ldg Seaman Alf Wooldridge killed 22-5-41.

'When I got there I saw the Stukas coming down and I could actually see one of the pilots turn his head round to look at the ship. The planes were coming in across the ship amidships and I felt sure that I would be hit. I went over the side and soon found a wooden plank with six or seven others hanging on. My pal, Johnny O'Brien was among those men and he said to me, "We won't last long on this plank of wood. We've got to make for one of them carley floats". We both set out but that was the last I saw of him. When I reached a float it was already full of men but I managed to hang on to the side until, eventually I was hauled aboard'.

Stoker Bill Howe, Survivor 22-5-41.

Bill Howe, who had been a farmer's boy on Dartmoor, was at his action station on the main deck;

'A bomb came through the other side of the superstructure and exploded. The pressure of the blast was terrific and it felt as though someone had punched me in the ears. Many men were killed, especially on the deck below, as they had no means of escaping. Everything seemed to happen at once; more bombs dropped and it was impossible to assess the damage before fresh reports came in. All over the ship there were loud explosions and eventually the engines and boilers were put out of action. I heard someone shouting, "Abandon ship, abandon ship", so I went up

on deck where the surgeon grabbed me and a couple of others and we set about looking for wounded men to tend. Some of them were very badly wounded, with legs and arms gone. Others were just lying there and if there was any sign of life, the surgeon gave them morphine.

'Eventually I had to leave the ship, she was keeling over so much that I just stepped off her and onto a carley float. There were about a dozen men on the float and we were among the last to leave the ship'.

Lieutenant Hugh Singer, a New Zealander, was the ship's junior surgeon. He survived the sinking and, after the war, wrote an account of his experiences;

'Before the ship was detached with Fiji, *to give covering fire for the rescue of* Greyhound's *survivors,* Gloucester *had been reduced to about twenty rounds of anti-aircraft ammunition per gun. By the time she was isolated, the 4-inch guns were only firing spasmodically and although the pom-poms kept up a*

Lieutenant Hugh Singer, survivor 22-5-41.

brisk fire, they were insufficient to cope with the whole squadron of dive bombers whose concerted attacks became bolder. When the order was given to abandon ship, Gloucester *was listing heavily to port. The starboard whaler was lowered but it was so badly damaged that it sank immediately. The port whaler was also unseaworthy. HMS* Fiji *was steaming past at that time, dropping her carley floats in the water for survivors. After performing this task of mercy,* Fiji *left the scene'.*

Lieutenant Singer, without any apparent concern for his own survival, did not abandon ship immediately, but instead established an emergency dressing station on the starboard side, next to the bakehouse. Together with Bill Howe and the rest of his medical party he administered help to injured men, many of whom were close to death. With the pom-pom magazine on fire, shells exploding all around them and low-level attacks from the air, the action of Lieutenant Singer and his party was one of incredible courage and humanity.

Most of the men they treated were from the gun crews and the two most serious cases were strapped on to 'Neil Robertson' stretchers before being passed into one of the carley floats which Ernie Evans had helped to bring alongside the ship.

Lieutenant Singer recorded;

'No more than first aid could be attempted as speed was essential. Dressings were applied and fractures splinted. Those not too gravely

wounded were given gr¹/₄ of morphine, only in order that they might help themselves as much as possible. Others who were more dangerously wounded were given a minimum of gr¹/₂, as their survival under these conditions seemed highly unlikely and there seemed no point in allowing them to suffer unnecessarily'.

Surgeon Lieutenant Commander R G Dingwell joined Singer and his party, told them not to delay abandoning ship for much longer, and reminded them to take their shoes off before they left the ship. Lieutenant Singer, however, still did not abandon ship but continued with his work until the situation was completely hopeless;

'Soon after Dingwell had left us, a number of German aircraft flew over the ship and bombs fell among the survivors who were swimming near the starboard side. After placing the last of the casualties in a carley float, I took the party aft but we were obstructed by a fire that was out of control. I returned to the waist where I found a small party of officers throwing loose wood into the sea for the benefit of survivors. At this moment another man was brought to me with a badly wounded leg. After splinting his leg I lowered him in to a carley float which was about to leave the side of the ship. By now this carley float was full to capacity and the men were up to their chests in water. Some of them were in a critical condition'.

Lieutenant Singer praised the ship's chaplain, the Reverend William Bonsey, and Leading Sick Berth Assistant Brian Priestly, for their valuable assistance in tending the casualties;

'At 1715, I could find no more men needing attention and so we abandoned the ship. By this time the port gunwales were awash and it was simply a matter of stepping down into the sea. Captain Rowley was the last man to leave the ship. Shortly after, HMS Gloucester slowly turned turtle and sank by the stern'.³

Notes

1. There is no record that the order to sink *Gloucester* was countermanded therefore it is presumed that Cpt. William-Powlett made the decision himself not to sink the ship.
2. Pryce J E, *Heels in Line*, Arthur Barker, 1958, p.16 Many other men must have done the same thing as Ordinary Seaman Jim Pryce recalled seeing a row of boots and shoes placed along the guardrail.
3. *Experiences of a Naval Surgeon* by Surgeon Lt H Singer.

CHAPTER SIXTEEN

Aftermath: 'Devastated at the Things I Saw'

T ed Mort, was eighteen-years old when *Gloucester* went down. His ordeal was terrifying for one so young;

> *'The time came to abandon ship. Me and a boy called Donald Allen grabbed a canteen door, which was hanging off, threw it in to the sea and dived in after it. The next thing I remember was the planes machine gunning us and we both dived under water but Allen didn't come up again. I saw a patch of blood in the sea and knew he was gone. I was convinced that I too would be killed. The planes kept coming in at such low levels that at times you could see the pilot's faces. I saw some bombs dropped that I think were incendiaries, which were intended to set the oil alight. I was about half a mile from* Gloucester *when she went down. She turned over for some time, then stood on end before she finally sank. It was a horrible feeling, watching my home going down and being alone, floating on the canteen door'.*

Victor Parsons, nineteen years old at the time of the sinking, gave his account to the Imperial War Museum in a taped interview;

> *'We had run out of anti-aircraft ammunition and in the end we were firing starshells and practice projectiles, until there was nothing left. When the order came to abandon ship, I went over the side without a life jacket on. I saw the ship burning and explosions going off. I swam as far away as possible from* Gloucester, *and then* Fiji *came by dropping carley floats. I managed to hold on to one, a few hundred yards away from* Gloucester. *The ship looked as though a giant had hit her with a hatchet; the gun turrets were hanging over the side; the funnels were*

split and the upper deck was smashed. I could see a big black mass of survivors near the bows of the ship and then a dive-bomber came down and dropped his bombs right in the middle of them. He didn't attempt to hit the ship. When the ship finally sank the explosions from the boilers sent shock waves through the sea and I thought my lower body would fall off. Then I got onto the carley float and there were about forty men in the sea clinging to the raft, or to each other. Then we were strafed by the Luftwaffe's machine guns'.

Frank Teasdale, from *Liverpool*, was twenty-four and an experienced rating when *Gloucester* sunk;

'As the ship tilted over, I slid from the pom-pom deck, over the side and into the sea. I had my Mae West on and swam to a trough that was used by the baker for making dough and was now floating in the water. I was quickly joined by others and soon there was no room, so I swam away and reached a carley float where I held onto the rope around the side. When Gloucester went down it was a terrible feeling. The crew really loved that ship'.

Royal Marine Ken Macdonald, who had managed to scramble aboard *Gloucester* as she was leaving Alexandria, was at his action station in the Transmitting Station for the 6-inch guns;

'At around midday there was a brief respite in the attacks which allowed the exhausted men to get some soup and corned beef sandwiches from the galley. The action soon began again and as the raids increased in intensity the ship suffered several hits until she was dead in the water, on fire and sinking. The Transmitting Station was flooding but I managed to get up on deck where I could see what a wrecked state the ship was in. I quickly abandoned ship but was machine-gunned in the water by enemy aircraft before I managed to get to a carley float'.

Ken was the only survivor from the men in the 6-inch gun Transmitting Station.

Chief Petty Officer Bill Wade had served on many ships before being drafted to *Gloucester* and he was an experienced sailor. Constantly concerned for the welfare and safety of the young seamen under his command, those on board who knew him held him in great affection;

'I knew we had no ammo left and I told my men to keep under cover. The first bombs to hit knocked the after director out of the ship and that is where I would normally have been. When we got into the sea we were machine-gunned and I saw a lot of men killed. The things I saw devastated me'.

Yeoman Petty Officer Bob Wainwright, from Newcastle, had already seen plenty of action whilst serving on *Gloucester's* sister ship, *Liverpool* where he had narrowly escaped death when she was hit by two bombs which failed to explode. Later he was drafted to HMS *Kent* and was on board when she was torpedoed in September 1940. Three days later he joined *Gloucester*.

Bob was stationed on the bridge of *Gloucester* and had a grandstand view of the attacks that took place prior to the sinking;

'When we ran out of ack-ack ammunition we finished up firing the 6-inch guns or starshells, it was a waste of time really. Wave after wave of Stukas were concentrating on us. By the time the order came to abandon ship we had gone another half mile from where we were first hit. I saw men in the carley floats, and men who were swimming, being machine gunned by the enemy planes. I decided it might be safer to remain on the ship for as long as possible. A bomb hit the ship aft and the aft Director Control Tower went up in the air, then toppled over the side, it also took half of the main mast away. The aerials came crashing down and I took cover. One of the aerial insulators hit the captain's steward and it took the top of his head clean off. I went back to the bridge and assisted a Sub Lieutenant to throw the Cypher books over the side. All the time pom pom shells were exploding. Fiji was off the starboard side and Captain Rowley told me to make a signal to Fiji and ask her to come alongside but before I could do so, the captain took the flags from me and sent the signal himself. The reply came back, "Sorry but I will drop carley floats". I made my way to the forecastle, where I saw a Royal Naval Reserve Lieutenant bravely directing men into the water, between air raids. The ship was listing so much that I just walked into the sea where I joined up with signalman Len 'Al' Bowley. We both knew that we could suffer severe internal injuries if the boilers exploded so we decided to swim as far from the ship as possible. The ship was wallowing in the water and I couldn't believe she was about to sink. After Gloucester went down we were swimming from one piece of flotsam to another. Bowley kept asking me if we were going to make it. I told him, "of course we are", but in truth I didn't think that we had a hope in hell'.

The sinking of *Gloucester* was a success story for the Luftwaffe pilots. Gerd Stamp was one of those who attacked *Gloucester* and *Fiji*. He said that 22 May 1941 was;

'A day of historical meaning. Sailors only, in battle against air crews only, focused on one day and on one spot'.[1]

Stamp was correct in his appraisal of the situation, since the Royal Navy had never before, nor have ever since, had to endure such a sustained attack from the air.

Also flying a JU88 was Lieutenant Gerhard Brenner, from Ludwigsburg, the most senior and experienced pilot of the wing.

The German press recorded the sinking of HMS Gloucester.

He and Stamp were two of the pilots who attacked *Gloucester* and *Fiji*.

Stamp recalled that as they prepared for their third raid of the day the runway at Eleusis was like a rush hour, with a constant flow of aircraft coming and going;

*'The briefing officer had told us to fly to Kythira. There, and west of
the Kythira Straits, we would find enough targets and among them
would be two battleships'.*

Taking off in the early afternoon Stamp surveyed the scenic views
against a cloudless sky, became excited when he spotted the two
battleships and thought that they were a majestic sight. He endured
a tremendous barrage from the fleet that was making for the open
sea, south west of Crete;

*'They had left two cruisers near Kythira and we assumed that they
were to go to Crete and bombard the area where our parachutists had
been dropped two days earlier'.*

*'We concentrated our efforts on preventing them from going there.
One was sunk, a few miles from the southern end of Kythira. She had
been burning and the pile of black smoke could be seen from far away.
Brenner and I then attacked the other cruiser closer to Anti Kythira.
We made near misses only and Brenner was furious at himself'.²*

Brenner later secretly took off by himself on a fourth raid and
located *Fiji* by an oil slick from her stern. He dropped a 500lb bomb
so close to the ship that it blew in her bottom and she later sank.
Although 523 men were rescued later that night, 295 men lost their
lives.³ From the original four ships of Force B; *Gloucester*, *Fiji*,
Greyhound and *Griffin*, only *Griffin* survived the day.

Throughout the day of 22 May, many people on the island of
Kythira were watching the battle from the hilltops. George
Kalligeros and his teenage friend Nikos Sotorchos spent the whole
day watching the spectacle of the Stukas attacking the British ships;

*'At first, the ships were shooting against the planes and some of them fell
into the sea in pieces. Later, the planes concentrated on one ship only, while
the other ships sailed away. I had a pair of binoculars and we took turns to
use them. We were just young and it was very exciting to us, we had a
grandstand view of everything. Eventually, the sky became so black with
the smoke from the ships that the sun was blocked out: it was like night'.⁴*

The survivors from *Gloucester* had abandoned ship under the
worst possible circumstances. The one hope, which many of them
had, was that they could see the hills of Kythira and Anti Kythira
and even the mountains of Crete were visible in the far distance.
Some of them thought that they could swim to land, others felt
certain that rescue would be swift. After nightfall, they reasoned,
the destroyers would return and take them from the sea.
Meanwhile it was just a question of hanging on to the sides of the
packed carley floats, or the pieces of flotsam; all that remained of
their beloved ship.

Notes

1. *Crete 1941 Eyewitnessed* pp.127–132.
2. Ibid.
3. Ibid. Lieutenant Brenner was killed in 1942 when his aircraft was shot down in the Mediterranean.
4. Personal interview with Ken Otter 20-5-1998 Kapsali Bay, Kythira.

CHAPTER SEVENTEEN

The Longest Night: Where is our Navy?

Once the ship had gone down, the men in the water had to fend for themselves. Bob Wainright came across two midshipmen desperately clinging on to an upturned motor boat. Realising the precarious position of the young officers, Bob tried to persuade them to leave the wrecked motor boat and swim with him to the main group of survivors. Unfortunately they refused and were never seen again.

None of the ten midshipmen who were aboard *Gloucester* survived the sinking. They included Peter Wyllie, who was making his first voyage after recovering from a fractured skull, which he sustained when *Gloucester* was hit on 8 July 1940.

The men of *Gloucester* paid a heavy price for the destruction of the enemy convoy by Admiral Glennie's squadron during the previous night. Exactly how many *Gloucester* men died from the bombing and machine gunning whilst they were in the sea will never be known but the numbers must have been considerable, especially as those in groups around the carley floats attracted most attention from the German pilots.

Electrical Artificer Albert 'Tubby' Revans wrote an account of his experiences;

'After the ship had finally disappeared I began to feel very lonely. Whilst she remained on the surface there seemed to be something solid that I could go back to if necessary. Then there was nothing in sight except the mountain top of Kythira in the far distance. Nothing, that is, except the heads of a few other men in the same terrible position as myself. I thought about trying to swim to Kythira but guessed that it was too far away so I swam through the oil-covered sea to a carley float. It was manned by Regulating Petty Officer Albert Herniman and several other ratings. I hauled myself aboard

and felt much better off. Inside the raft was the Gunnery Officer, lashed up in a straitjacket stretcher and suffering from a very severe wound in the neck. The only sign of life he showed was a faint gasp now and then and it was obvious that he did not have long to live. The float became more crowded but we came across another one, which was empty although badly damaged. Stoker Bill Hollett and myself decided that we would be better off on the other float. As soon as we boarded it, it sank at one end and I went in to the water up to my neck again. However, we found that we could keep it on an even keel by keeping our weight at one end. We paddled around and found three more men; a South African, Henry McCarthy, a Maltese steward and a boy. The raft, in its water-logged condition, was a poor support for five and we were up to our waists in water but the sea was calm and we managed to make our way towards the larger group of rafts which we could see converging on each other. We were gathering in order to facilitate rescue operations if any of our ships turned up. Just as we reached the others, an incident occurred not calculated to increase our hopes of rescue. Three Messerschmitt 109s came zooming towards us, low over the blue sea. I saw their yellow painted noses dip and swing dead ahead, in our direction. They approached us at a terrific speed then, at about two hundred yards range, I saw twin streams of tracer bullets leave the leader and come streaking toward us. I dived and struggled to get below the surface with my life belt on. Somehow I managed to get a couple of feet under and heard the bullets from the second machine coming, thud, thud, thud, into the water. I came up, gasping for breath, as the third machine opened fire. I was too late to duck but fortunately the bullets landed several yards from me. Three times those machines came for the rafts with blazing guns. It was a most fearful business. There were about twenty of our men killed and wounded. I guessed that the time was then about six o'clock in the evening. We saw no more aircraft, except in the distance, so after lashing several pieces of floating wreckage to our carley float we set off to try and paddle to Kythira'.

Lieutenant Singer, one of the last men to leave the ship, got into the sea;

'I found the water agreeably warm but I soon found that water which is pleasant for bathing is not necessarily a suitable medium in which to spend a day and night. After swimming for about one hundred yards I came across the head of a torpedo but my attempts to get onto it proved useless as the head began to spin round. As I swam away I looked back and saw Sub-Lieutenant Hay attempting the same exercise'.

That was the last recorded sighting of the Sub-Lieutenant.

Singer continued to swim away from the ship, until he came across another group swimming around two fenders, which were loosely connected with a wire rope. They told him that they had been instructed to keep together in as large a group as possible, presumably to facilitate the location of survivors in any rescue operations;

'While I was with this group I watched Gloucester sinking. I felt very lonely in the water after the ship had gone'.

Lieutenant Singer, a water polo player and strong swimmer, thought that Kythira seemed reasonably close so he set off to swim to the island. In fact he was about fifteen miles from land and when he realised that he could not reach the island he returned to the group around the fenders. Soon after his return, the ship's padre, Reverend William Bonsey, decided to set off on his own despite advice from the others to stay together. His body was never found.

Singer gave an unequivocal account of how men were machine gunned in the water;

'Several aircraft came down and machine gunned survivors, both in the water and on rafts. It was one of the more unpleasant minutes, watching a JU88 dive straight for our party and seeing the spurts of water coming at us in a straight line. Fortunately he stopped firing just before he reached us. I believe a number of men must have been killed in this way and I subsequently looked after the blacksmith, who had been wounded while on a raft'.

Petty Officer Jack Donnelly, from Jarrow, was the ship's blacksmith and although he survived the sinking, he sustained a serious bullet wound to his stomach. He was hauled onto a carley float and the following day, picked up by a German rescue craft. Jack eventually had his wounds treated in hospital and survived the war. He died in 1958.

Boy Seaman Peter Everest had a particularly bewildering experience following the destruction of the ship;

'I ended up in a carley float with about fifteen other survivors. My leg was very badly damaged but it wasn't broken. Most of the others in the raft were also injured. One man had lost an arm and he died in the night. We paddled the float about three hundred yards away from the ship and watched her go down. It was an horrific sight and I felt very lonely as a stillness crept over the scene. We were machine gunned when a plane flew low over us. Most of the men in the raft were covered with oil and there were others in the sea, hanging on to the raft. One chap in the raft had nothing

Petty Officer Jack Donnelly, survivor 22-5-41.

on and had a terrific gash in his flesh. He never made a single utterance before he died in the night. He must have been a very brave man. I was so bewildered that I didn't really seem to fully know what was going on. I remember that the salt water in the carley float, which I was sitting in for almost twenty-four hours, helped to disinfect my wounds'.

Fellow boy seaman, John Bassett, said that after he and two other boys got into the sea, they could see land. They attempted to swim ashore but after he had swallowed a few mouthfuls of foul seawater, John decided to swim back to the carley floats. He never saw the other two boys again.

Ernie Evans was on a carley float when three or four yellow nosed Messerschmitts came down;

'I could see the pilots clearly. The planes swung round and came back, firing on us. I could see tracers as they were hitting the water so I got off the float and swam away. Two men were left on the float, one of them was the blacksmith and how he survived the machine gunning I just don't know. The other chap hung onto the side of the float and was shot in the hand. His fingers were hanging off and he died later. I got back on to the float, which was shot to pieces and barely afloat. Many men who had been on the float were killed by the machine gunning. Those of us who were still able restored some order and made the best of it but many more men died during the night'.

John Stevens was helping others to row a cutter away from *Gloucester* but they had only gone about two hundred yards when they discovered that the boat had been damaged by shrapnel and was rapidly filling with water;

'John Mayer, the Petty Officer told us to grab some beams together and make a raft. We found three of the ones that I had earlier helped to throw overboard. The Petty Officer did a great job of lashing them together in an 'H' shape. Then he sat in the middle, to steady it, and told the rest of us to hang on to the sides. How he did it I still don't know. I later found out that he'd also done a great job getting men off the ship and into the cutter. While we were struggling to survive in the water, we were continually machine gunned by the German planes so I pressed my head against the beams for protection. I saw carley floats with fifty or sixty men on and around them and I remember to this day those planes coming at the lads and watching them diving under the water, only half of them coming back up'.

John was a strong swimmer and had represented Ilford before the war. He saw some stepladders floating nearby and thought his chances of survival would be better if he swam to them. Unfortunately the ladders kept tipping over so he returned to the improvised raft;

'At that point we were still confident that we would be picked up later. I saw a messmate of mine, Ebenezer Voakes, floating by with his Mae West on and I called out to him to come and join our raft. He shouted back that he was all right but I never saw him again'.

Nightfall blackened the already dark sky and Albert 'Tubby' Revans recorded what happened on his raft;

'By eight o'clock it was dark, very dark, with no moon and only faint starlight. We could see, or fancied we could see, the dark bulk of the island, looking to the north. But after a while the wind rose dead off the land and raised an icy, chopping sea, which made clean breaks right over us. In addition to chilling us to the bone, it made it most difficult to cling to the raft and we were capsized several times. At about ten o'clock Bill Hollett showed signs of weakening. His breath came in rattling, liquid gasps and there was white foam coming from his mouth and nose, showing against his black beard. We supported him between us and encouraged him as best we could but after about an hour his head fell back and quite peacefully, without a struggle, he died. We took off his lifebelt and released his body, which sank like a stone. Who next? I thought. I soon found out. The Maltese, called Joe Simlar, was already very weak but he clung on doggedly and kept on saying that he was all right. About an hour after midnight we were capsized again and when we got the raft righted, poor Joe was gone. This left three of us. I was quite fit but McCarthy and the boy had gone blind with oilfuel in the eyes. Poor devils, they could do nothing. I tried, nearly all night, to paddle towards where I thought the island lay, but it was hopeless and I suppose I knew it really'.

As dawn broke, Tubby's fears were realised and he knew his efforts to reach Kythira had been in vain, even though the sea was calmer and the raft was now floating better with fewer men on it;

'So we drifted all that miserable morning. McCarthy's lungs were full of oil and water he had breathed in the night before, he died at about 1100. I put him over the side and saw his body sinking down and down through the clear water. I could still see him fathoms deep, sinking slowly with his dead eyes open and rolled up, only the whites showing. The boy was in a bad way now, blind and very weak. I could see that he would not last long. About midday he began speaking wildly and a little later raved incoherently for about half an hour, then suddenly he fell quiet and died at about two o'clock in the afternoon. By then I was too weak to take off his lifebelt, so he drifted away on the surface, his red hair resting on the water'.

During the night many men died from sheer exhaustion, from the events of the previous twenty-four hours and the incredibly demanding itinerary of the previous months. Some died from the wounds they had sustained during the attack on the ship and some died from being machine gunned in the water. As the night wore on more and more men died as they were waiting to be rescued.

Billy Grindell described his long night;

'The carley float could hold perhaps thirty or forty men inboard. When one died he was put over the side and somebody who was in the water was pulled on board. Eventually I got pulled on and there were two other stokers in the raft, Jimmy Henshaw and Billy Doyle. We were sitting in the float with water up to our necks. Fatigue was our worst enemy at that point but if you went to sleep it was fatal. Both Doyle and Henshaw fell asleep and drowned in the float at my feet. The following morning there was only six of us still alive'.

Bill Howe was on a float, parts of which had been shot away, and men were hanging onto the sides and paddling with their free hand;

'Later we joined up with some other rafts and after dark an officer attempted to navigate by the stars, although by morning we hadn't moved more than a mile from our original position. One young rating was so demented with thirst that he kept taking mouthfuls of sea water until his tongue swelled so much that he choked to death'.

John Stevens recalled more horrors of the night;

'I was clinging onto the beams which we had lashed together to make a raft. In the early evening the body of marine Ken Mawby floated by and I saw that he had two lifejackets, which a first aid party must have attached to him. I realised that if I was to survive I badly needed one of them, but I couldn't undo the knots. Suddenly a messmate of mine grabbed hold of me. His eyes had a glazed look that we later termed, "the glare of death" and the next thing I knew was that he was taking me down with him. I managed to get his grip off me and get back to the surface. I reached the float but by that time Mawby's body had floated away'.

During the night, some of the men with John Stevens started singing songs in an attempt to keep their spirits up but as the time wore on their singing died away;

'Later John Mayer, the Petty Officer, started to get 'the glare' and then the beams broke apart and he just floated away. That left eight of us and through the night most of the others faded away, one by one, without saying anything. Dawn broke and only me and Hugh 'Ginger' Connolly were still alive, although we were dangerously tired. We were

John Stevens, survivor 22-5-41.

feeling very cold so we climbed onto the beams and urinated on ourselves in an attempt to get warmed up a bit. Later we got back into the sea, but we got cramp and so we spent the rest of the morning getting on and off the beams. The sea became choppy, then suddenly Ginger said to me, "I've had enough mate". I told him, "Hang on Ginger. You can make it", but he just let himself go under. I tried desperately to keep him afloat but in the end I had to let go of him and he drifted away'.

John, now completely alone, faced his own ordeal to stay alive as he slipped towards unconsciousness;

'There was only me left and I had two voices in my head. One was saying "You're going to die, you're going to die" and the other voice saying "You mustn't die, your mother says you mustn't die". My widowed mother idolised me. I was her only son and all the time I kept thinking of the effect my death would have on my mother. The two voices kept up a constant battle with each other but gradually the voice that said I was going to die began to dominate. I thought then that if I was going to die it would at least be peacefully and I leaned over the beam and put my head in the sea. As I did this the other voice screamed at me, "You mustn't die, you mustn't die"'.

Other survivors had similar experiences of hallucinating during the long hours after *Gloucester* had been destroyed.

Bob Wainwright and his friend, Len 'A1' Bowley were also in the water all night. Bob recalled what happened to them;

'We reached a group of men who were gathered around a raft made up of two barrels, which were lashed together. There were three or four men on each side so we stayed in the water. During the night there was a bit of panic as some men tried to get onto the raft for a rest. I told young Bowley that we should swim away and let them get on with it and that's how we spent the night, just swimming to and from the raft. It turned over a few times in the night as men tried to climb on to relieve their tiredness, but by the morning there were only three men left alive on the float so we were able to get aboard and rest. It was then that I started hallucinating and saw what I thought was a Martian in the sea with long hair that drifted out to point in the water. Later I thought I saw a Maltese fishing boat behind us and I couldn't understand why the man sailing it didn't pick us up so I started shouting to him'.

Bob Wainwright's raft eventually went alongside a carley float, which he and Bowley scrambled into.

Eighteen-year old Ted Mort stayed in the sea for five hours before he was pulled onto a carley float to take the place of a man who had died. On the float he met up with the officer in charge of the Royal Marines, Captain Richard Formby. In his letters home to his wife, Pam, Richard Formby had written that he hoped the war would not go on for much longer and that he would soon be reunited with her and their three children. Even though he was a tough man and very fit from being a champion boxer, Richard Formby died during the night.

Ordinary Seaman Victor Parsons was covered in oil, like most of the other survivors. He ended up on the same float as Petty Officer Jack Donnelly, the ship's blacksmith. Jack, who was in extreme pain from the machine gun bullet wound in his stomach, survived the night in the float, sitting hunched over and uncomplaining. Others, hanging on to the sides around the float, just drifted away in the night. Vic recalled;

'Those of us in the float kept our spirits up by chatting and singing but as the night wore on my spirits dropped and I thought I was going to die. I tried to cling to the hope that we would be rescued, which always happened after a ship went down'.

Most of the men expected a rescue operation to be mounted during the night and Douglas Hall recalled an officer on his float giving him a whistle to blow. But as dawn broke those who had survived the night realised that the likelihood of rescue was remote.

Surgeon Lt Singer was intrigued that so many uninjured men had died during the night;

'One of the most astonishing features of this unfortunate business was the ease with which some men gave up the struggle for existence and allowed themselves to drown without apparently making any effort at all. Admittedly the "Mae West" proved a most unsatisfactory form of lifejacket, but it did give valuable support and was effective if the swimmer helped himself a little. And yet from the time I abandoned ship until far into the night I saw men, among them several first class swimmers, just give up. There was no panic. They died very peacefully. Two of them actually smiled to me and said "good bye". I think they must have been affected sooner, and to a greater degree, by a sort of lethargy, which one had to fight. I found that even I could contemplate drowning without any qualms, and at times I had an overwhelming urge to let down my "Mae West" and give up what seemed an unending and pointless struggle'.

Lt Singer spent most of the night hanging onto some fenders with about twenty other men. Nearby he saw Commander Tanner supporting himself on a drawer but after dark the Commander disappeared and was never seen again. Singer and the diminishing number of men around him still hoped that they would be rescued during the night;

'Throughout the night our hopes were falsely raised many times and in retrospect the situation had comic elements. We all hoped that a destroyer might come back to look for us after dark and we were keenly on the lookout for one. In the distance we saw the searchlights on Crete and mistook them for those of a ship. Accordingly we raised a shout. Some distance away in the dark, Lt Cdr Heap was in a carley float, heard our shouts and mistaking them for hails from a rescue ship, blew his whistle. We heard his whistle and optimistically assumed that we were about to be picked up. So began a vicious circle which was broken only when we were too tired, or too full of water, to shout any more but which began all over again if either of us got a false alarm'.

Only six of the original twenty men clinging to the fenders with Singer were alive when dawn broke and one of those men drowned soon afterwards. Lt Singer and Chief Petty Officer Evans collected a couple of pieces of wood to use as paddles in an attempt to reach the island of Kythira which still appeared to be tantalisingly close. They didn't make it, nor even get close, but the effort of trying helped to keep their minds focused.

In the early morning light of Friday 23 May it became painfully obvious to the survivors that there would be no rescue by the Royal Navy. The safety of darkness had gone and no operation would be carried out in daylight when there would be a danger of further attacks from the Luftwaffe.

Ken Macdonald summed up the feelings of the survivors;

'Again and again we asked ourselves what had happened to the destroyers. Why hadn't they returned to pick us up after dark?

Lt Cdr Stitt, in 1944, suggested that a message had been sent to the Naval Officer in Charge at Suda Bay, asking for rescue craft to be despatched but that there were none available. However, the Letters of Proceedings submitted after the battle of Crete, do not mention any such signal being sent.[1]

The records show that a rescue operation was mounted, albeit a brief half-hearted one, on the evening of Thursday 22 May, by two ships of Lord Louis Mountbatten's 5th Destroyer Flotilla, which had arrived west of Kythira at about 1600, just after *Gloucester* was first hit. The movements of Mountbatten's flotilla need to be closely considered to understand why the destroyers rescued no survivors from *Gloucester*.

Mountbatten's 5th Destroyer Flotilla, made up of *Kelly, Kashmir, Kipling, Kelvin* and *Jackal*, had been operating in the waters around Malta. On Wednesday, 21 May, Mountbatten had been ordered by Cunningham to proceed east towards Crete and rendezvous with Rear Admiral Rawlings' Al force, west of Kythira, not later than 1000 on 22 May.

On the voyage east, Mountbatten became involved in an unsuccessful search for a submarine and after being ordered by Cunningham to break off the search, his flotilla finally joined Rawlings' force.

Rawlings' report on the battle stated that the air attacks had ceased at 1810, when his force was 60 miles southwest of Kythira. At 1928 Rawlings received a report that *Fiji* had been hit and was sinking. Cunningham said that at 2030 *Kelly, Kipling* and *Kashmir*, were ordered to search for survivors and that the destroyers, *Decoy* and *Hero* were despatched to embark the King of Greece and members of his government, from Agriarumeli on the south coast of Crete. At 2100 *Kelvin* and *Jackal*, Mountbatten's two other destroyers, were deployed to the Kythira Channel to pick up *Gloucester* survivors.[2]

As darkness fell and the threat of further air attacks diminished, the obvious question to be asked is why a search for *Gloucester* survivors wasn't mounted until 2100, which was over half an hour after the rescue ships had been sent to *Fiji's* survivors. If *Kelvin* and *Jackal* had been deployed to search for *Gloucester* survivors at 2030, they would have reached *Gloucester's* last known position at around 2230 and certainly no later than 2330. This would have given them three or even four hours to carry out the rescue and still have at least three hours to steam south before dawn broke.

The deployment of *Kelvin* and *Jackal* would seem to have been an afterthought following the sinking of *Fiji*, which had gone down some three and a half hours after *Gloucester* had been hit. *Kelvin* and *Jackal* were ordered by Rawlings to abandon the search at 2143 when they were already steaming towards *Gloucester's* last known position. They were then ordered to proceed to Kissamo Bay and Canea Bay to patrol the area. Rawlings states in his report that he was becoming increasingly concerned about how scattered his forces had become and that he wished to have them in a position where they could rendezvous south of Crete, by dawn.

There is no evidence to suggest that any enemy convoys were en route to Crete, which would have justified *Kelvin* and *Jackal* being called back from the search. It was known that there were no more convoys on their way to Crete, as a result of the German Enigma code having been broken. In fact, *Kelvin* and *Jackal* spent the rest of the night on a futile patrol during which they failed to locate or sink any enemy shipping.[3]

Mountbatten's other ships, *Kelly, Kashmir* and *Kipling*, failed to locate the position of *Fiji* or to pick up any survivors. They were subsequently deployed to patrol off the north coast of Crete where *Kipling* developed a steering fault but *Kelly* and *Kashmir* went on to destroy two stray caiques and shell the airfield at Maleme.

The survivors from HMS *Gloucester* continue to feel aggrieved that *Kelvin* and *Jackal* were called back from the search before they had reached *Gloucester's* last position. Furthermore the fact that two destroyers could be found to rescue the King of Greece has reinforced their belief that ships could also have been found to rescue the *Gloucester* men.

Notes
1. *Under Cunningham's Command 1940-43*, George Stitt, Allen & Unwin 1944.
2. PRO ADM 199/810 110319 and *London Gazette* 24-5-99.
3. Ibid.

CHAPTER EIGHTEEN

Picked up by Germans: Caiques and Kythira

On Friday 23 May, during the late morning and throughout the afternoon the surviving *Gloucestermen* were eventually rescued.

Ken Macdonald recalled his rescue;

'It must have been late in the forenoon that we heard the sound of aircraft and then sighted two planes flying low over the sea, dropping flares. As they got nearer we recognised with a feeling of dread, the yellow painted noses of our adversaries of the day before, but to our overwhelming relief they soon disappeared. Shortly after this encounter we sighted a small vessel which, after executing frequent alterations of course, causing acute anxiety and frustration with every movement, finally and to our immense relief it came alongside the raft and we were hauled aboard'.

Sam Dearie was soon rescued;

'When I saw a caique coming towards my float I stood up, intending to wave but instead I fell into the sea. I remember how cold I was and that I couldn't stop my teeth from chattering. I was pulled onto the caique and told to take off my overalls. I didn't have a stitch on underneath. I was given a cigarette and sent below, where I found a bunk and immediately fell asleep. When I woke up there were around forty or fifty other survivors down there with me'.

Victor Parsons also recalled the desperate state that he was in when he was rescued;

'We didn't realise that they were Germans who were rescuing us. I was covered in oil and I think, at first, they thought that they were

picking up their own survivors. I was exhausted and from the waist down I was like a jelly and couldn't stand up'.

Bob Wainwright also recalled that the rescue crew thought that he was a German soldier;

'All I had to my name were my underpants, a money belt containing a 'French letter', five cigarettes, some matches and the top of a matchbox'.

Throughout the morning and afternoon the half-dead survivors were picked up. It is ironic that they were eventually saved by Germans who had commandeered Greek caiques and were in fact searching for their own men from the ill fated convoy which had been decimated by Glennie's force the previous day. Had the convoy not been destroyed there would have been no search and it is probable that none of the *Gloucestermen* would have survived.

Lt Singer, who was still with CPO Evans, described his excitement at sighting his rescuers;

'Finally, in the afternoon, we saw a small ship cruising and stopping at intervals to pick up survivors. As she drew closer we shouted until we were hoarse and to our great relief the ship suddenly altered course and came straight for us. I was assisted on board with a boat hook. Our rescue ship was a small vessel, probably used for trading among the Greek islands. The Greek crew had been replaced by Germans'.

After stripping off their wet clothes, Singer and Evans were sent below to a large cabin, which occupied most of the aft of the ship;

'We had not seen another soul in the water all that day so we were very glad to find other survivors from Gloucester in that cabin. There were double tier bunks all round the bulkhead and although there were not nearly enough to go round, we all managed to pile in somehow. I slept at once and only woke when we reached harbour. Then the first thing I did was to take a drink of water which made me, and all the others who drank water, violently sick'.

Frank Teasdale was on the same float as Petty Officer Ellender, Royal Marine Bert Ham and able seaman 'Tubby' Salter;

'When we saw the rescue craft we didn't know whether to wave at it or not. Petty Officer Ellender decided to take a chance and so we were rescued'.

Ernie Evans was in such a state of shock by the afternoon that he didn't even realise that his rescuers were German until he was aboard the boat. John Stevens was in no doubt as to who his rescuers were;

'I'd almost given up hope when I saw a plane circling low over the sea. I thought I was about to be machine gunned again but the plane

fired flares and flew off. Then I thought I'd been left to die. About half an hour later I saw a caique coming. It was flying a flag with a swastika on it. Two German sailors threw me a line but I didn't have the strength to hold it. They steered the caique round to me and leaned over the gunwales to pull me from the sea'.

John was one of the last men to be rescued. In general the attitude of the rescuers towards the survivors was good. They were given water and bread and Lt. Singer said that he was given a blanket to keep himself warm.

CPO Bill Wade however, was concerned about the lack of medical treatment given to ordinary seaman Kenneth Bickell, who had celebrated his eighteenth birthday only two weeks earlier. Bill recalled that the boy was alive when he was passed from the float to the rescue craft, although he was in a bad way. Bill said that the Germans would not allow Bickell to be attended to and that he was left on the upper deck, where he soon died. John Bassett, a boy seaman, had been on the same float and confirmed that Bickell was still alive when he was picked up by the rescue craft.

From HMS *Gloucester's* total company of 810 men, only eighty-five survived the sinking of the ship and the subsequent twenty-four hour ordeal in the water. The body of Kenneth Bickell and seventy-seven survivors were taken to the island of Kythira in one of the German commandeered Greek caiques. Seven survivors, who were picked up in other boats, did not go to Kythira but were eventually taken to Athens.

Ken Ayers, a twenty-eight year old supply assistant had been on *Gloucester* for only ten days. It was his first ship and he had not had any time to forge friendships on board. In civilian life, Ken had been a schoolteacher in Luton from where he had volunteered to join the navy. By the time he was rescued he had drifted away from the other survivors and was picked up by a small boat and taken to the tiny island of Anti Kythira. From here he was transferred to Athens.

Lieutenant Commander Roger Anthony Heap and Surgeon Lieutenant Hugh Singer were the only survivors from fifty-one officers and midshipmen on board *Gloucester*. Only nine of the ninety-six Royal Marines and four of the thirty South Africans survived. All five of the civilian NAAFI men were killed along with nine Maltese stewards and cooks.

Admiral Cunningham was deeply upset at losing so many ships in the battle of Crete. Captain E T L Dunsterville RN, was a survivor from HMS *Kelly* who was taken back to Alexandria where he spent some time in Cunningham's company;

'He had a tremendous talent and was known to us as the 'Red Eyed Tyrant', yet he was most upset at our losses in the battle and evacuation of Crete. He and Lady Cunningham used to walk up and down at night, distraught at what was happening'.

Cunningham later told Mountbatten that when he heard of the losses he felt like;

'getting onto a destroyer and going out and getting myself killed'.[1]

When the losses were totalled up, it is little wonder that he felt so grieved. Of the fifty-four ships engaged in the battle for Crete and the subsequent evacuation of troops from the island, eleven vessels were lost, twenty-two were damaged and two thousand, two hundred and sixty-one men were listed as killed or missing.[2] Cunningham described it as;

'a disastrous period in our naval history'.[3]

The loss of *Gloucester* stands out as a particular tragedy since over 30% the total naval personnel killed were lost from that one ship. Of all the British warships that were sunk or damaged during the battle of Crete, *Gloucester* was the only one from which the Royal Navy picked up no survivors.

Captain Rowley's body was washed up four weeks later and found by fishermen on a beach near Mersa Matruh, on the North African coast, four hundred miles away from where *Gloucester* had gone down.[4]

On 17 August 1941, Admiral Cunningham wrote to Captain Rowley's mother, Christina;

'He died as he had always lived, most gallantly and the Navy mourns the loss of grand officer and fine man who, had he lived, would have gone very far'.

Cunningham paid tribute to the extraordinary service that *Gloucester* had given under his command;

'Thus went the gallant Gloucester. *She had endured all things and no ship had worked harder or had had more risky tasks. She had been hit by bombs more times than any other vessel and had always come up smiling. As she left Alexandria for the last time, I went alongside her in my barge and had a talk with her captain, Henry Aubrey Rowley. He was very anxious about his men, who were just worn out, which was not surprising, as I well realised. I promised to go on board and talk to them on their return to harbour, but they never came back. I doubt if many of them survived as they too were murderously machine gunned in the water. Rowley's body, recognisable by his uniform monkey jacket and the signals in his pocket, came ashore to the west of Mersa Matruh, about four weeks later. It was a long way to come home'.[5]*

17ᵗʰ August
COMMANDER-IN-CHIEF,
MEDITERRANEAN STATION.

My dear Mrs Rowley,

Your letter only arrived today.

I fear that by this time you must have been informed by the Admiralty that what was almost certainly the body of your son was washed up at Alexandria about a month ago & buried there.

I cannot tell you with what deep regret, I & indeed the whole fleet learnt that he had died in that action off Crete. He died as he had always lived most gallantly & the navy mourns the loss of a grand officer & fine man who had he lived would have gone very far.

You will have seen that for his work at the Battle of Cape Matapan he was awarded a very well deserved D.S.O. & I hope that this recognition of his sterling worth & the fact that he died most nobly for his country may be of some comfort to you.

My deepest sympathy & that of the whole fleet is with you in your tragic loss.

Yours very sincerely
Andrew Cunningham

Admiral Cunningham's letter to Captain Rowley's mother.

Cunningham was in no doubt that the loss of *Gloucester* could have been avoided. The golden rule which he and his captains had learned was that in encounters with enemy aircraft in the confined waters of the Mediterranean ships must keep together for mutual defence and never be deployed for individual tasks. He said;

'*The fleet should remain concentrated and move in formation to wherever any rescue or other work had to be done. The detachment of* Greyhound *was a mistake, as was that of* Gloucester, Fiji *and the other ships. Together, the fleet's volume of anti-aircraft fire might have prevented some of our casualties'.*[6]

Cunningham believed that, had he been at sea, *Gloucester* would have been saved and he put the loss down to the inexperience of some of those at sea.[7] Officially, Cunningham recorded;

'*The junction of Forces A & C on the afternoon of the 22 May left the Rear Admiral Commanding, 15th Cruiser Squadron, (King) after a gruelling two days, in command of the combined force. Before he had really time to grasp the situation of his force, a series of disasters occurred, the loss of* Greyhound, Gloucester *and finally* Fiji. *Past experience had gone to show that when under heavy scale air attack it is essential to keep ships together for mutual support. The decision to send* Kandahar *and* Kingston *to the rescue of* Greyhound's *people cannot be cavilled at but in the light of subsequent events it would probably have been better had the whole force closed to their support. The Rear Admiral Commanding, 15th Cruiser Squadron (King) was however not aware of the shortage of AA ammunition in* Gloucester *and* Fiji'.[8]

However in private correspondence, Cunningham was far more scathing about the inadequacies of Rear Admiral King and went so far as to highlight the fact that, irrespective of how much ammunition *Gloucester* and *Fiji* had, they should never have been deployed away from the group safety of the fleet.

On 30 May 1941, he wrote to Sir Dudley Pound, The First Sea Lord, expressing his personal views;

'*Some mistakes were certainly made in the conduct of our operations, the principal one being the failure of CS 15 (King) to polish off the caique convoy in the morning...I could cheerfully put up with our losses had we had some thousands more Hun soldiers swimming in the Aegean. The sending back of* Gloucester *and* Fiji *to the* Greyhound *was another grave error and cost us those two ships. They were practically out of ammunition but even had they been full up I think they would have gone. The Commanding Officer of* Fiji *told me that the air over* Gloucester *was black with planes'.[9]

Pound replied, expressing similar doubts;

'*19/6/41 Are you satisfied with King as CS 15. If you are not, let us shift him. We cannot afford to use second class material when first class is available'.[10]

King was soon removed from his post and given a desk job at the Admiralty. Cunningham's private correspondence to Pound continued;

'*18/9/41 I was not very happy about him. I was much upset that he failed to utterly destroy that convoy full of Hun soldiers, south of Milo, particularly when his destroyers and the two little a/a cruisers* Carlisle *and* Calcutta *were getting in well among the caiques...I have always had the feeling that he was a better office wallah than sailor. He wants everything cut and dried and most precise orders, doesn't exhibit much initiative at sea'.[11]*

King never went to sea again and was placed on the Retired List on 15 June 1944.

In the months following the sinking of *Gloucester,* the awful fact that the rescue had been aborted, and the survivors left to their own fate, was clearly on the minds of both Sir Dudley Pound and Admiral Cunningham. On 19 June 1941, Pound wrote to Cunningham;

'I had hoped very much that most of the Gloucesters *would have got ashore on Kythira Island'.[12]*

On 25 July 1941 Cunningham replied;

'I have not heard one word about any of the Gloucester's *ship's company though there is a rumour, that the Germans broadcast, that 75% of them had been rescued'.[13]*

The belief that many of *Gloucester's* men have survived has been incorrectly handed down as fact by some researchers. David A Thomas wrongly states;

'But the Germans had rescued more than 500 Gloucestermen, *many by air-sea rescue aircraft'.[14]*

C A Macdonald claims;

'Although it was at first thought that Gloucester *had gone down with all hands, nearly 500 were picked up after the battle by Italian destroyers or German float planes and became POWs'.[15]*

The Royal Navy's own historian, Captain S W Roskill DSC RN, in his official history, was mistaken about the events following the sinking of HMS *Gloucester* when he wrote;

'That night destroyers searched for survivors from Gloucester'.[16]

That search never took place, as we have learned, since *Kelvin* and *Jackal* were recalled before reaching the area in which *Gloucester* had gone down.

Whilst the lack of clarity about the abandonment of *Gloucester's* ship's company has been misleading, the lack of adequate recognition for the bravery of Captain Rowley and his ship's company is disturbing.

On 8 January 1942, The Lords Commissioners of the Admiralty wrote to Christina Rowley, the Captain's mother;

'On May 22nd 1941, this gallant Officer handled and fought his ship with exemplary courage, skill and devotion to duty throughout a day of heavy and frequent air attacks, until, in the afternoon, she was put out of action, and at 1600 she sank.

Despite this acknowledgement of his *'exemplary courage'*, and bearing in mind that *Gloucester* was deployed on an impossible task, it is surprising that their Lordships did not award Captain Rowley, at the very least, a bar to the DSO which he was awarded following the battle of Matapan. Instead he received no more than a, 'Mention in Despatches'. No other member of *Gloucester's* ship's company has ever been given any award in connection with their action in the battle of Crete.

Such bravery against hopeless odds should surely have merited a far higher award for the Captain at least, in recognition of the action of the whole ship's company.

Notes

1. Zieglar Philip. *Mountbatten: The Official Biography*. Collins 1985. p143.
2. *Crete 1941 Eyewitnessed*, appendix.
3. *A Sailor's Odyssey* p390
4. Captain Rowley's body rests in the Alexandria (Hadra) War Memorial Cemetery; plot 2, row A. grave 21. From the 723 men who lost their lives on board *Gloucester* during the battle of Crete, only two others have known graves: Mr C F Williamson, the ship's schoolmaster who was aged 41, and Supply Assistant Kenneth Higgins who was aged 25, are both buried in the Commonwealth War Graves Cemetery at Suda Bay, Crete.
5. *A Sailor's Odyssey* p.371.
6. Ibid p.373.
7. Warner, Oliver. *Cunningham of Hyndehope, Admiral of the Fleet*. John Murray. 1967. p.154.
8. Para. 7&8, Cunningham's Despatch 4 August 1941. Pub. 21/5/48 London Gazette.
9. Cunningham's private letters, B.Lib ref: MSS 52561.
10. Ibid.
11. Ibid.
12. Ibid.
13. Ibid.
14. *Crete 1941 Eyewitnessed*. p.164.
15. Macdonald CA. *The Lost Battle - Crete 1941*. p.249.
16. Roskill, Captain S W. *The War at Sea 1939-1945*. HMSO 1954. p.442.

CHAPTER NINETEEN

Death And Daring: Two Young Greek Heroes

The main group of survivors from *Gloucester*, plus the body of Kenneth Bickell, were taken back to the island of Kythira by their German rescuers. Tired and hungry, the prisoners were brought up on deck as the caique moored in Kapsali Bay. When they

Kapsali Bay, Kythira 1941. The survivors were landed on the mole and moved around the bay. They were held for ten days in the house on the extreme left.

were rescued, the Germans had stripped the men of most of their scant clothing. Some were completely naked others wore only a pair of underpants. The prisoners were mustered, counted and then marched around the bay to a large house that had been occupied by the Germans.

A Company of German troops was stationed on the hilltop at Hora, directly overlooking Kapsali Bay. Among them were some Mountain Troops who had been rescued from the invading convoy that had been decimated by Glennie's force in the previous thirty-six hours. The reaction of the Germans on coming face to face with British sailors, whom they held responsible for the massacre of their comrades, was predictable.

The terrified prisoners were made to stand against a high wall: they were facing a squad of German soldiers who had their guns trained on them. Bob Wainwright heard a German officer order his troops to prepare to fire. John Stevens remembered that Lt Cdr Heap, who could speak some German, jumped forward and told his captors;

'We are not destroyer men. We are cruiser men'.

All the survivors remembered this terrifying incident vividly: at the time they were convinced that after their struggle to survive for so long in the water, they were about to be shot. Lt Singer described the incident;

'An enormous bull-necked Lieutenant came and delivered a harangue. The substance of this, when thoughtfully translated, was that as our troops in Crete had consistently mutilated their enemies, the British prisoners were to be shot in revenge'.

Fortunately a German military doctor was present and he intervened. The prisoners heard the words, 'Geneva Convention' spoken, after which the guns were eventually put away.

Ken Macdonald was one of the prisoners who had faced the German guns;

'A German captain came up to us after the guns had been lowered and said in perfect English, "You are lucky that the German navy picked you up. If it had been up to me I would have had you shot." I found out later that this German officer had survived Glennie's attack on his convoy and the next morning had sent out the caiques to search for any of his men who might still have been in the sea. It was one of those caiques that found us.'

The prisoners remained continually wary of their German guards following the terrifying ordeal in front of the firing squad. The survivors remained on the island of Kythira, in a house that Lt Singer described as;

'being in bad repair, but the conditions were quite tolerable'.

Ken Macdonald remembered that immediately after the dreadful experience in front of the armed Germans, he and the rest of the prisoners were herded into the house where they collapsed on bare boards and slept until the following morning.

The burial of Kenneth Bickell now had to be arranged. The Germans directed that the body should be interred in a dry creek behind the house. Nikos Sotorchos, one of the boys who had watched the battle from the hilltops, recalled that the villagers in Kapsali Bay told the Germans that the creek flooded in winter and that if Kenneth Bickell was buried there his body would be washed away. The Germans eventually took the body and laid it to rest in quiet spot on a nearby hillside. A few stones and a wooden cross, with the boy's name inscribed on it, marked Kenneth Bickell's resting-place.[1]

Surgeon Lt Singer treated those men who were injured. Most of them had swallowed oil and the doctor made up a solution to make them sick. Others were allowed to bathe their wounds in the sea and used small pebbles from the beach to scrub most of the oil off their bodies and out of their hair. With the help of the warm sun they gradually regained some of their strength.

Food was in very short supply. The Germans made it clear that they would share none of their food with the prisoners. Fortunately, however, some local people were sympathetic to their plight and arranged to get food to the prisoners despite the risk to their own lives.

Nikos Sotorchos and two of his friends, who were all about fifteen years old at the time, devised a plan to feed the prisoners. They collected some eggs, together with milk and bread. One of the boys, who could speak some German, occupied the guards at the front of the house by offering them the eggs. Meanwhile, Nikos and his other friend crept along the dry creek and managed to smuggle the bread and milk to the prisoners, via the courtyard at the back of the house.

After a few days, word spread across the island that Nikos and his friends were struggling to supply the British men with small amounts of food. People from nearby villages soon offered some of their own food and provided a donkey to carry it down to Kapsali Bay and the young boys were able to continue feeding the prisoners.

John Stevens never forgot the risks that those boys took to get food through to the men;

'It was an incredible act of kindness, which put their own lives in danger. Had it not been for them I have no idea where we would have got food. I doubt if many of us would have survived long without it'.

TWO YOUNG GREEK HEROES

The survivors remained on the island until the fall of Crete, ten days later. The more seriously wounded men, including Blacksmith Donnelly, still with a machine gun bullet wound in his stomach, a rating with a fractured skull and Royal Marine Noel Haines, who had inhaled oil into his lungs, were flown by seaplane to Athens. Eventually Noel Haines was sent to Klagenfurt, Austria where he died from the effects of the oil on 16 October 1941.

On 4 June, the prisoners still scantily dressed and without footwear, were taken in caiques from Kythira to Piraeus. Before he left the island, Len Bowley had found a few small sheets of note paper and he began to record a diary of events which happened to him;

'Wednesday June 4th 1941. Left Kythira in 3 boats (Greek) on way to Athens'.

John Stevens, wearing only a pair of calico shorts with a length of wire as a belt, recalled that during the voyage he and Royal Marine Bert Ham found some tins of pineapples in the hold. They went to a lot of trouble to steal some of the tins but then realised that as they had no way of opening them they had made a pointless effort.

During their journey north, Petty Officer Ellender had been entrusted to steer the caique for a while. The crew of only four German sailors would have been easily overpowered at this point and suggestions were made to commandeer the boat and sail for Alexandria. The chances of them making a successful journey through four hundred and fifty miles of hostile water were extremely unlikely so the idea was not pursued.

On the morning of 6 June, they arrived at Piraeus where they were amazed at the devastation they encountered. They had been to the Port on numerous occasions during the previous months and had seen some damage during the evacuation of the Allied troops, but the full might of the German offensive was now apparent to them as they surveyed the bombed port. As soon as the men were put ashore however, the triumphant enemy diverted their attention.

Noel Haines, died in POW camp 16-10-41.

Ken Macdonald recalled;

'The reception committee of German Military wasted no time in showing their hostility and enforcing it with their rifle butts'.

John Stevens said that the prisoners were broken up into groups of about a dozen men and made to march around, while being watched by crowds of tearful Greeks. The men were photographed and filmed for use in propaganda newsreels. The Germans also broadcast that 75% of the ship's company had been captured after the sinking.

Royal Marine Ernie Evans remembered being marched through Piraeus and Greek people throwing cigarettes to them, much to the annoyance of the Germans. A register was made of the prisoners' details, including their dates of birth.

When Peter Everest said that he was just sixteen years old, the Germans jeered and took the opportunity to declare that Britain must be losing the war if they had to send sixteen year olds out to fight for them;

'I felt very vulnerable at that point. Big German soldiers, all laughing at me for being so young, surrounded me. I had been through such a lot but their taunting reinforced the awful plight I was in'.

The next day the prisoners were taken in lorries, to the outskirts of the City of Corinth, sixty miles east of Athens, where a temporary prisoner of war camp had been built. Conditions in the camp were appalling; there were no toilets or medical facilities.

Len Bowley made an entry in his diary;

'June 7th taken by road to Prison Camp at Corinth. Terrible conditions. Slept out in the open air'.

Ken Macdonald recalled the camp;

'We had a food ration of a loaf of bread between ten men, a cup of ersatz coffee and a bowl of cabbage-water soup. It was no surprise that many men were showing signs of dysentery and other medical problems. We also learned that some trigger-happy guards had been responsible for numerous deaths'.

Bob Wainwright said that while he was in the camp his group were told by a German officer that, because of the atrocities committed by British troops on Crete, every tenth prisoner was to be shot. Bob spent a restless night but next morning the officer said that he had changed his mind. This all may have been part of a psychological game being played out against the prisoners; many of the survivors recount stories of being taunted by their captors.

In the camp the prisoners were given their first opportunity to write home. They were supplied with a sheet of flimsy paper, almost like tissue paper, and a pencil stub. Len Bowley, who was twenty-one years old and had been married for just five months, wrote to his young wife in Broadstairs, Kent;

L.H.BOWLEY C/JX211740 7 June 1941 A Prisoner Of War Camp. O/SIG

My Own Darling Wife,

I am afraid that when you heard that my ship had been sunk, I was the cause of you having a lot of worry. Well darling, eight days after your twenty-first birthday my ship went down fighting! We were very unlucky because the Royal Navy could not pick up any survivors. There are very few of us left out of a large crew. We spent 19 hours in the water and oil-fuel, hanging on to pieces of wood and one or two rafts. Of course I lost everything when the ship went down, and I had so many souvenirs that I was going to bring home to you sweetheart. When I was picked up I had just my pair of overalls on. But my own darling Beryl, I had your letter with the two snaps of yourself and one of your mother and Marge, in my pocket. They got soaked in the sea, but I have dried them off, and I treasure them very much. As soon as I get to a proper camp I will be able to send my address to you so that you can write. It will take a long time for letters to travel, but it will be so lovely to hear from you again. Please have a lot of snaps taken and save them until I come back to you. Please put the date on the back of each snap. I am only allowed to use one sheet of paper so I must soon say goodbye. Please remember me to all, and let my mother know that I am a Prisoner of War and I and not wounded. To you Beryl darling I send all my love, I can put up with anything knowing that you are waiting for me.

Your ever-loving husband,
Len
xxxxx

P.S. When I am able to send my address please send a snap or two in each letter.[2]

The seventy-eight prisoners who had been held on Kythira were now waiting to be transferred from Corinth. The smaller group of seven prisoners, who had been taken straight to Athens, was detained there in an army barracks. 'Tubby' Revans described the conditions in the Athens camp;

'Here we made our first acquaintance with the hardships of POW life. The place was crawling with bugs and the food was meagre and hardly fit for human consumption. It was several days before I became hungry enough to eat anything. We had biscuits that were green with mould, black peas crawling with weevils and ersatz tea. In time, we all got used to it somehow'.

Meanwhile, the main group of prisoners was marched from their camp to Corinth railway station. Len Bowley's diary records some details;

'Sunday June 8th 3am 1600 of us walked 7 miles to station, then by rail to Athens, arrived at noon. Meal at 3pm. Still got no boots'. At the station they were herded into cattle trucks for a long journey north to Salonika. Len wrote more details in his diary; *'Long train ride. Arrived 2.30am. Started 25mile walk to? Left 3am and arrived 2.30pm Blisters!'*

After twenty hours they were forced out of the trucks and made to continue the journey on foot.

Ken Macdonald described the conditions on the train;

'We were issued with a loaf of bread and a small tin of meat paste. We were crammed into cattle trucks, fifty men to a truck. The doors were locked and we set off in conditions where we had no space to lie down and without even room for everyone to sit down at the same time. There were fourteen men from Gloucester in my truck and we were fortunate in being together in one corner. We devised our own system of watch, with seven of us sitting down while the other seven protected us from the crush. After four hours we would change places. The only ventilation was from four small grills, set high up in the sides of the trucks. The temperature inside those compartments, travelling under the hot sun in southern Greece, was unbearable. Two large bins had been provided; one contained drinking water and the other was intended as a toilet. Several of the prisoners were suffering from dysentery and the stench inside the trucks was disgusting. After almost twenty-four hours in the cramped, foul smelling and unbearably hot trucks, the train stopped and the doors were opened. A tunnel through the Braillos Pass had been damaged by retreating Allied troops and the train had been forced to terminate its journey. We were ordered to get out of the trucks'.

The men were then forced to march over mountains, to Salonika, in the intense heat. They still had no footwear and many of them had no more clothing than a scant pair of shorts. There

Telegram from the Admiralty to Ken Hooper's family.

were many casualties on the march and the prisoners were under constant threat of being shot if they fell behind or tried to escape. Lieutenant Singer spent much of his time doubling back and forth among the men, treating prisoners who had been overcome by heat or were suffering from the debilitating effects of dysentery. Many of the *Gloucester* survivors remember other prisoners dying on the march to Salonika although many were sustained with food and water given by Greek people as the column passed through villages.

During the next few days the column slowly moved north, through the Thermopolae pass. They slept in fields or beside the road at night, and passed under Mount Olympus on their journey, before eventually reaching Salonika. They had walked over 150 miles.

From the day news reached home that *Gloucester* had sunk, families of the ship's company were left to speculate on the fate of their loved ones. In fact a full list of *Gloucester's* casualties was not published until the war had ended and even then most of the ship's company were listed as 'missing presumed killed'.

Ken Hooper's family, at home in Plymouth, were sent a telegram from the Admiralty telling them that the ship had gone down. Ken's girlfriend, Audrey, who was serving in the WRNS at the time, was on duty when the message came through and she had to arrange for the sad news to be delivered to his parents. Understandably, they

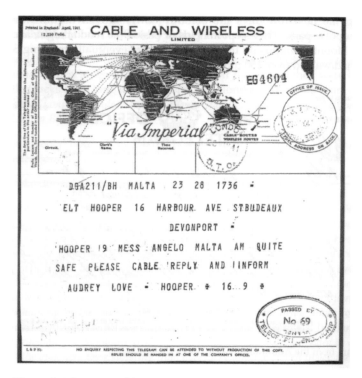

CABLE AND WIRELESS
LIMITED

EG4604

"*Via Imperial*"

DGA211/BH MALTA 23 28 1736 =

ELT HOOPER 16 HARBOUR AVE ST.BUDEAUX

DEVONPORT =

HOOPER 19 MESS ANGELO MALTA AM QUITE

SAFE PLEASE CABLE REPLY AND IINFORM

AUDREY LOVE = HOOPER + 16.9 +

PASSED BY
No 69

Ken Hooper's telegram to his parents.

were all distraught at the news and Audrey, unable to contemplate staying in Plymouth any longer, immediately volunteered to go to work in the British Embassy in Washington DC. She was given embarkation leave and prepared to set off on the journey across the Atlantic, with five other WRNS who had also volunteered to go.

Meanwhile, news of *Gloucester's* fate had reached the hospital in Malta, where Ken was still recovering from the operation to remove an abscess from his back. Realising that his family would think that he was on board when she was sunk, he quickly sent a telegram to his home informing them that he was alive.

When the good news reached Audrey she was about to leave for America. She went to her commanding officer, explained the situation and asked for her posting to Washington to be withdrawn. The commanding officer was sympathetic to her request and she returned to her previous duties.

The ship on which Audrey would have sailed was torpedoed by a U-boat on its journey across the Atlantic. The five other WRNS who were on board all lost their lives.[3]

Notes

1. The wooden cross is no longer there and the exact location of the grave has not been traced.
2. The original of this letter is too fragile to have risked trying to reproduce a photograph of it for inclusion in this book. The letters that Len refers to having in his pocket when he was in the water were dried out and he managed to keep them with him throughout his captivity. He still keeps the fragments of paper and some of the original writing can just be made out, although it is very faint from being in the water for so long.
3. Both Ken and Audrey had a fortuitous escape from death. They later married and still live in Plymouth.

Prison Camps: Salonika to the Stalags

S urgeon Lt Singer described the camp at Salonika and the awful circumstances in which the prisoners found themselves;

'*Dulag 183, Salonika, was a camp closed to the outside world. No representatives of the protecting powers, or of the International Red Cross, were ever allowed inside. The Commandant, Oberleutnant Schmidt, a middle aged officer with greying hair, cold eyes and a Himmler chin, delighted in the misery which he caused and was always baffled and enraged that he could not break the spirit of the British prisoners. The camp sergeant major shared this feeling and used to revenge himself by beating and kicking his charges. Of the two doctors, the senior officer, himself a caricature of the traditional German, appeared to know nothing of medicine and enjoyed despotic rights over the fate of everybody in the camp. His assistant, though generally well disposed, had no authority. The camp itself had been built for the Turkish army during its occupation of Salonika. It was distinguished mainly by a commodious bathhouse; when not disqualified by the shortage of water this was the best place in the camp. The camp was always crowded; between eight and twelve thousand prisoners might be in it at any one time. The main parade of the day began at 0600 and often went on till well into the afternoon. Officers were not called upon to work but everyone else, even if they were genuinely ill, had to go out on working parties. Rations of between 900 and 1,200 calories a day were quite insufficient for men who had to do hard manual labour and those who entered the camp in good shape very quickly became no more than skeletons of their former selves. The day began with ersatz tea, dirty pink in colour. At lunchtime unpalatable soup of greasy water, flavoured with lentils and barley, was served; sometimes as a treat the normally inedible parts of a horse or water buffalo were added to this. Later in the day one fifth of a Greek loaf was issued to each man, varied twice a week by the addition of some bad cheese. The evening issue of soup was, as a rule, not quite so good as the morning one. After some weeks the privilege was granted of buying a little fruit and cheese in the local market on two days a week.*

'*Meanwhile the guards amused themselves by throwing occasional scraps of food over the wire and watching the scramble that followed. On other occasions when a condemned issue of cheese had been thrown into the dustbins, the prisoners fought with each other and with a tribe of giant rats for any fragments which might be edible. The physical conditions of life were humiliating to the most extreme degree. Sanitation was scanty and primitive; the prisoners slept on the floor in overcrowded rooms and were there assailed by bugs of quite exceptional number, size and ferocity.*

'*Newcomers were often almost unrecognizable after their first night in the camp. Dozens of the creatures would drop from the deckhead and crawl freely over each sleeper. Mosquitoes, lice, fleas and flies were also a perpetual scourge. For those who were demonstrably very seriously ill a hospital existed. This was kept very short of both food and medical supplies; although there was at Salonika an enormous dump of captured British medical equipment very little of this ever got through to the camp.... epidemics of beri-beri and diphtheria had to be treated without any of the essential remedies. There was no aspirin for the scores of men who suffered constantly from sandfly fever. There was no soap and there were no towels'.*

Whilst at Salonika, Lt Singer worked tirelessly to alleviate the suffering of the prisoners. His day started at 0530 and he was often called out at night to deal with injuries sustained by prisoners from

Marlag Milag Nord. Back row: (L to R) Tubby Revans, Duke Ellender,Unknown,Froggy Morrellic, Bob Wainwright, Tubby Sanderson. Middle row: (L to R) Ken Macdonald, Bill Wade, Paddy Walsh, Taff Evans, Sgt Laverick, B Williams, George Lofthouse. Front row: Butch Wade, Rattler Morgan, Freezer Frost, Ginger Stewart, Spike Maloney.

stray bullets that the guards fired into the prisoners' accommodation for no apparent reason.

Ken Macdonald summed up the feelings of all the *Gloucestermen* towards the camp;

'We hated the place. It was full of despair and depression, hunger, sickness and death. Dysentery and other diseases were rife and the death toll was high'.

The camp was, however, the eventual rendezvous point for the two groups of *Gloucester's* survivors although the joy of the reunion was dampened by the realisation that so few of the men had survived.

The smaller group of seven men, which Tubby Revans was in, had arrived at Salonika before the main party got there on 12 June. It was a happy reunion although Jim Pryce, who had come in with Revans said that when he approached 'Butch' Wade, a South African who had served on *Gloucester*, Wade did not recognise him because he had lost so much weight. Ken Macdonald described Pryce as being, 'like a match with the wood scraped off'.

Len Bowley's diary records how he reached Salonika and what happened to him during the next few days;

'Monday 9 June 7pm. Left by train for Salonika. Arrived Tuesday 10th June 4pm. Last part of journey I was in truck with army ratings. Went to another prison camp. Went into hospital with my blistered feet. Wednesday June 11th. Rest of party left for another camp. Saturday June 14th. Left hospital at Salonika. Stopped in Prison Camp. Monday 16 June. Went to another camp (5 miles)'.

The prisoners were moved from Salonika after twelve days with the exception of Lt Singer, who remained there until 28 August, when he was sent to Germany in an ambulance train.

On 24 June, the prisoners were once again herded onto cattle trucks to be transported north to Wolfsberg in Austria. Ken Macdonald described the ordeal;

'To this day I do not know how I survived that dreadful journey. Apart from a short break every twenty-four hours, for the issue of bread and water, we were incarcerated in that filthy hell on wheels for an unbelievable thirteen days. In our truck alone there were two deaths and in spite of our protests, their bodies were not removed for several days. We were never to know the total death toll of that horrific journey'.

Ernie Evans also remembered the horrors of that journey;

'The journey in the cattle trucks was a dreadful experience. I was with Reg Wills and Peter Everest. Peter was very ill with dysentery. The train stopped and Peter was in a bad way, so Reg lifted me up to the bars at the top of the truck. I could see a guard and I shouted to him for water, but he just raised his rifle and fired into the roof of the truck, causing splinters to hit my face'.

Heydebreck POW camp. Back row (L to R) Len Bowley, Bert Ham, Chas Watters, Maurice O'Leary, Joe Reid. Front row (L to R) Frank Teasdale, Nichols, Tubby Salter, John Stevens.

Ted Mort had more recollections of the journey;

'When we left Salonika all we had was a small tin of meat, a bottle of water and a piece of black bread. It didn't last long and once it ran out it was about a week before I had anything to eat again.'

Ted said that when he was onboard *Gloucester* he weighed about eight stones but by the end of the war he had lost three stones due to the lack of food.

Len Bowley put down his experiences in his diary;

'Tuesday 24 June. Left Transit Camp by train to another camp in Austria arriving after a terrible journey in cattle trucks. No air, water or food. When it rained I borrowed a spoon from Army lad and caught the rain, through grills in cattle wagons, to drink'.

Eventually the starving and exhausted prisoners reached the end of their journey. Some of them, including Ernie Evans and Peter Everest, had been put off at Marburg in Yugoslavia. The rest arrived at Wolfsberg, in southwest Austria and were told that they were about to be marched to the POW camp.

John Stevens recalled that many of them were too weak to stand any longer and a group of them sat down in the road;

'A German officer came along, waving his pistol and we thought we would be shot. We let him know that we were too ill and weak to march. The other POWs were marched off and some time later trucks came and took us to the camp'.

Stalag XVIIIA was an established POW camp, mainly occupied by French prisoners, and a few British soldiers who had been captured at Dunkirk. It had recently been extended to cope with the influx of prisoners taken after the fall of Greece and was better than the appalling conditions of the camps at Corinth and Salonika.

It was not until the men reached this camp that they were officially registered as prisoners of war and issued with a POW number. They were each given cards, which they could send home to their families, showing their POW details. They were issued with clothing and some were given tetanus injections. The clothing was very welcome since most of the *Gloucestermen* were still wearing only shorts. Many were also without footwear, although the Red Cross had given some men triangles of cloth which they were able to tie round their feet.

Ken Macdonald described the issue of clothes they received, which were bits and pieces of uniforms captured from countries that Germany had overrun.

'I was given a pair of powder blue cavalry breeches, complete with a two inch gold stripe down each side. A pair of wooden sabots were issued for my feet and a vivid green tunic, with scarlet facings, completed the ensemble'.

Sam Dearie was issued with a Yugoslavian officer's jacket, which was a pearl grey colour;

'I got a pair of very wide riding breeches which looked quite comical'.

The prisoners were detailed off into working parties and it was an additional blow to many of the *Gloucestermen* to find that they were now split up from their shipmates after they had all endured so much together.

The working parties did road construction or relaid railway sleepers. Many of them had to work for twelve hours, with only a wash in cold water and some basic food to look forward to at the end of their day. It was hard work. John Stevens remembered that he once had to remove the decapitated body of a young girl who had committed suicide on the railway line that he was working on.

In his small battered diary, Len Bowley continued to write down his experiences;

'1 July 1941 Camp at WOLFSBURG. Inoculated at 2pm. Thursday 3 July left WOLFSBURG for another camp in Austria. Went by train arriving next morning July 4th. Then on to another camp high up in the hills. Working 10 hours a day on roads with 2 mile walk to job. Saturday half-day, no work Sunday. Sunday 20 July moved to another camp about 18 miles away. Went by lorry'.

The prisoners, who had been sent to the camp at Marburg in Yugoslavia, went through a similar registration process to the men at Wolfsberg. They were deloused, photographed, inoculated and issued with clothing and their POW numbers.

Tubby Revans had lost about forty pounds in weight since his capture only three months before and found that he was too weak to cope with the work;

'I had to unload 200lb sacks of flour from lorries and I just couldn't manage it. Then they gave me a job as a cleaner at an Army Cadet School, where I managed to get some scraps of food'.

Blackhammer POW camp. Back row (L to R) Nichols, Doug Hall,
Happy Day, Dolly Gray. Front row (L to R) Leverton, George Friend,
Jim Pryce, Sammy Brown

By September of that year, Revans and some of his fellow
prisoners were billeted out to work on farms collecting the harvest.
Revans recalled that the farmer and his wife looked after him very
well. On his first evening they fed him a meal of pork, chicken,
beetroot, cake and plenty of wine. Although the work was not hard,
the hours were long and each night he was so exhausted that he
just fell into his bed. With sufficient food, fresh air and manual
work, together with proper sleep, he began to rebuild his strength
and regain his personal dignity. Only a few prisoners enjoyed such
a comparatively easy life, but the majority was not so lucky.

Billy Grindell was at Marburg and was detailed to a work on road
building. Despite being fit, he didn't like the work and managed to
convince the authorities that he had dysentery. After a period in the
camp's sick bay Billy was sent to work on a farm but to his disgust
found that he was expected to work seven days a week. The truculent
Welshman, together with three Australian soldiers, decided to take
the matter into their own hands and on the following Sunday
morning they stayed in their bunks. The men's revolt went horribly
wrong however and ended in tragedy when an enraged guard came
into the hut and sprayed it with bullets, killing two of the Australians.
Billy got fourteen days in the cells on a diet of bread and water.

Sam Dearie recalled how he was also in a road building party
when he and five Australian and New Zealand soldiers refused to
work beyond the limit which their guard had set for that day. The
arrival of six German soldiers with fixed bayonets soon settled the
strike however. Sam, like most of the survivors, had to carry out
heavy manual work whilst existing on a starvation diet.

Len Bowley recorded a long awaited and very welcome arrival;
'September 3rd. Received 1st Red Cross Parcel. Scottish branch British
RC Society. Sunday 7th had my first shave. There was a concert. Monday

Sept. 8th. The whole camp threatened to strike because of the food rations. Officer came on Tuesday. 3 men sent away from Camp. Friday Sept.12th 1.30pm myself and 3 other naval ratings were given 1 hour to pack kit and leave for Wolfsberg. All naval ratings called to Wolfsberg. Spent night near Spittal. Left station 7am Saturday Sept.13th arrived Wolfsberg 7.30pm. No food rations all day. Monday Sept. 15th received 2nd Red Cross parcel (Scottish branch) and new British Battledress. Friday Sept. 26th. Tea meal has been cut out. Threats by men not to work. We were due to leave for naval camp on Wed.23rd Sept. then on Sat.27th departure postponed again. After another 2 or 3 postponements, left Stalag 18A Wolfsberg 5am Saturday October 4th 1941 (I have known Beryl 5 years)'.

The *Gloucester* survivors who had been deployed away from Stalag XVIIIA, at Wolfsberg, had all been recalled to the camp by early October. It was a happy reunion for them particularly as they were given food parcels from the International Red Cross and were issued with British battle dress, shirts, socks and boots which had just arrived at the camp.

On 4 October 1941, the *Gloucestermen* were marched to Wolfsberg station to be transported to the naval prison camp, Marlag, in Northern Germany. John Stevens recalled;

'A German officer told us that we were about to be repatriated in exchange for German sailors who were being held in Britain. Because we had just been given proper British uniforms, we believed the story'.

Ken Macdonald recalled that as they made their way to the station their morale was higher than at any time since the sinking of the ship, four months earlier. The train journey north was luxury in comparison to the nightmares of their previous train journeys, although at one point the train stopped while an Allied air raid took place. The men were terrified because they could not get out of the carriages.

The journey took three days but before they could be taken to the naval POW camp, they were interned at the German naval barracks at Wilhelmshaven. Here they were interrogated about the radar equipment that *Gloucester* had carried. The men were determined not to be cooperative with the Germans but many didn't know much about the radar anyway. Their stay extended to several weeks and for much of the time the prisoners were cooped up in the barrack rooms day after day. It became evident to them that they were being held to punish them for their lack of cooperation during the questioning.

They had to face further danger from an unexpected quarter whilst at Wilhelmshaven, which was a key German naval port. It came when the RAF carried out bombing raids on nearby dockyards and although the raids were frightening for the men, fortunately the barracks were not hit.

Len Bowley recorded details of his journey from Wolfsberg to Wilhelmshaven and some of the events that he experienced there;

'Travelled by Cattle Truck (seats 30 in a truck). Arrived Bremervorde 2pm Tuesday Oct.7th. By bus and trailer to Camp at Sandbostel Sailns in Marlag. Merchant navy in Milag Internment Camp. We went there. First class concert on Wed. night by Henry Mollison, Merchant Seaman. One hour notice to pack kit and leave Sandbostel on Friday Oct.10th 11am by bus to Station then from noon by train (carriages) to WILHELMSHAVEN arriving Oct.12th 6.20am. By lorry to RM barracks. From window could see damage done by RAF. Clock stopped at 9.58pm!!! 29 of Glos. Crew in one small room, (attic).

Wed. Oct.29th. I went to RAF (7men) funeral at Wilhelmshaven cemetery with 15 other ratings from Glos. Raining and sleet all the time. Bodies washed up from sea. German Air Force band and 10 in party which fired 3 rounds at burial. White ensign laid over graves. Bodies already buried.

Wednesday Nov.19th. I was questioned by a Commander from 3.30pm to 6.30pm about Gloucester, then again on Thursday morning.

My 1st Wedding Anniversary on Sunday Nov. 23rd. My own darling Beryl. Tuesday Dec.9th 1941 left Wilhelmshaven, arriving 4pm same day. Wed. saw concert: '2 Smart Girls'. Pantomime in Christmas week. Heavy snow Christmas Day and freezing hard.

28/12/41 Received 2 pairs of socks from rating from 'Undine' who lives Kitchener Ave. Chatham. First pair in 7 months prisoner of war'.

On 9 December 1941 the *Gloucester* survivors were transferred to Marlag und Milag Nord. It was the same day that Britain declared war on Japan, joining the United States as an ally. From now on Germany would be fighting against not only the British Commonwealth but also the might and wealth of America.

Christmas Card from POW Camp.

POW Camp postcard sent from Bert Ham to Jack Ivey.

CHAPTER TWENTY ONE

Four Years of Hell: Liberation at Last

The naval POW camp that the men joined was split into two sections; Marlag, where the Royal Naval officers and men with the rank of Petty Officer and above were detained, and Milag, where men of the Merchant Navy were held. Despite the snow and freezing conditions of winter in Northern Germany the men were pleased to be back among naval prisoners. Lt Singer and Lt Cdr Heap were already in the camps and were delighted to meet up with the men who they had last seen in Salonika.

The accommodation was cramped but tolerable. Lt Singer and other naval medical personnel manned a sick bay and each camp had an orchestra and theatre for entertainment. Boxing and football matches were organised and there was an educational centre with a well-stocked library. Red Cross parcels, together with parcels from relatives at home, ensured that the prisoners' rations were supplemented. The food parcels did however depend upon the ease with which they could be transported and as the Allied bombing of Germany intensified, so the supplies dried up and the conditions under which the prisoners were held worsened. The men settled into a routine but some became very depressed and Billy Grindell recalled at least one prisoner who committed suicide.

In Marlag camp, most of the *Gloucestermen* had been passing themselves off as Chief and Petty Officers, as men with those ranks did not have to do work, in accordance with the Geneva Convention. A few months later the Germans managed to verify the true ranks of the men through the International Red Cross and as a result some were moved to other camps where they would have to do work.

Ken Macdonald managed to get himself appointed as a batman to Lt Rogers, the leader of the camp orchestra and so avoided transfer. While Macdonald and those above the rank of Petty Officer remained at Marlag, the other ratings were sent on a 600-mile train journey east, to Stalag VIIIB in Poland, where they were to remain for the next two years.

Stalag VIIIB was situated at Teschen, just east of the border with Czechoslovakia. It was a bleak, hard existence for the men as they endured the long, cold winters with the quality and quantity of their food diminishing as the war slipped from Germany's grasp.

There were still some ratings from *Gloucester* who remained in Stalag XVIIIA at Wolfsberg for most of the war, although they were seconded out on working parties.

Ted Mort, for part of the time he was a prisoner, had to work at an iron ore works. He suffered from bronchitis and pneumonia during the war and ended up with emphysema in later life, which was attributed to the dust he inhaled during his work as a prisoner.

Most of the prisoners recalled freezing temperatures, hard work and a poor diet. Bill Howe was on a working party clearing a railway tunnel which partisans had blown up. The food was sparse and as the contractor only had to provide food for them on the days they worked, the prisoners were not fed on Sundays. For most of the time they lived on bread, ersatz coffee and potatoes. Bill worked on roads and railways until the end of the war without any contact with the other survivors from *Gloucester*.

Some prisoners recalled tales of their efforts to sabotage the German war effort by pouring sand or grit into the petrol tanks of lorries. Victor Parsons was once caught shovelling grit into the machinery at a quarry where he was working and was punished with daily beatings in the cells following the incident.

Several attempts to escape were made, although most were of short duration. Petty Officer Bill Wade managed to escape with a New Zealander and the pair rowed a boat down the Danube. They were picked up after forty eight hours and spent ten days in solitary confinement existing on bread and water. Douglas Hall escaped whilst on a working party in Poland but without maps or currency his freedom was short lived.

Ted Mort made several attempts to escape but each time he was recaptured and spent a lot of time in special punishment camps. He recalled one such camp at Landeck, in Austria where the most persistently troublesome prisoners were made to carry stones in backpacks to the top of a mountain, drop their load and return to carry another load. During one escape Ted almost got to Yugoslavia where he hoped friendly partisans may have looked after him but to his dismay he was recaptured and sent to Klaggenfurt gaol, for collection by the German military.

Ernie Evans met Petty Officer 'Jumper' Collins in one of the prison camps. This was an amazing coincidence as before the war they had lived only three doors from one another in Plymouth. Collins had earned his nickname in the camp because of his numerous attempts to escape. It was not long before he invited Ernie to join him on yet another attempt but the guards thwarted their plans. Evans and Collins were sent back to Stalag XVIIIA where they spent a period in solitary confinement. During an Allied air raid in 1944, Ernie's legs were shattered when the roof of his POW hut fell in. He was treated for his injuries at the time but due to a lack of calcium in his diet, his bones would not knit together and he remained in plaster until he returned to England.

When the Allied landings took place in Normandy, on 6 June 1944, it was three years and two days since the *Gloucestermen* had left the island of Kythira. Now, spread through various prisoner of war camps in Germany, Austria, Yugoslavia and Poland, they picked up scraps of information about the Allies' progress across Europe. They knew that their release must come eventually but they still had to face the harshness of yet another winter, with further diminishing supplies of food.

POW work party with German cook. Ernie Evans and Peter Everest, far right.

Towards the end of December 1944, the Russian army was advancing westward and the Germans decided to abandon some of their POW camps. Prisoners held in a camp at Blechammer, halfway between Cracow and Breslan, were made to leave on 23 December. The prisoners, including some *Gloucestermen*, set out in freezing weather, supplied with only one blanket each. Marching through desperately cold winter storms they struggled to survive on sugar beet, stale black bread and occasional issues of potato soup. At night they slept wherever they could find shelter but Victor Parsons remembered men freezing to death on the forced march.

Jim Pryce suffered from frostbite on the journey and later he wrote;

> *'It seemed as if we were doomed never to get away from the eternal snow and the bodies that lay motionless beside the road. There was no longer an element of luck in survival, it was simply a case of fitness and ruthless determination. It was every man for himself.'[1]*

In three months the men had marched over four hundred miles, through the bleak winter, existing on a starvation diet until they reached Stalag VIIA at Moosburg, twenty miles north of Munich.

John Stevens was marched from Poland, in a group of about 250 men, through Czechoslovakia to Moosburg. He recalled the horrors of that march and the number of bodies of Jews, Russians and Poles who had been shot or died whilst being forced to march west along the same route. When the American forces reached Moosburg on 29 April, John weighed only 8 stones 5lb. He had weighed 13 stones when he was on HMS *Gloucester*.

Len Bowley tried to escape three times during his captivity. On his third attempt he met up with advancing American forces in Bavaria. From there he was taken by road to Paris where he was kitted out in American Army uniform and was able to send a telegram to his wife, Beryl who was at home in Broadstairs. From Paris he went to Le Havre where he boarded a ship to Southampton and then caught a train to Broadstairs. Len arrived home one month before the war ended.

Frank Teasdale recalled that Bert Ham hid himself away in the camp. He wanted to stay behind with Tubby Salter who was too sick to make the long march that Frank and the other prisoners were forced to undertake. Bert and Tubby didn't have to wait too long before the advancing Russian guns could be heard and the few remaining German guards abandoned their prisoners. The jubilant POWs took their first steps towards a long awaited freedom.

Bert and Tubby left the camp and joined a procession of refugees who were struggling along the narrow road, pushing their possessions in handcarts and prams. Suddenly, they saw a Russian fighter plane swoop down towards the column of people. Bert dived for cover as the plane strafed the road, killing and injuring many of the defenceless civilians. When he recovered himself after the plane had gone he found that his fellow shipmate, Tubby Salter had been killed in the attack. It was a tragic end for the sailor who had endured so much and Bert could do no more than bury Tubby at the roadside.

Prisoners detained in Marlag camp, near Bremen, had their hopes of being rescued raised as the advancing armies' gunfire came closer on the morning of 2 April 1945.

The Germans told the men that they were preparing to abandon camp and would leave only a few men behind to hand over to the advancing Allies. The prisoners were delighted and rejoiced at the news but during the afternoon a detachment of SS soldiers ordered the prisoners to pack up and leave the camp. A few prisoners, among them Bob Wainwright and Bill Wade managed to hide and avoided being moved on. The rest of the men, walking as slowly as they dared, stretched out in a long column heading east. At midnight they halted for rest and set off again at dawn, hoping that the advancing Allies would soon overtake them. During the morning some RAF planes flew overhead and the men were confident that they would be recognised as POWs. To their horror however the planes opened fire, killing and injuring many of the POWs.

Ken Macdonald dived into a ditch when the firing started and he remembered the bravery of a senior British naval officer who stayed on the road marshalling the men to safety. The officer was killed along with other prisoners, some of whom had been captive since 1939.

The euphoria of the previous day now turned to bitterness as the men witnessed their fellow prisoners being killed and wounded by 'friendly fire'. The main core of their anger however, was directed at the Germans who had made them leave the comparative safety of the POW camp to embark on a senseless march east. The dead and wounded were taken to a nearby hospital and the grim march continued. They faced another three air attacks that day.

The prisoners spent the night in a wood and were terrified by planes flying overhead and dropping flares to help them search for the enemy. The following day a senior naval officer got the Germans to agree to let the column rest during the day and march at night under cover of darkness. The Germans were in as much danger from the planes overhead as the prisoners were and they seemed relieved by the plan. After ten arduous days the column reached the River Elbe and was ferried to the other side. Their march continued until 28 April when they reached the city of Lubeck on the shores of the Baltic Sea. They had been marching for four weeks with little food, shelter or medical facilities.

At Lubeck the men were lodged in an army barracks. In the distance they could hear what was the last artillery barrage of the war, as the River Elbe was crossed at Lauenburg and Allied forces occupied the last barrier in north-west Europe.

The men spent the next two days in excited anticipation, which was heightened on 1 May, when news reached them that Hitler was dead. On 2 May the prisoners woke to the sight of thick smoke rising from the outskirts of the city of Lubeck. They heard gunfire during the morning but this stopped just after midday and soon they saw tanks and jeeps of the 11th Armoured Division heading along the main road into the city.

The special unit dealing with liberated POWs were given a tumultuous welcome when they entered the barracks where the *Gloucestermen* were being held. Official registration took two days before the men were taken south to Luneburg. Here they had a frustrating wait for three more days before transport could be arranged for their flight home.

On VE Day, 8 May 1945, most of the *Gloucester* survivors, who had been held at Marlag, landed in Buckinghamshire. It had been six years and three months since *Gloucester* had sailed from Plymouth.

Note
1. *Heels in Line* p.218.

CHAPTER TWENTY TWO

Homecomings: Church Bells and Babies

S am Dearie was eventually flown home following his release. His father had died in 1943, while Sam was being held prisoner but his mother made sure that he had a traditional Glaswegian welcome. Sam kept a newspaper cutting from the *Glasgow Times*, which recorded his homecoming;

> *'On active service repatriated; Dearie.*
> *Mrs S Dearie wishes to thank Newbank*
> *Welcome Home Fund committee for the*
> *social evening and gifts to her son*
> *Samuel on his return from Germany.*
> *49 Glammis Road, E1.'*

Peter Everest, the young boy seaman who had joined *Gloucester* as his first ship, just four days before her sinking, remembered the joy of his liberation;

> *'We were in a camp near Salzburg when the Americans reached us. They gave us Lucky Strike cigarettes and chocolates. It was wonderful although the next day everybody was ill with stomach upsets and had to be given castor oil'.*

A few days later he was flown to England and arrived home just before his 21st birthday. Peter's mother did not know that he was due to arrive and was amazed to see her boy, who had left home when he was only sixteen, standing on the doorstep.

Bob Wainwright eventually reached his home in Newcastle Upon Tyne and had an emotional reunion with his family.

Gloucester *survivors at the war memorial, Plymouth Hoe, 1992. (L to R) Frank Teasdale, Billy Grindell, Ernie Evans, Maurice O'Leary, Bill Howe, Bill Wade, John Stevens.*

Tot time with the Mayor of Plymouth, 1990. (L to R) Reg Wills, Frank Teasdale, John Stevens, Fred Farlow, Maurice O'Leary, Bill Wade, Billy Grindell, Ken Macdonald.

John Stevens was flown home in a Wellington bomber;

'As we approached England the pilot invited us to go up to the flight deck to see the white cliffs of Dover. It was a most emotional sight and when we landed at Oxford all I can remember seeing was lads getting down to kiss the ground'.

John travelled to his home in Essex where he was greeted by the sight of *'Welcome Home John'* banners strung across the street. He recalls that people who he had never met before came up to shake his hand.

Billy Grindell flew back with Lt Cdr Heap and Surgeon Lt Singer both of whom were delighted to see him again. Billy later travelled to Wales by train, with Ted Mort. Ted left the train at Newport while Billy continued on to Cardiff where he saw his daughter, Margaret, for the first time: she had been born after *Gloucester* sailed in 1939.

In Newport, Ted Mort got off the train and set out on the happy walk to his home. He knocked at the door and was perplexed that there was no answer. A neighbour, seeing him at the door, came out and broke the terrible news that his mother had died and his father had moved to the Cotswolds in order to get work. It was a dreadful homecoming for the young sailor.

Ernie Evans had a delayed homecoming as he was detained in hospital for a while because of the injuries to his legs which he had sustained in Stalag XVIIIA. When he did arrive in Plymouth he couldn't believe the state the city had been left in by the bombing and he found it difficult to find his way home with so many familiar landmarks gone. When he eventually got there a 'Welcome Home Ernie' banner was flying across the street.

Bill Howe had spent most of his period as a prisoner separated from the other *Gloucester* survivors. He was released by American soldiers and flown back to England where he was issued with a travel warrant to Bovey Tracey, the nearest railway station to his home village of Manaton, on Dartmoor. On the journey he had to change trains at Newton Abbot and he took the opportunity to telephone a friend of the family and inform her that he was on his way home. When Bill arrived at Bovey Tracey, the lady was waiting to drive him home in style in her Austin Seven. Bill's father had been the sexton at the village church and, as a boy, Bill had learned to ring the bells. When the car drove into the village the road was packed with people to welcome him and the church bells were ringing out;

'My mother was in tears when she saw me. I had weighed 12 stone when she had last seen me and I was only eight stone when I got home'.

There were 810 men aboard HMS *Gloucester* when she was
destroyed on 22 May 1941. Only 83 survived to come home at the
end of the war in 1945.

The men and boys who lost their lives continue to be
remembered by the remaining survivors and their families who
gather each year at the Royal Naval War Memorial on Plymouth
Hoe on the anniversary of the sinking of their ship;

HMS Gloucester: *'The Fighting G'.*

CHAPTER TWENTY THREE

The Story Continues

Since the publication of the first edition of this book I have received many letters from families and friends of the men and boys who lost their lives on *Gloucester*. The sinking of the ship devastated over 700 families and it is hardly surprising that so many of them were keen to learn how their loved ones had lived and died. Many wanted to share more stories, and personal letters, which illustrated the personalities of the men who served on *Gloucester*.

Some of the stories are heartbreaking. Reg Bull is still trying to trace the whereabouts of his father's body. In 1941 Reg Bull's mother received a letter from a man living on Crete saying that he had found a body on a beach and that correspondence in the pockets indicated that the body was Leading Stoker Reg Bull of HMS *Gloucester*. The Cretan said that he had buried the body, as he didn't want the occupying German forces to dispose of it. After the war the Cretan wrote again to Mrs Bull asking if she wanted the authorities informed so that the body could be interred in the Commonwealth War Graves Cemetery at Suda Bay. Contact was then lost with the man who had found Leading Stoker Bull's body. His son, Reg, continues to make numerous enquiries in his search for more information but, so far, without success.

Joyce Jenkins sent me a copy of a poignant letter from her brother, Fred Hunt, who was lost when *Gloucester* went down:

I hope everyone at home are alright and in the best of health, and I'm longing for the day when I see you all again, you might write in your next letter what's to do at home whether or not your rations are cut down any more than when I was home, and stuff like that, something to give me an idea.

Joyce still treasures the last birthday card her brother sent to her.

Mrs Sheila Mansell-Barlow, widow of Lieutenant Commander J O Mansell, was anxious to find out more about her husband who piloted *Gloucester's* Walrus aircraft. Survivor John Stevens, an air mechanic, contacted her and spoke at length about her husband's life and the circumstances of his death. After 60 years of unanswered questions John's recollections were a source of long awaited comfort.

Mrs Angela Spencer-Harper, a local historian from Henley-on-Thames, wrote to me that Stoker Basil Lambourne's parents had owned the bakery at Highmoor and that they had waited through four years of anguish before being told that their son would not return home.

I was especially delighted to make contact with the Reverend William Bonsey's family. William Bonsey was *Gloucester's* padre and his sister, Jean Elliot of Groton, Suffolk was able to provide me with a copy of a poignant letter which he had written to the grieving parents of two of his school friends. Both boys had enlisted into the RAF; one had been killed in a flying accident and the other had been missing for over a year.

> HMS *Gloucester*
> May 19 1941

I have been meaning to write to you for simply ages - ever since I heard that dear ... was missing – and I've put off writing because I've been waiting to hear the good news that he was alright – that lovely news doesn't seem to be forthcoming yet and I can't put off writing any longer. You know how I feel for you – and you know also how I admire you both- I can't say more. But I do hope that, if my mother and father have to go through what you have gone through during these past few years, they will be as brave.

If anything happens to me I want them just to carry on as usual, and please help them to do so. I'm not afraid to die except for the thought of the grief of those at home – that, to me, is the only tragic side of death because I feel we embark on a wonderful new adventure, full of joy and happiness, far greater than anything we have ever experienced on earth, and of course we are all going to be together one day – never to be parted from one another. I know you will do this for me, if it is ever necessary, please.

.... in one of her letters to me, thinking particularly of you both, says: "It makes one wonder how God can seemingly be so cruel and do these things to people" i.e. let their loved ones be killed. But He doesn't do it. I can't believe that it is any part of His Will that you and thousands of other poor dears should suffer so terribly. One must remember that war is something that man makes, not God; and God I believe is, in a sense, powerless to stop it, because if He did step in and put His thumb heavily on war makers then He would be taking away the great gift of freedom of will which He has given to mankind. Once having given us

that gift He can only leave us to use it for good or evil – He has, as it were, tied His own hands.

We all know what His Will is for His Creation - Love one another- and the more I think about that the more I feel how deeply and acutely He must be suffering Himself with all others who are suffering so greatly. As I see it all He can do is help us to endure our suffering by sharing it with us, and welcoming so kindly and tenderly all those who pass through the gate of death – securing them from all possibility of any pain or further pain and misery.

I hope you won't think this a cheek of me writing thus to you; it isn't a sermon or string of platitudes. It is a poor effort to put on paper my thoughts in case they may possibly help others as they help me (I think Isaiah, Chapter 63, verses 8–9 are wonderful).

Life in the Navy is very different from civilian life – I am awfully lucky as I have a lovely ship and a grand lot of men to live with. We are of course all longing to come home for a spell 2–1 majority have been away $2^1/_2$ years (myself almost $1^1/_2$ years) and we hope that that is not so far away. We've been kept very busy out here and have had some thrilling experiences especially of late, and every one of us realizes how truly lucky we are to be still alive and kicking. Rome radio has claimed us sunk seven times I believe – let's hope they will never be able to make those claims actual truth!

The battle of Matapan was one of our very lucky occasions as their 15" inch shells were dropping all round us for twenty minutes or so, sending up great splashes of water all over the ship and splinters

tinkling down on the decks – but no damage and no casualties to us or any of the Fleet. We all said a very sincere and humble "Thank God" after it was all over. I'm longing to see you both and my family, the sooner the better. Very much love to you both.

From William.

Three days after writing the letter, Reverend Bonsey lost his own life. After heroic efforts to aid injured men on the ship, the padre got into the sea just before *Gloucester* went down. He was last seen attempting to swim to the island of Kythira.

A plaque in St Bartholomew's church, Groton, Suffolk, where the Reverend Bonsey's father was the parish vicar, commemorates

The Reverend William Bonsey RN.

William's life. He is also remembered on the war memorial at St John's College, Cambridge where he read Divinity before the war.

Surgeon Lt Hugh Singer is still remembered by the survivors for his amiable nature and excellent medical skills, both on the ship and in the POW camps. After the war he was 'Mentioned in Despatches' for his efforts in POW camps where he worked tirelessly to alleviate the suffering of Allied prisoners. Dr Singer, a New Zealander, has since passed away but his daughter, Sally and her husband Hugh live in Dorset, England with their family. Many other members of Lt Singer's family still live in his hometown of Gisborne, New Zealand. In November 2000 Judy and I visited Gisborne and were wonderfully entertained by members of Lt Singer's family who related accounts of his early life. Following Lt Singer's survival of *Gloucester's* sinking, his father, Dr AL Singer, donated a trophy to the Gisborne branch of the Royal Lifesaving Society in gratitude for the lifesaving lessons which the young Hugh had received as a boy in Gisborne. The Singer Trophy, which was competed for annually until 1986, is now on display in the Gisborne Museum and Arts Centre.

Clive Simmons wrote about his uncles, James and George Simmons from County Mayo, Eire, who lost their lives when the ship went down. Four brothers of the Simmons family served in the Royal Navy during the war. Alf Simmons met his brothers, James and George, for the last time when *Gloucester* was in Malta. Clive's father Charles, who served as a Chief ERA, recently passed away but often recalled with sadness the loss of James and George. He always treasured the memory of his own last meeting with them in Greens Hotel, Durban, whilst he was serving aboard HMS *Dorsetshire*.

An amazing coincidence led me to a relative of Royal Marine William 'Sharkey' Ward. Ernie Evans, a Royal Marine survivor, was on a flight to Italy a couple of years ago when he struck up a conversation with Beryl Mulroy, who was sitting next to him. Before long Ernie was describing his wartime experiences to Beryl and mentioned that he had been a POW following the loss of his ship. Beryl's partner, Adrian Roberts, overheard the story and asked Ernie which ship he had been on. Adrian was amazed when Ernie said, *Gloucester*. "My uncle, Sharkey Ward, lost his life on that ship", Adrian replied.

Ernie had known Sharkey very well and was able to tell Beryl and Adrian many stories about the popular Royal Marine. Adrian, in turn, related to Ernie the harrowing story of what had happened to Sharkey Ward's family during the war. Sharkey had grown up, with his two brothers and four sisters, in Salford, where his mother and father owned a shop. In a bombing raid, on 22 December 1940, the shop received a direct hit and Sharkey's mother and six other members of the family were killed. Jack Ivey, another friend of Sharkey's, remembers that, following this tragedy, his friend was offered the opportunity to return home on compassionate grounds but opted to stay on *Gloucester*. Jack recalls Sharkey Ward's grief, and his words, *"I've got no home to go to now. The Gloucester is my home from now on."* Exactly five months later Royal Marine William 'Sharkey' Ward lost his life when the ship went down.

Tubby Salter.

Bill 'Tubby' Salter was another great character aboard *Gloucester* and I was pleased to put his nephew, Ray Casey, in touch with John Stevens who remembered Tubby with fond memories. John told Ray how his uncle had survived the sinking aboard a raft with Bert Ham, and how the two men had stayed together as POWs, in the same hut in Heyderbreck, Poland. Tubby made two escapes from working parties and when recaptured he was put in detention, on a diet of bread and water. According to John Stevens, Tubby loved to dress up and entertain other prisoners at concert parties and his cheerful nature, and constant teasing of the German guards, did much to keep up the prisoner's spirits during their long period of captivity.

Near the end of the war, as the Russians advanced towards Poland, the POWs from Heyderbreck were marched west. Tubby Salter, however, being too ill to march was left behind and his friend, Bert Ham, decided to hide away in the camp in order to stay and look after his sick pal. Eventually the few remaining guards fled from the camp and Tubby and Bert joined a column of refugees trying to

escape from the advancing Russians. Whilst on the road the refugees were strafed by a Russian fighter plane and Tubby's legs were shattered. He died in the arms of Bert Ham, who buried him by the roadside where his body still rests. A few weeks later the war ended.

In September 1999 Captain Rowley's daughter Betty Birkby, and her husband Geoff led a small party of members from 'The Fighting 'G' Club' to the island of Kythira, when *Gloucester's* survivors had been landed in May 1941. The group visited the tiny

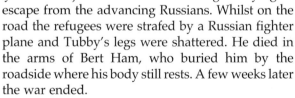

AB Melvin Baker – South African Navy. He survived the sinking and now lives in Port Elizabeth.

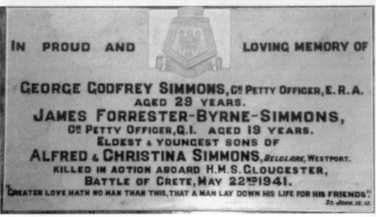

IN PROUD AND 🦅 LOVING MEMORY OF

GEORGE GODFREY SIMMONS, C⁰ PETTY OFFICER, E. R. A.
AGED 29 YEARS.
JAMES FORRESTER-BYRNE-SIMMONS,
C⁰ PETTY OFFICER, G.I. AGED 19 YEARS.
ELDEST & YOUNGEST SONS OF
ALFRED & CHRISTINA SIMMONS, *Belclare, Westport.*
KILLED IN ACTION ABOARD H.M.S.GLOUCESTER,
BATTLE OF CRETE, MAY 22ND 1941.
"GREATER LOVE HATH NO MAN THAN THIS, THAT A MAN LAY DOWN HIS LIFE FOR HIS FRIENDS."
St. John. 15. 13.

chapel above Kapsali Bay where there is a plaque commemorating *Gloucester's* loss. The ancient chapel looks out across the Kytherian Straits where the dreadful events of 1941 took place. Whilst on the island the group also met Nicos Sotorchos, one of the three Greek boys who smuggled food to the starving survivors. The group was also taken, by boat, to hold short a act of remembrance and to cast wreaths on the sea for their loved ones.

Many people have contacted me with stories relating to men who served on *Gloucester* and I was delighted to make contact with three more survivors from the ship. Bill Draper from Leeds was put in contact with me this year. I interviewed Bill at his home where he recalled that he and his twin brother, John, had both served in the Royal Navy during the Second World War. Bill remembered seeing

Captain Rowley in the sea after the sinking and the captain trying to keep up the spirits of the survivors by calling out, "Carry on ashore boys. I'll see you when you get there!"

Later, as a POW, Bill worked on a farm in Austria and in common with most prisoners he learnt to speak German. He fell in love with an Austrian farmer's daughter, Fredericka and the pair vowed to marry after the war. Fredericka was unable to obtain a visa to Britain, due to family connections with the Nazi party and so the romance never matured although the pair did correspond for some time after the war.

Ken Ayres wrote to me about his memories as a survivor and I later visited him at home in Canterbury. After training at HMS *Royal Arthur* he was sent to Alexandria when he joined *Gloucester*, only ten days before she sank. Following the sinking,

Lt Cdr R J Robertson DSC.

Ken was picked up the next day and taken to the small island of Anti-Kythira and therefore did not make contact with any other *Gloucester* survivors, most of whom were taken to Kythira. After war Ken returned to teaching and retired as a deputy head-teacher. It was not until 1999 that he met other survivors from the ship, at their annual reunion in Plymouth. Sadly, Ken passed away on 26 July 2001.

The most recent survivor who came to light was Melvin Baker from Port Elizabeth South Africa. Melvin was one of thirty South African Navy men who joined *Gloucester* in April 1940 whilst the ship was in Simonstown. Melvin, aged 19 when the ship went down, was one of only four South African's who survived. I was especially pleased to make contact with Melvin as he is the last of that four still alive. It was therefore a special trip for the 'The Fighting 'G' Club' members when he, his wife Cynthia and his daughter Marian, joined them in Devonport, Plymouth, for their annual reunion in May 2001. Melvin and his family extended their visit into June 2001 so that they were able to join a large party of 'Fighting 'G' Club' members on an emotional commemorative visit Kythira, which I will deal with in a following chapter.

Soon after his return to South Africa from the commemorative visit to Kythira, the present HMS *Gloucester* was at the port of Durban. Melvin and Cynthia were invited to go aboard and went to sea for a day, during which *Gloucester* took part in an exercise with the South African Navy. They were given VIP treatment and South African TV and newspapers covered the event with great interest. It was a wonderful gesture by Commander David Heley RN, Captain of *Gloucester*, and typifies the ship's continuing awareness of the history of the men who sailed in her predecessor sixty years ago.

Throughout Britain in 1945 there must have been a number of obituaries to the men who lost their lives on *Gloucester*. In *The Times* newspaper on 8 May 1945, tribute was paid to Lt Cdr Edward Daniel DSC. After a dazzling career, which included service on HMS *Warspite*, HMS *Cornwall* in China, and in submarines, he joined *Gloucester*. Lt Cdr Daniel, who was married to Diana Bonham-Carter, was awarded a DSC for, "Courage and coolness", when *Gloucester* was attacked by enemy aircraft on 11 January 1941.

The same edition of *The Times* carried an obituary to Lt Cdr Robert John Robertson DSC. Lt Cdr Robertson distinguished himself at Dartmouth by winning prizes in maths, navigation and seamanship. Later he won the Goodenough medal for gunnery and five firsts whilst on his course for promotion to Lieutenant. He saw service in destroyers, HMS *Cornwall* (at the same time as Lt Cdr Daniel) and also the battleship HMS *Hood*, before being drafted to *Gloucester*. Lt Cdr Robertson was awarded his DSC following the battle of Matapan.

Lt Cdr Robertson's daughter, Rosemary Bodger, lives in Canterbury with her husband, Dr Hugh Bodger. Rosemary sent me copies of two of the letters her father sent home. Lt Cdr Robertson wrote about the attack on the Italian Fleet at Taranto and also of seeing the aircraft take off and return after the raid;

One of the chaps who actually took part in the raid, we fished out of the ditch ourselves only the morning before the show actually happened. He, poor chap, hasn't been so lucky since that day for he lost a leg when Illustrious *was hit by bombs the other day. I gather, however, that he is getting on quite well. On our return to harbour after the Taranto party, this chap came over to see us and say "thank you" for fishing him out of the pond, and he gave us a most vivid description of the whole show. I must say I take off my hat to these Fleet Air Arm chaps. They really are superb.*

The letter also gives an indication of the effect of Sir Winston Churchill's speeches on the morale of the fleet;

We listened to Winston Churchill's broadcast this morning and loved it. He does speak well and is always such a tonic to listen to! He gave us some wonderful laughs particularly in his choice of adjectives when describing Mussolini. What always makes us feel not a little proud is the matter of fact way in which he refers to the Royal Navy and just what he expects from us. To hear him speaking you would think that he never asked much from us and that naturally we shall do whatever is wanted! He is right too, for we can and will do whatever, and more, than is asked even though the task may seem almost impossible sometimes.

Lt Cdr Robertson was concerned about his loved ones during the bombing raids over Britain. He continues;

Lu's letter was a great joy to read and gives one a little idea of what individuals are going through at home. All of you at home are a constant source of pride and wonder to us for you have been simply magnificent. No wonder the Germans, and Hitler in particular, have been so charry about trying out the invasion for they know jolly well what a very poor time they are going to get when they do try their luck.

Lt Cdr Robertson, the ship's gunnery officer, also wrote of his enthusiasm to take on the Italian fleet. Four weeks after writing this letter his wish would be granted at the battle of Matapan, where he won his DSC;

Now that the Germans are beginning to take a part in the war in the Mediterranean, I have no doubt that things will warm up a lot for us too. I wonder if they will persuade the Italian navy to take a rather more active part. I hope so and that we shall get our chance to have a really good scrap with them! I am keen, though, that we should wait another fortnight or so for there are certain preparations which I have still to make and which I should like to complete before that day comes.

Many men on the lower deck of *Gloucester* shared Lt Cdr Robertson's confidence in the ability of the Eastern Mediterranean Fleet. In a letter dated 1 April 1941, Able Seaman Richard Brown of Wootton, Norfolk wrote;

Dear Bet and Ted

I suppose by now you have heard about the big fleet battle, which has happened at last in Musso's duck pond. I am very pleased to inform you that we were there doing our bit, we certainly had some exciting times, too exciting in fact, still now it is all over we can look back and say "it was worth it" don't you think?

His letter ends in confident mood;

I am still keeping in the best of health, after several trying days that we have been through out here. We are in harbour at the present time getting ready to give that spaghetti eater some of the old roast beef of England.

I still remain one of the gang,

Dick.

Longing to be back home was a constant subject in Lt Cdr Robertson's letters but he could only imagine what the reunion with his children would be like;

Darling mine, I am getting so fed up with being a grass widower and am simply aching to be with you again. Why must these infernal dictators force us to fight this war and so keep you and me apart. I just long to be with you and spend a lot of time each day wondering what you are doing, thinking about you and the children, and picturing my return to you again when this business is all over ... I wonder what Rosemary and John Richard will think of me when they see me again. It would be so glorious if Rosemary could just look at me out of those big brown eyes of hers and say "Daddy". I'm afraid, though, that that is too much to expect at first as she is still a very little girl and I cannot be anything more than at most a very faint memory to her. Bless you my darling. I love you so dearly. God bless and keep you safe.

Bob XXX

In his last letter home, Lt Cdr Robertson voiced his concern over the conflict in the Balkans but remained optimistic about *Gloucester's* chances of dealing with the Luftwaffe;

We are all wondering what this war in the Balkans is going to develop into. I fear that the Yugoslavs are going to have a pretty thin time of it for some time to come but, at any rate, we have at long last got a footing on the mainland of Europe again and a chance of fighting the Germans directly on land. If we can succeed in rolling up this party I think we shall have gone a long way towards winning the war .... however, quite apart from these considerations, my main hope is that this outbreak of war with the Germans may ease the pressure at home very considerably and keep you from bombing attacks .... but meantime I can see that ourselves out here are going to have no easy time of it! However, there are quite a number of German aircraft who are also going to come in for a mighty thin time and are going to get a great deal more than they bargained for!

In this final letter, Lt Cdr Robertson writes again of yearning for his home and family;

In peacetime one could at least say that one was nearly half way through but one cannot say that in wartime for commissions abroad do not run to any set time these days. Well, I suppose that one can do no more than get on with the job and go on hoping that one will be able to get home again in the not too remote future. It would help so much, though, if one could get a glimpse of one's wife and family occasionally. I wonder what Rosemary and John Richard will think of their Daddy when they see him for the first time again?

With all my love to you, darling mine, and a special big hug for Rosemary and John. I love you always, Bob XXX

   Rosemary also sent me the following letter from Lt Cdr Roger
Heap who was one of only two officers to survive *Gloucester's*
sinking; the other officer was Surgeon Lt Singer. The letter was sent
from Milag und Marlag POW camp and was addressed to
Rosemary's mother;

28 August 1941

Dear Mrs Robertson,
   The whole tragedy, as you can imagine, is simply ghastly, and I am
doing my best to get things sorted out and everybody informed of what
information I can tell. Your husband was a great friend of mine & as
navigating officer, I suppose, my work was more closely linked with his
than anybody else's on board. I am only too sorry to tell you that I can
confirm that he was drowned during the night after we had abandoned
ship. He was in the water with me for several hours - I personally saw
him go. Surgeon Lieut Singer is the only other officer that I know has
been saved and he is a POW.
   As I am limited to the number of letters that I can write, I should be
most grateful if you could let Miss Faith Cooke of 103 Gordon Avenue,
Camberley, Surrey, know that her brother Instr Lieut Cdr Cooke
suffered the same fate as your husband. I can confirm this as well. I
have also heard from Mrs Robertson, your mother-in-law, and would
be most grateful if you could inform her of the circumstances. I am sure

Lt Cdr R A F
DSC OBE.

they will understand my difficulties and forgive me for not answering their enquiries personally.

We are all quite comfortable here and are also very hopeful. Yours sincerely,

Roger AF Heap.

During my research it became clear to me that a book could be written, in its own right, about any one of the *Gloucester* survivors. This is certainly true of Lt Cdr Roger Anthony Fortrey Heap DSC OBE and I am most grateful to his son, David, for sending me letters and papers left by his father.

Born at St Asaph, Wales, in 1911, Roger was the younger son of Edith and Dr Edward Heap. After being educated at Epsom preparatory school he entered Dartmouth Naval College as a cadet and later served as a midshipman on the battleship, HMS *Queen Elizabeth*. His first duties in the war were aboard HMS *Newcastle*, on North Atlantic protection duties, but as the situation in France deteriorated he was seconded by the Admiralty to take an old cargo ship to Dunkirk. The ship, laden with stones and concrete, was ordered to be sunk at the entrance of the harbour to prevent the port being used by the Germans. The mission was successfully accomplished and Lt Cdr Heap was one of the last men to get away before the advancing German forces overran Dunkirk.

Following the first attack on *Gloucester*, in July 1940, Lt Cdr Heap was sent to the Mediterranean where he joined *Gloucester* as the Navigating Officer. David recalls his father telling him about his narrow escape when a bomb passed through the Director Tower without exploding. Lt Cdr Heap had been climbing the ladder to the Director Tower when the bomb came through the roof. Lt Cdr Heap was awarded his DSC following the battle of Matapan.

Lt Cdr Heap was among those survivors taken to Kythira after *Gloucester's* sinking and later marched to Salonika. It was here that the Germans realised that he may have valuable information about the ship's radar. The decision was made to fly him to Berlin for interrogation after which, Lt Cdr Heap was sent to Milag und Marlag, the POW camp where Royal and Merchant Navy men were detained. Roger's parent's still had no information about their son at this point. Their first news came via an old friend, Tony Rolt, who was already detained as a POW. He wrote this letter home;

Oflag VB
June 23rd 1941

Dear Mum,

*Big news this morning, Roger Heap has arrived here with about 250
from Greece. I expect you have already heard that he was one of the ten
[sic] survivors from the* Gloucester *and had the most amazing
experiences, including 23 hours on a water-logged raft. He has recovered
and considering what he has been through is in excellent spirits. Have
fixed him up with clothes and food for the time being.*

All my love, Tony

In a letter to his sister, Lt Cdr Heap describes some of his ordeals
following the sinking, and as a POW;

Oflag VB
11 August '41

My Dear Barbara,

*So pleased to get a letter from you and Tress. I agree with you I don't
want to be sunk again! It's a long story which contains a 23 hrs swim,
being too ill or weak to eat for 9 days during which we had a 26 mile
march- I had no boots! A week with 34 others in a cattle truck and
finally arriving here .... Of course I lost everything and now am
in khaki .... Life is very dull here and it is hard to pass the time
.... I am longing for parcels, food and cigarettes are scarce ....
Goodness knows when I shall get any parcels from England .... Tell
mum Tony Rolt is here.*

Despite the Spartan conditions as a POW, Lt Cdr Heap found life
in Oflag VB a vast improvement on the appalling conditions he had
endured whilst held in Salonika. As time passed, Lt Cdr Heap set
up a system for sending and receiving coded messages in his post.
The code system, given to only a few officers, enabled Lt Cdr Heap
to communicate with the Admiralty. Heap's son, David, sent me
this 'nonsense' coded letter, sent from the Admiralty to his father:

When not sending coded messages back to the Admiralty, the
young Lt Cdr was busy digging tunnels in an attempt to escape. Lt
Cdr Heap was eventually made 'Escape Officer' in charge of
coordinating escapes.

By May 1943 the German commanding officer at Milag und
Marlag had enough of Lt Cdr Heap's escape attempts and the
young naval officer was transferred to Oflag IV C, better known as
Colditz Castle. He spent the rest of the war inside the bleak castle,
although this did not deter him from planning escapes. Identity
papers in the name of Jan Scep were prepared for him but his escape
plans never came to fruition due to coded instructions which he
received from the Admiralty in London.

Lt Cdr Heap's forged escape papers.

Colditz Castle housed many prominent prisoners, including King George VI's nephew, Lascelles the Earl of Harwood, and the British Government was particularly worried about their fate, especially if the Russians reached Colditz first. Having a system of communication with the prisoners therefore became most important and Lt Cdr Heap was instructed to stay put rather than attempt an escape. On his return to Britain at the end of the war,

Lt Cdr Heap was awarded an OBE for 'Fortitude whilst a prisoner of war'.

In 1953 Lt Cdr Heap married and in the same year was appointed as the Queen's Harbourmaster at Trincomalee, Ceylon (now, Sri Lanka). After leaving the Royal Navy he took up employment with Esso, serving on tankers for about ten years, before working for many years at the Hydrographic Office. In common with many of *Gloucester's* survivors, who had spent long hours in the sea, Lt Cdr Heap had swallowed oil and the effects caused him problems in later life. In 1960 he needed an operation to remove a damaged section of his intestine, from which he successfully recovered and eventually retired to Oban

The letter confirming Lt Cdr Roger Heap's OBE.

where he enjoyed sailing off the west coast of Scotland. This remarkable man passed away 9 January 2001, aged 89, having suffered from Parkinson's Disease for some years.

Ken Macdonald, the only Royal Marine Bandsman to survive the sinking, was also a prisoner in Marlag und Milag. Almost as soon as Ken arrived at the POW camp he set about organising a band and taught many prisoners to play musical instruments. After a few months those *Gloucester* prisoners who were below the rank of Petty Officer were moved to other camps but the Senior British Officer at Milag made representations to the Camp Commandant for Ken to stay in Marlag. The German officer agreed, no doubt only too pleased that Ken's musicians might have a positive effect within the camp. He was later transferred to the officers' orchestra but in order to remain at Marlag the Germans insisted that he carry out some work each day. He was given the task of cleaning out the toilets, for which his fellow prisoners nicknamed him 'Captain of the Heads'.

After the war Ken went to Africa and became the Rhodesian Army Director of Music. His superb account of *Gloucester's* sinking and his subsequent imprisonment, 'Bandsman and Barbed Wire' is kept for posterity at the Royal Marine Museum, Southsea, where it can be seen on request.

John Stevens, President of the 'Fighting 'G' Club', recently related to me yet another amazing episode in *Gloucester's* story. A few years ago a number of British War veterans had returned to Germany to revisit the areas where they had seen action during the war. Whilst staying in a guesthouse in the Frankfurt area they came across Erich Wergner, a German war veteran. Erich Wergner, who spoke excellent English, asked the British visitors if they had ever heard of HMS

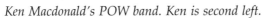

Ken Macdonald's POW band. Ken is second left.

Gloucester, as he was interested in finding out what had become of the survivors of the ship. It transpired that he had been in charge of one of the caiques that had picked up some of *Gloucester's* survivors.

After returning from Germany, the leader of the British party contacted the *Navy News* and was put in touch with John Stevens. John struck up a correspondence with Erich and was invited to travel to Germany to stay with Erich and his wife, Ingmar. Sadly the meeting was never able to take place.

Bill 'Froggy' Morellic, was a *Gloucester* survivor whose widow, Mary, lives on Guernsey. She read about Erich Wergner in the *Navy News* and subsequently wrote to him to thank him for saving her husband's life. Erich and his wife Inger eventually travelled to Guernsey to meet Mary and they became good friends. Mary remembered that Erich always maintained that in rescuing the survivors he was only doing what any sailor would do for another sailor.

Information came to me from Martin Brett, the son of Lt Cdr John Brett who lost his life when *Gloucester* went down. Martin was baptised when he was two months old, in *Gloucester's* ship's bell, before the ship left Devonport in 1939. For the Coronation of Queen Elizabeth in 1953, Admiral Cunningham requested that his two pages should be sons of men who had lost their lives in the Mediterranean during the Second World War. As a particular tribute to *Gloucester*, Martin Brett was chosen to be one of the pages. Clearly Admiral Cunningham still held the memory of the loss of *Gloucester* close to his heart and he remained in contact with Martin for several years.

The loss of *Gloucester* was more recently remembered at Thetford School, Norfolk, on 11 November 1999. Leading Telegraphist Victor Lovick, a Thetford School old boy, lost his life when *Gloucester* went down

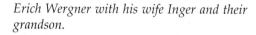

) Bill Wade 1909–1999. ashes were scattered over position where Gloucester

Erich Wergner with his wife Inger and their grandson.

and the school's present head of History, David Seymour, decided to dedicate that year's Remembrance Service to Victor's memory. By coincidence, CPO Flint, also a Thetford Grammar School old boy, was serving on the present HMS *Gloucester* and he led the Service of Remembrance. Also present at the service were members of the Lovick family, including Victor's brother, Don; Captain Rowley's daughter, Betty Birkby, and her husband, Geoff; Jean Elliot, sister of the ship's padre, Rev William Bonsey; and Peter Everest, the ship's youngest survivor. The service was highly emotional, particularly when the school choir sang 'Eternal Father Strong To Save'.

Admiral Cunningham is the pe in the middle of the three leadin the Queen out of Westminster Abbey. Martin Brett is immedi behind Admiral Cunningham.

A few weeks later, on Sunday 30 January 2000, the tenth HMS *Gloucester* was on her way to the Gulf when she stopped in the Mediterranean over the position where her predecessor lies. A Service of Remembrance was held at which a wreath was laid on behalf of 'The Fighting 'G' Club' together with a wreath from Thetford Grammar School, which was laid by their old boy, CPO Roy Flint.

The 'Fighting 'G' Club', under the Presidency of survivor John Stevens, continues to flourish and over 170 families are members of the club. John Stevens, together with fellow survivors Dolly Gray and Bert Ham, both of whom are now deceased, formed the club in 1982. The success of the club is a great tribute to the dedication and devotion of John Stevens. Each year on the anniversary of the ship's loss and again on Remembrance Sunday, John attends Gloucester Cathedral, to place a wreath under the stained glass window that is dedicated to the officers and men of HMS *Gloucester*.

Stained glass window in Gloucester Cathedral.

Rounding the Circle

I n the autumn of 1998 Jeff Wilkinson, producer for the BBC TV
South-West programme, *Spotlight*, took three of *Gloucester's*
survivors back to the island of Kythira. John Stevens, Ernie
Evans, and Bill Howe visited the house where they had been
imprisoned in May 1941, following their rescue by the Germans.
During their stay on the island the three men had an emotional
reunion with Nicos Sotorchos, one of the three Greek boys who had
risked their lives to smuggle food to the imprisoned survivors.
Nicos, a boat builder, still lives in Kapsali Bay just a stone's throw
away from the house where the survivors were detained. Later, on
the TV programme, John Stevens publicly thanked the people of
Kythira for their kindness in providing the food which Nicos, and
his two friends, gave to *Gloucester's* survivors.

The *Spotlight* programme was initially shown in the BBC South-
West region and a few months later it was shown nationally on BBC
2. Following its screening, and the attendant interest that it aroused,
the committee of 'The Fighting 'G' Club' organised a return to
Kythira to commemorate the 60th anniversary of *Gloucester's* loss.

On 12 June 2001 a group of 42 members of the 'The Fighting 'G'

Kapsali Bay, Kythira

Club', gathered at Heathrow airport for the visit to Kythira. Among them were six of *Gloucester's* survivors:

John Stevens, 83, of South Ockenden, Essex, President and founder of the Club.

Len 'Al' Bowley, 81, a signalman on the ship, now living in Normandy, France.

Ernie Evans, 78, one of *Gloucester's* Royal Marines, from Sevenoaks, Kent. As a schoolboy living in Devonport, Plymouth, Ernie had seen *Gloucester* launched.

Billy Grindell, 84, a stoker from Cardiff, Wales.

Ken Macdonald, 84, from Gosport, Hampshire, and the only Royal Marine Bandsman to survive the sinking.

Melvin Baker, 82, an ordinary seaman from the South African Navy who had made the journey from his home in Port Elizabeth, South Africa.

On arrival at Kythira the group were wonderfully surprised when Nicos Sotorchos met them at the airport. He was evidently as pleased to see the survivors, as they were him. Although Nicos speaks no English it was plain from his handshakes, kisses and hugs that he was honoured and overwhelmed that the old men had returned to his island. Throughout the following week Nicos was never far away from the group of survivors.

At the small village of Kapsali Bay all the villagers, several of whom remembered watching the battle of Crete in May 1941, made the group most welcome. Commodore John Milnes RN, and his wife Sally, had also made the journey to Kapsali Bay. Commodore Milnes, the Military Attaché at the British Embassy in Athens, had been told of *Gloucester's* story and had come to represent the British Ambassador at the commemorations.

HMS *Northumberland*, under the command of Commander Stuart McQuaker RN, arrived in Kapsali Bay early on the morning of Friday 15 June to attend the weekend ceremonies. The ship was en route for operational duties in the Persian Gulf. That evening the

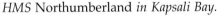

HMS Northumberland *in Kapsali Bay.*

ship's company laid on a barbecue in Kapsali Bay, for 'Fighting 'G' Club' members and local villagers. The conviviality of the evening set the scene for the following two days ceremonies and it became evident that the men and women of *Northumberland* would do all in their power to make the weekend a huge success.

At 10.30am the following morning, Saturday 16 June, the six HMS *Gloucester* survivors assembled at the quay where they had been landed sixty years before. Then they were naked, covered in oil and suffering severe shock. Now they stood proudly wearing blazers bedecked with medals glinting in the sun. Behind them a guard of twelve men and women from HMS *Northumberland* paraded in their immaculate tropical white uniforms. Immediately behind the guard, the relatives of those lost on *Gloucester* gathered, many wearing the medals of their loved ones. At the rear of the parade the local Greek band assembled to accompany the procession.

Meanwhile, at the other end of Kapsali Bay, a number of people gathered on the balcony of the house where the survivors had been held captive following their rescue in 1941. Commodore John Milnes and Commander Stuart McQuaker represented the Royal Navy, Mr A Kalligeras, the Mayor of Kythira, represented the people of the island together with two Greek Orthodox Church priests; Father P Megalokonomos and Father D Froumentios. The most important guest at the house was Nicos Sotorchos, 75, waiting patiently to formally welcome the survivors back to the house where he had helped to smuggle food to them sixty years before. Mr Sotorchos was accompanied by his son and daughter-in-law.

Between the procession forming up at one end of Kapsali Bay, and the official greeting party waiting on the balcony of the house at the other end of the bay, many villagers and other visitors from other parts of the island, who had heard of the event on local TV, were lining the narrow road around the bay. Cameras clicked and flashed: emotional tension heightened, as the time came for the ceremony to begin.

At 10.45am the band struck up and the survivors led the march around the bay. In 1941 they had been marched naked and exhausted at gunpoint: today they were upright and so proud to be able to say thank you to the Kytherians. Loud applause accompanied the smiling men as they made

Cdr S McQuaker, Ken Otter, Nicos Sotorchos, Commodore J Milnes.

their way round the little changed waterfront towards the house which had been their prison. At one point along the route an elderly Greek lady stepped out among the survivors and cast rose petals on their heads.

When the survivors reached the house they were greeted by yet more applause, before taking their places on the balcony. A crowd of several hundred people had gathered in front of the house, including schoolchildren who had come dressed in traditional Greek costume. Each survivor was introduced to the crowd through an interpreter, and the exploits of Nicos Sotorchos and his two friends, Manolis Katsoulis and Panayiotis Kassimatis, were told to the British and Greek audience: Nicos is the only one of the trio still alive. John Stevens presented a medal to Nicos, on behalf of the survivors, in gratitude for his bravery and kindness. The medal was inscribed, *'For He Who Dared'*. It was a highly emotional moment as the two old men held each other in a warm embrace and a tearful Nicos waved to the onlookers.

The Mayor of Kythira made a speech stressing the importance of remembering the tragedy of war and the necessity for all nations to live in peace. A brief memorial service followed, conducted by the Greek priests. Commodore Milnes then unveiled a brass plaque which had been specially engraved and brought by the 'Fighting G Club' to be placed on the house. The plaque, which is in both Greek and English, reads;

> *In this house, with its surrounding garden, German forces detained survivors of the British Cruiser HMS Gloucester, sunk in the Kythira Straits on 22 May 1941.*
>
> *Landed on this beautiful island of Kythira, the local population fed and clothed them. Otherwise they would surely have perished.*

John Stevens and Nicos Sotorchos.

The HMS *Gloucester Association extends their everlasting gratitude for the help and sustenance given to them during their captivity here.*
June 2001

At the conclusion of the ceremony the local band played both the Greek and British national anthems and the guard from HMS *Northumberland* marched off to great applause from the crowd. Greek schoolchildren, in their national dress, danced as the Greek band played on. The band concluded their programme with 'Colonel Bogey', to the great delight of the survivors and the rest of the British contingent. An open-air lunch followed, during which, framed pictures of HMS *Gloucester*, signed by the survivors, were presented as a momento of the occasion. A presentation was also made to the Mayor of Kythira on behalf of the Mayor of Gloucester.

On the morning of Sunday 17 June HMS *Northumberland* put to sea with the six survivors, and the group of 'Fighting 'G' Club' members. *Gloucester* had been sunk at a position of 36. North and 23.1 East: slowly HMS *Northumberland* made way to the position where a memorial service would take place that morning.

At 10.45am, the ship's company assembled on the flight deck, at the stern of the ship. Commander McQuaker told us that so many officers and ratings had volunteered for the ceremony that they could not all be accommodated in the space available and some had to be turned away. As the White Ensign was hauled down to half-mast, Commander McQuaker led the service by a number of officers and ratings leading prayers and giving readings. The Duchess of Gloucester sent a message, which read,

'I am thinking of you today as you honour your comrades who lost their lives in the last Gloucester'.

Commander David Heley RN, Captain of the present *Gloucester* also sent a message that his thoughts, and those of his ship's company, were with those gathered for the act of remembrance.

Royal Marine Shakespeare sounded the Last Post across the silent sea and the poignancy of the notes brought forth much emotion. The six survivors stepped up to the rail at the stern of the ship to cast their wreaths onto the sea where they had fought for their lives and where so

C'dore J Milnes unveils the plaque, watched over by Nicos, Ernie Evans and Len Bowley.

School children in traditional dress.

many of their shipmates had perished. They had never forgotten their friends and now they had come back to pay their last respects. The relatives, who had travelled to honour their loved ones, then stepped up to cast their wreaths over the stern. Many of them felt that it was the equivalent of a funeral, albeit sixty years after the tragedy. Finally, the circle had been rounded.

HMS *Northumberland* sailed back for Kythira as Commander McQuaker hosted a buffet lunch for everyone, at the end of which, Nicos Sotorchos read a moving poem which he had specially written for the occasion. After saying their farewells, the six survivors and the members of "The Fighting 'G' Club", gathered on the quay in Kapsali Bay to wave goodbye to HMS *Northumberland* and to give three cheers for Commander McQuaker and his ship's company. The ship's company lined the port side waving back as she sailed out of sight.

Wreaths to be cast on the sea.

Members of HMS Northumberland's *ship's company attending the memorial service at sea.*

NICOS' POEM

Welcome.
On my small island I welcome you.
You are all my friends,
Those of you I know and those of you I don't know.
We first met each other in difficult times
And thus kept our friendship hidden deep in our hearts.
Time, and the years, passed and I said, "All were like memories".
But good friends you never forget.
From the alleyways of life,
With the winds from the north,
God brings you back here again, here to these old places.
You are a proud people, with a great history,
That is why we have held on to this friendship of ours.
You came, and you came again.
Welcome, yet again.
I hope you are all well now,
And will be so when we meet again.

HMS Northumberland *17 June 2001*

Len Bowley, Billy Grindell, John Stevens, Nicos, Ernie Evans, Melvin Baker, Kapsali Bay, June 2001.

Roll of Honour

HMS *Gloucester*

8 July 1940

Capt F R Garside CBE RN
Lt Cdr Churchill RN
Sub Lt Murray RN
Midsh Atkins RN
Ldg Sig C Hyde
AB H Ward
Ord Sea Foster
Ord Sea Allison RNVR
Boy Sea E Rodda

Cdr J R D'Aeth RN
Lt Cdr M Lindsay RN
Sub Lt V Layard RN
Ch Yeo Frazer
Ldg Sea K Hensby
Ord Sea E Owens
Ord Sea F Knight
Ord Sea F Nolan RNVR
Boy Bugler J Godliman

11 January 1941

Ldg Sea J Phelan
Cpl H Walker RM
Marine W Burgoyne
Marine E Green
Marine R Basset-Burr

Marine M O'Leary
Marine R Whitely
Marine A Lewis
Marine A Jesson

22 May 1941

Officers Killed:

Capt H A Rowley DSO RN
Mr D Cull Gnry Off
Midsh J Hutton-Attenborough RN
Lt Cdr W A Timmons RN

Lt Cdr C R Barnett RN
Capt R Formby RM

Lt W B Setton RN

Missing Presumed Killed:

Mr F A Bond Gnry Off RN
Lt Cdr J Brett DSC RN
Cdr H C Brown DSO RN
Lt J Chedwode RN
Lt Cdr J H Cooke RN
Lt E O Daniel DSC RN
Wrt Off Mr Dalling RN
Lt Cdr R Dingwell OBE RN
Midsh P A Espeut RN
Lt W C F Grant-Dalton RN
Sub Lt R G E Haynes RN
Lt E G Hughes RNVR
Lt Cdr J O Mansell RN
Wrt Off Mr A E G Northcott
Midsh R E M Pole RN
Lt Cdr R J Robertson DSC RN
Sub Lt H Q Rose RN

Wrt Off Mr T R G Scutt RN
Midsh G L Stevens RN
Lt RN Weir RNVR

Midsh P N Wyllie RN

Rev W T Bonsey Chap RN
Lt R S Brooke RN
Midsh A L Browning RN
Lt M C Brown RM
Wrt Off Mr J Costelloe RN
Midsh J R D'E Darby RN
Midsh Hon J W Darling RN
T/Midsh E D F Elliot RNR
Midsh L W Evans RN
Sub Lt R O C Hay RNVR
Mr E E Houshold Gnry Off RN
Sub Lt G F Kebble RN
Wrt Off Mr J E Mitchell RN
Sub Lt R G Orck RN
Sub Lt N Q Reading RN
Lt I M Robertson-Walker RN
Midsh C A M
Rumbulow-Pearce RN
Sub Lt P E Starmer RN
Cdr R P Tanner DSC RN
Mr C F Williamson
(Schoolmaster) RN
Wrt Off Mr A Young RN

Ratings Killed:

Ord Sea K M Bickell
Boy Sea J A Raiker

Boy Sea D Mooney

Missing Presumed Killed:

Boy Sea H Adams
Ldg Sto C Alexander
Ord Sea D Allen
R P O H Allen
AB A Allsopp
A/PO Sto MF Antonucci
Ord Sea A Atkins
AB G H Avery

CPO A Aldcroft
AB H Allcock
AB F Allen
Sto J Allen
AB G P Andrews
AB J B Armstrong
Sto J Atkinson
Ord Art4 V T Avery

Ldg Sto AG C Back RFR
AB J F Bailie
AB J T Baker
Tel B N Barton
AB T Bates
Tel J Bell
Boy Sea J A Benstead
PO E E Binning
Sto G F Bishop
Ord Sea D A Blakemore
Ch Sto J J Boak
Ldg Sea J T Boggie
Shipw 3 C Bone
Mechl W H Bostock
AB RJ Boucher
Ord Sig A F Bowden
Ldg Sea W F A Bowgen
Air Fitter J Boyle
A B T Bradley
Ord Sea J C Branney
AB P F Bressington
AB J F Broadley
AB T C Bromfield
AB D Brown
AB P R Brown
AB W Brown
Ord Sea W Buckley
AB F R Bullen
Ldg Sto W T J Bunney
Joiner 3 K C Burrage

Boy Sea D A R Bacon
AB G D Baird
P O Sto R Baldwin
AB J Bastin
Sto W A Beavis
Ldg Sea S W S Bennett
Boy Sea J F Betterly
AB E Birtwhistle
Ord Art5 R Blackshaw
AB G Blewitt
ERA 4 T Boardman
Sig C Bond
P O Sto J W Boote
Ord Sea J W Bosward
Ldg Sea J D Bovey
ERA4 J G Bowyer
Ldg Sto H T A Boyce
AB N A F Bradley
POAirm P J Branford
Ldg Cook(S) D G Brayley
AB W A Brinkworth
PO Sto G Brocklehurst
Sto W F Broomfield
AB J Brown
AB R A Brown
Sto 2 W B Buchanan
Ldg Sto R C Bull
Supply Asst C B Bunce
AB W Bunton

AB M E Callan
CPO H J Calton
AB A F Cannings
Sto T Carlon
PO C Carter
AB W R J Casson
AB T C Chambers
EA 1 H Chapman
Ldg Sto R Chegwin
AB T F Churchman
AB G P Clark
Ord Sea E S Clarke
PO E S J Cleal
AB F Coates
PO Sto J G Cockiling
AB L Collins

Sto J H Callow
AB G O Campbell
EA 4 J Carberry
AB P Carmody
Ldg Sto PW Case
AB N J Catlin
AB T Channer
Sto J Chapman RFR
Ldg Cook (S) L J Chudley
Boy Sea M M S Clancy
P O A S Clarke
AB L Clarke
Ch Shipwt F W Clift
Ldg Sto G C Cock
Ord Sea P J Collins
ERA 1 R Collins

AB R Colishe
AB H Connolly
PO R Convers
CPO Supply S E Cook
AB G V Cookman
Mech 1 H W Cox
Boy Sea J M Craig
Shipw 4 P N Cross
AB J A Curtis

Sto L Daley
Boy Sea E W Dalton
Cook R L Daniels
Ch Sto A L Davey
AB G H Davies
CPO Writer R C Davies
Ldg Sea W Davies
Ch Ord Art M J W Day
PO Sto J J Desmond
CPO W H Dickens
Sto J Dodds
ERA4 E C Down
Sto W B Doyle
SupplyAsst A W Driver
AB W Dunkerton
Boy Sea T H G Dunne
Ldg Sea H Dyson

Ldg Sea J H A Eggleston
Ord Tel J J Edmonds
AB C S Elkins
AB G N Ellis
Shipw 4 R C Edmond
Ldg Sea J T Esau

CERA W T Fear
Sto J Fedrick
AB A Fenney
AB H G R Findlay
Ord Tel W G M Fittus
Ldg Sea G A Floyd
Sto P J Flynn
Sto B H Foster
Boy Sea E Frail
Cook F J Frost
AB G J Fyffe

Ord Sea C E Gale
ERA 3 J Garner
Sto D Gillon
AB R H Glasson
EA3 P F Glover
Air Fitter W G Godwin
AB F Gravell
AB W D Gregg
A/PO S Griffiths
PO Sto G G M Grist
Shipw 4 E J Gwyther

Ldg Sea R E Hall
Sig V J T Hallett
PO R H Hamlyn
Boy Tel J Harden
Boy Sea V Harnwell

Ch EA T G A Comiskey
AB J C Conway
AB A T Cook
AB W F Cooke
AB F Copeland
Joiner4 R Cox
AB A R Cross
PO Tel A C Crossman
AB J M Curtis

Ldg Sto G H Dalley
AB L J Daniels
Sto L Davenport
Ldg Sea A W Davies
A/PO J Davies
AB R J Davies
A/PO Airm C A Day
Sto A E Desmier
Sto B V Dewdney
Ord Sea J E Dodd
Ord Sea G E Dowding
AB M Doyle
Sto E H Drake
ERA4 R C Duggan
AB J Dunkinson
Sto F Dutton

AB H A Eaketts
AB A Edge
AB D F Edwards
AB J W Elliott
Ch Sto H C S Ellis
Sto E T W Ennor

Sto C Farrell
Sto J Fear
Sto K W Feltham
Ord Art 2 E V Fidler
Ldg Sto D K Finlayson
Sto W E E Flood
A B K Flynn
Sto W J Foot
Ldg Airm C A Foster
SupplyAsst E H Francis
CPO Cook S Furzey

Sto R Gallaway
Ldg Cook (S) T Gaynon
Ldg Sto T Gilson
AB A H Glen
AB T C Godfrey
AB E Grantham
Tel T Greer
AB TA Gregory
PO F G Grimshaw
AB P F Grove

PO J F Hall
Sto C W R Hallam
Sto W G B Hamilton
Sto C Handcock
AB H J Harfoot
Sto J Harris

AB C A Harrison
AB T Hart
AB A H T Hawkins RFR
Ch Mech G Haywood
Ord Sea E C Hennessey
Sto J Henshaw
Ord Sig I J Herd
AB G Hessey
CPO Cook E W Hicks
Supply Asst K D Higgins
PO W H Hill
Sto W H Hilton
CERA R Hobbs
AB J Hockey
Sto L C Hocking
Sto J C Hodgson RFR
Boy Sea E Holdsworth
Sto W Hollett
Master at Arms F H Hooper
CPO J C E Horn DSM
ERA3 B G Horwell
AB D A Hudson
AB B L Hughes
CPO Tel TG Hughes
Sto F J Hunt
PO A Hutton

Supply Asst R R T Isaac
A/ Ldg Sea W E Ives

Sto A Jackson
Sto W H Jackson
AB G R James
AB Stephen G Jennings
Ch Sto W M Jeremiah
A/Ldg Sea W J Johnson
Ldg Sto A K M Johnstone
Sto C Jolley
AB C L Jones
Sto G Jones
Ldg Sig J G Jones
AB R A Jones
CERA C H Jope

Sto W Kay
PO J H Keates
AB W J Kelly
PO Sto R S Kevern
Sto E A King

Sto B Lambourne
AB P K Lane
Sto T R J Lauristan
PO/ SBA HM Lean
A/Ldg Sea H J Lee
Sto J L Leslie
A/PO Cook D B Lewis
AB L Lewis
Ldg SBA D Linderman
AB W Littler
Boy Sea T Lockhart
Sto A E Lough
Ldg Tel V A R Lovick
Sto D Lynch

AB H Harrison
Sto S Hartley
AB F E Hayes
ERA3 W H Hazelton
Ord Tel R Henshall
Sto W A Heppell
RPO H T Herniman
Ldg Cook(S) E L Hickman
Ch SBA G H T Hicks
Boy Sea G Hill
Ord Artv 4 F Hillyard
Yeo Of Sigs C W Hines
PO Sto R R V Hobbs
Shipw 4 G H Hockin
Ch Sto H D Hodgson
ERA4 J W Hodkinson
Sto R Hollands
Ord Sea A H T Hook
ERA 4 G A C Hopping
Ldg Cook(S) R W Horn
AB J W Howell
Sto L Hudson
Ldg Supply Asst H J Hughes
A/PO Sto L A A Humphries
Boy Sea J P Hunt

Ldg Sea T A Irwin
Sto A E Ison

Ldg Supply Asst R D M Jack
AB F Jackson
Ord Art A L James
AB T W J Jenkins
AB Sydney G Jennings
A/PO Tel C H Johnson
Boy Tel W Johnston
Boy Sea A Jolley
Sea A Jones
AB E A Jones
A/Ldg Sea H Jones
Ord Sea N H Jones
AB W E Jones
Shipw 2 W J Jury

Ldg Cook C Keates
Sto J S Kelly
Sto W Kerrigan
Asst Cook N H Kiddier

ERA4 R C M Lambert
AB C Lane
AB W T Larcombe
Ldg Sto J O Laverick
Boy Sea A C Lear
C Sto H Leeson
Sto A H Lewis
Ch OA H R Lewis
AB C H Lilleker
CPO J Lindsay
Sto H Lloyd
Ord Sea J Logie
ERA 5 E J Lover
Sto W V Ludlam

A / Ldg Tel F P McCabe
PO Cook WJ McClure
AB D R McDermott RNVR
Boy Sea J M McGilvray
Sto B McGregor
AB J Mcinnes
Boy Sea W K McKinnel
Sto T McQueen
Boy Sea R McSpadden
AB C F Mansfield
Sto A T Marsh
AB G I Maule
Ldg Cook J Mellor
AB J S Maloney
Ord Tel J G Moran
Sto A J Morgans
Boy Sea J M Muir
AB B W Munday
Sto A J Murphy
AB N Murphy

AB K S Nash
AB H Neill
Ldg Sto J Norris

AB J O'Brien
ERA3 B O'Donnell
AB A E Orr
Ch Yeo Sigs F J Otter

A / PO G W Parker
AB F Parkinson
AB H T Parsons
ERA3 F G Paterson
ERA5 L J Paulett
Writer C S Peddlar
AB C H T Perkins
Ch Sto S Perry
AB H Pickles
Boy Sea J H Poter
A/Ldg Sea C F Porthall
Ord Sea J Power
Ldg Sto NA Presley
Boy Sea I J Price
Ord Sea R C Pring
PO Sto E R Pritchard
Plumber 3 H J Pulsford

Ord Art4 H J Raisen
Ord Sea W K Rich
Ord Sea D E Richards
Painter 3 R Richards
Boy Sea G R Roberts
AB H E Roberts
A/Ldg Sto D Rodney
AB J Ruscoe
Sto A S Russell

Sto E W Sansby
Boy Sig L J Schofield
AB T J Sear

Sto T McBride
AB G H McCleary
Ord Sea W S McCulloch
Ord Sea D N McDonald
Boy Sea J McGrath
Ord Sea J McGuinness
A / Ldg Sea D McKay
Sto M McLoughlin
A/PO W J MacRae
AB F C Mannning
PO M W Mardhant
AB R F J Martin
Ord Art2 J Mayer
Sto D Mills
Ord Tel W H Moody
AB O P Morgan
Ord Sea S Morrison
A/PO H B Mummery
AB J S Munro
Tel D J Murphy
Boy Sea W B Murray

Sto W H Nash
Ord Sea T Nicholson
Sto N Notman

Sto J D O'Brien
AB E A Olsen
AB F G Osbourne

PO W F Pannell
AB L A C Parker
Boy Sea G Parsons
AB J D Pass
AB L F Patterson
CPO Cook A F Peddle
Cook C W T Penny
Boy Sea R M Perry
PO R E Philpott
AB S Platt
Boy Sea T Porter
A/Yeo Sigs F H Powell
PO Supply WH Powesland
PO S A Press
Ldg SBA B S Priestly
AB E Pritchard
Sto P H Pritchard

AB J Quirk

Boy Sea R Rawcliffe
AB A Richards
AB J Richards
Ldg Sto T Rimmer
PO Sto G G Roberts
AB C Rodgers
AB R A Rogers
AB A Russell
A B G Ruthven

Sto L F Scarr
Ord Sea E J Scoble
Sto W J A Searl

Blacksmith C F L Searle
Sto A J L Selby
Air Fitter R E Sharrock
Boy Sea C F Sheppard
Ord Sea A E Simmonds
A/PO J F B Simmons
Sto R Simpson
Ord Sea J Sloan
Sto M Smiddy
AB F W Smith
Sto H Smith
Boy Sea JL Smith
Ord Sig W A Smith
Boy Sea K Sparks
Air Fitter J Spraggon
Ord Sea J M Stanley
AB E R Steggal
ERA4 J A Stevenson
Ord Sea R F Stockton
AB J H Sturt RNVR
Sto J Swindells

EA 4 H Taylor
AB A D Thomas
Sto J J Thomas
ERA 2 F H Thompson
Ord Sea L Thompson
A/Ldg Sea R S Timpany
A/Ldg Tel L J Toogood
AB T T Tueart

Sto G L Urquhart

Air Mech E N Voakes

PO G B Walker
Ord Sea R F Ward
AB W J Watson
A/PO W Wedlake
SupplyAsst W J R Westlake
A/PO Sto G Whell
AB S Whitaker
Boy Sea R A Whyte
Ldg Wtr W G R Wilkins RNVR
A/Ldg Sea W J Willox
AB J T Wiscombe
AB A H J Wooldridge
ERA 4 R Worth
Ord Art 4 G B Wright
AB W J Young

Sto J Seary
Ldg Sto W H Sharland
Boy Sea L Shattock
Ord Sea A E Shields
ERA4 G G Simmons
Ord Sea W Simnor
Boy Sea A J Slade
Ord Sea A Sloss
Ldg Sea E J Smith
Boy Tel G Smith
PO Sto J R Smith
A/PO R S Smith DSM
AB L Snape
A/Ldg Sea R S Spillane
AB J C Stacey
Ord Sea E R N Steer
AB J Stephenson
AB R Stobbs
A/Ldg Sto P A Stratford
Ldg SupplyAsst T D Sullivan

A/Ldg Sto F A Tanner
ERA 4 R T Thatcher
Ord Sea D Thomas
A/Ldg Sea R M Thomas
A/Ldg Sea J Thompson
PO Sto T Thornton
A/Ldg Sto A Todd
A/Ldg Sea T A Toyne
Ldg Sto J Turner
Sto A D Vincent

Sig W P Walby

Boy Sea F Waller
AB F Watson
Sto S Webster
PO P H Welch
A/Ldg Sea E H Westle
AB R Whitaker
Ord Sea C G Whyte
Sailmaker F A Whiting
Sto F Williams
Ch Shipw W E Wilson
Tel G A Woodbridge
Ord Art 4 E C Woolsey
AB D Wright

Ord Tel E C A Young

MALTESE

Killed:

Steward P Gatt

Missing Presumed Killed:

PO Steward G Borg
PO Cook(O) D Cini
Asst Steward V Demicoli
Asst Steward J Simlar

Ast Cook(O) C Cachia
Asst Cook(O) C D'Andrea
Ldg Steward J Micalaff
PO Steward E Xerry

SOUTH AFRICANS

Missing Presumed Killed:
(All RNVR)

AB W J Angel
Ord Sea P R Bagshaw-Smith
AB E F Barber
Ord Sea B H D Chilton
Ldg Sea E R Elliott
AB G B Grogan
AB M P Jensen
AB A Moore
AB B M Slatem
AB A W Sonderup
A/Ldg Sea C A Stokoe
AB W E H Thompson
AB R Webber

Ord Sea J Austin- Smith
Sto S Q Bagshaw-Smith
AB F G Carter
Ord Sea R E Edwards
AB H C Geraghty
Ord Sea V F James
Ord Sea H F McCarthy
AB J Roose
AB M S Smith
Sto R C Stadtlander
AB M M Symonns
AB C G Van Dyk
Ldg Sea D P Williams

NAAFI

Missing Presumed Killed:

Canteen Asst W Black
Canteen Asst J C Kibble
Canteen Manager H W Poole

Canteen Asst R J W Kerby
Canteen Ast R H Knowler

ROYAL MARINES

Missing Presumed Killed:

A A Adams
J Baxter
R J J Bressent
L H C Brown
R Collingwood
C E Davey
Sgt G H F Davis
T C C Dowding
N B Fallowell
Musician R A Fisher
A F Foster
Musician T Gledhill
W H C Grimson
Musician W F Hacker
J R Hamilton
D W C Hayler
J Jarvis
M Kane
Musician R McAvady
G F McDermid
E G M McLaren
F C Marshall
K R Mawby
Musician W D Muir
E J Nelson
Cpl E C Parsons
F J Pickford

H Baines
Musician C Bell
C E Brown
F Burke
Musician H O Columbo
C Davies
Band Cpl R Dillon
Musician W G E Ellis
W Findley
T Ford
F A Freeman
D Glendening
J M Guyan
Musician R G E Hamill
Musician R E Hamson
T Hyden
Cpl L W Jerret
J N Lamont
M McCann
Cpl I McGowan
C R Marshall
F V Martin
W Moynihan
P W Murphy
Sgt F R Packwood
H M Perrin
Cpl N J Plumb

G O Porter
Cpl F E Pritchard
J Reynolds
F T Ringrose
S J Roberts
Band Major H G Rogers
Musician J E Scott
F H Smith
E R Spencer
C C Thompson
H T Turner
A Waits
A Wells
Boy Bugler S Wild
W C Williams
Musician H G Woodhatch

F F Portlock
Musician B E Quantrill
Col Sgt C G J Richards
Sgt J C Richards
W A U Roberts
W G Saunders
D R Selley
H B Smith
Cpl E J C Sulley
Cpl A J Thomson
M G Turner
A Ward
F W Wilcoxon
A E Williams
I Woodhall

DIED IN CAPTIVITY:

Royal Marine N T J Haines (1941)
AB W Salter (1945)

HMS GLOUCESTER SURVIVORS

Officers:

Lt Cdr R A F Heap DSC OBE

Surgeon Lt H Singer

Chief & Petty Officers

Chief ERA Chadwick
CPO Evans
PO Jacobs
PO E A Revans
PO Walsh

PO Blacksmith Donnelly
Chief ERA Garland
PO Stoker Maloney
PO Yeoman Wainwright

PO Ellender
PO Hutton
PO Morellic
CPO Wade

Ratings

Supply Asst Ayers
Ord Sig Bowley
StoresAsst Butler
OD Collins
Stoker Dearie
Boy Seaman Everest
Ldg Stoker Garside
Stoker Grindell
Stoker Howe
Boy Seaman Leverton
Ldg Stoker Marsdon
AB Nichols
AB Price
Ldg Stoker Sandell
Ldg Seaman Smith
Stoker Stuart
Boy Seaman Thompson
AB Weatherden
Leading Seaman Williams

Boy Seaman Bassett
AB Brown
SBA Cable
Boy Seaman Coxell
AB Draper
Tel Farquason
AB Gittus
AB Hall
AB Jones
Ldg Tel Lofthouse
Ldg Seaman Morgan
Ldg Seaman O'Leary
OD Prosser
AB Seatory
Air Mech Stevens
AB Teasdale
Stoker Vickery
AB Western
AB Yarrow

AB Boddy
AB Browne
AB Cochrane
Ldg Stoker Darnton
Ldg Seaman Evans
Ldg Seaman Friend
AB Gray
Stoker Hambly
Ldg Seaman Kerr
Ldg Seaman Lowden
Boy Seaman Mort
OD Parsons
AB Reid
AB Shuker
AB Stirling
AB Tolan
AB Watters
Stoker Williams

Royal Marines

Mne Day	Mne Evans	Mne Frost
Mne Ham	Sgt Laverick	Mne Roberts
Mne (Musician) Macdonald	Mne Wills	

South Africans

| AB Baker | AB Nicholas | AB Wade |
| AB Webster | | |

BIBLIOGRAPHY & SOURCES

Bibliography

BEEVOR Anthony *Crete-The battle and the resistance*, John Murray, 1991
BUCKLEY Christopher *Greece and Crete-1941*, HMSO, 1952.
CHURCHILL Winston *The Second World War*, Bantam, 1971.
CLARK Alan *The Fall of Crete*, Anthony Bland, 1962.
CUNNINGHAM OF HYNDHOPE, Admiral of the Fleet, Lord *A Sailors Odyssey*, Hutchinson, 1951.
FLOWER Desmond & REEVES James (Editors) *The War, 1939–1945*, Cassell 1960.
GILBERT Martin *Finest Hour* Heineman, 1983.
HADJIPATERAS C.N. & FAFALIOS M.S. *Crete 1941 Eyewitnessed*, Efstathiadis (Athens), 1989.
KEMP Peter Lt Cdr *Victory at Sea*, Frederick Muller, 1958.
MACDONALD C.A. *The Lost Battle – Crete 1941*, 1993.
MACINTYRE Captain Donald *The Battle for the Mediterranean*, Purcell, 1964.
PACK Captain S.W.C. *The Battle for Crete*, Ian Allen, 1973.
PACK Captain S.W.C. *The Battle of Matapan*, Macmillan, 1961.
PEARCE Frank *Sea War*, Robert Hale, 1990.
PLAYFAIR Major General I.S.O. with FLYNN Captain F.C. MALONEY Brigadier.
C.J.C., TOOMER Air Vice Marshall S.E. *History of the Second World War - The Mediterranean and Middle East*, HMSO, 1956.
PRYCE J.E. *Heels in Line*, Arthur Barker, 1958.
ROHWER J. & HUMMELCHEN G. *Chronology of the War at Sea 1939-1945*, Greenhill Books, 1972.
ROSKILL Captain S.W. *The War at Sea 1939–1945*, HMSO, 1954.
SPENCER John Hall *The Battle for Crete*, Heineman, 1962.
STITT George *Under Cunningham's Command*, Allen & Unwin, 1944.
STUDENT General Kurt *Crete, Kommando*, South African Ministry Defence, 1952.
THOMAS David *A Crete 1941. The Battle at Sea*, Efstathiadis (Athens) 1980
WALKER Ernest *The Price of Surrender 1941: The War in Crete*, Blandford, 1992.
WARNER Oliver *Cunningham of Hyndhope, Admiral of the Fleet*, John Murray, 1967.
ZIEGLAR Philip *Mountbatten. The Official Biography*, Collins, 1985.

SOURCES:

Battle of Crete. Admiral Cunningham's Despatch. Supplement to the London Gazette 24-5-48.
East of Malta, West of Suez. Official Admiralty account of the Mediterranean Fleet, 1939-45 HMSO.
Letters of Proceedings. Rear Admiral HB Rawlings, Rear Admiral I Glennie, Vice Admiral HD Pridham-Wippell PRO ADM 199/810 110319.
Letters of Admiral Cunningham. British Library. MSS 52561.
Naval Operations of the Battle of Crete: 20 May-1 June 1941. Admiralty 1942.

UNPUBLSHED:

Lt Singer's account of his survival and time as a POW-Experiences of a Naval Surgeon.
Air Mechanic John Stevens' account of his survival and time as a POW Royal Marine Bandsman Ken Macdonald's account of his survival and time as a POW.
ERA 4 Tubby Revans' account of his survival and time as a POW.
Captain Richard Formby's letters.
Ord Signalman Len Bowley's letters and original diary notes.

INDEX

Page numbers in *italics* refer to illustrations.